Rational Choice

READINGS IN SOCIAL AND POLITICAL THEORY
Edited by William Connolly and Steven Lukes

Language and Politics *edited by Michael J. Shapiro*
Legitimacy and the State *edited by William Connolly*
Liberalism and Its Critics *edited by Michael J. Sandel*
Power *edited by Steven Lukes*
Rational Choice *edited by Jon Elster*

Rational Choice

Edited by JON ELSTER

New York University Press
Washington Square, New York

Selection and editorial material © Jon Elster 1986

First published in the U.S.A. in 1986 by
New York University Press, Washington Square,
New York N.Y. 10003

Library of Congress Cataloging-in-Publication Data
Rational Choice.
   (Readings in social and political theory)
   Bibliography: p.
   Includes index.
   1. Social choice.   2. Choice (Psychology)   I. Elster,
Jon, 1940-   .   II. Series.
   HB846.8.R38   1986   302'.13   86-5329

   ISBN 0-8147-2168-0
   ISBN 0-8147-2169-9 (pbk.)

Typeset by Katerprint Typesetting Services, Oxford
Printed in Great Britain by Billing & Sons Ltd, Worcester

Contents

Introduction

JON ELSTER

This introduction is intended to serve as a guide to the vast litera-ture on rational choice. The price to pay for the breadth of coverage is that each topic will be treated in a relatively superficial way. I hope that the summaries are nevertheless sufficiently informative to enable the reader to locate theories and applications that speak to his or her concerns. The structure of the exposition is as follows. Section I raises some general questions about the status of rational-choice theory. Section II surveys the basic concepts of the standard theory. Section III considers the structure of rational-choice expla-nation. Section IV looks at various limitations to, and explanatory failures of, rational-choice theory. Section V discusses some of the main alternatives to rational-choice theory. Section VI offers brief concluding remarks.

I THE NATURE AND SCOPE OF RATIONAL-CHOICE THEORY

The theory of rational choice is, before it is anything else, a normative theory. It tell us what we ought to do in order to achieve our aims as well as possible. It does not tell us what our aims ought to be. (At least this is true of the standard version of the theory. Some suggestions along non-standard lines are offered in sections III and IV.) Unlike moral theory, rational-choice theory offers conditional imperatives, pertaining to means rather than to ends.[1] For a further discussion of the relation between rationality and morality, I refer to Derek Parfit's essay below.

In order to know what to do, we first have to know what to believe with respect to the relevant factual matters. Hence the theory of rational choice must be supplemented by a theory of rational belief. Again, this is a normative theory before it is any-thing else. While the rationality of an action is ensured by its standing in the right kind of relation to the goals and beliefs of the agent, the rationality of beliefs depends on their having the right kind of relation to the evidence available to him. This suggests a further question: how much evidence is it rational to collect? The issue is further discussed in subsequent chapters.

Once we have constructed a normative theory of rational choice, we may go on to employ it for explanatory purposes. We may ask, that is, whether a given action was performed *because* it was rational. To show that it was, it is not sufficient to show that the action was rational, since people are sometimes led by accident or coincidence to do what is in fact best for them. We must show, in addition, that the action arose in the proper way, through a proper kind of connection to desires, beliefs and evidence. What is meant by 'proper' here is further discussed in section III.

On an alternative conception, rational-choice theory is, before it is anything else, descriptive. Choosing rationally means that one's observed choices fall into a pattern, characterized by the kind of consistency properties discussed in Amartya Sen's essay. On this view, rational-choice theory can yield prediction of actions, but not explanation, if by the latter we mean some kind of causal story. The basic objection to this behaviourist conception of rationality derives from its poverty of content (which its defenders would no doubt describe as its parsimoniousness). Again I refer to Sen's essay. I ought to add, however, that some forms of consistency are also desirable on normative grounds. There is a great deal of overlap between the normative and the descriptive conceptions of rationality, but the latter has too little structure to be really helpful.

What is the scope of rational-choice theory? Does it only cover the behaviour of individual human beings, or can it also be extended to other kinds of entities, which are either less-than-human or more-than-individual?

Consider first animal behaviour. Do animals possess the capacity for having beliefs and desires which is a necessary condition for ascribing rationality to them? Donald Davidson argues that they do not, since they lack language.[2] On his view, one cannot have a belief unless one also has the concept of a belief, which in turn requires having a language. This argument does not seem to be borne out by empirical studies of animal behaviour. The higher animals are capable of behaving in ways that are hardly explicable otherwise than by assuming that they form mental representations of spatially and temporally distant objects, and act on the basis of such representations.[3] Now someone might say that having a mental representation is not the same thing as having a belief; accepting the point, we might respond by saying either that animals are indeed incapable of rational choice or that rational choice does not require having beliefs. I am not sure it matters much whether we accept the alleged difference or, if we do, which of the two responses we make, as long as we recognize the fact that animals respond to their environment in non-automatic and non-myopic ways.[4]

If we limit ourselves to the descriptive conception of rationality, animals appear to behave rationally, or at least not less rationally than human consumers. Studies in experimental economics have shown that pigeons or rats, when placed in different choice situations, vary their choices in ways that conform to the standard consistency requirements of micro-economics. If an animal is allotted a fixed number of times he can press a lever (the budget constraint), and a good becomes available when the lever is pressed a certain number of times (the price of the good), his behaviour will correspond to a negatively sloped demand curve. The more times he has to press the lever to get access to one unit of a given good, the fewer units will he make available to himself (which is not to say that he will press the lever fewer times).[5] Deviations from rationality, such as inconsistent time preferences (see section II), correspond to similar deviations among humans. Even more strikingly, animals, like humans, are capable of coping rationally with their own irrationality. They can, for instance, pre-empt their own weakness of will by precommitting themselves to the choice of behaviour which gives the highest long-term benefit.[6] In these cases, however, the choice does not appear to rest on a mental representation of the outcomes of various courses of action. The underlying mechanisms – natural selection and reinforcement – are governed by actual outcomes of behaviour, not by intended outcomes.[7]

If we turn to more-than-individual units of decision-making, such as households, firms, organizations or political communities, not even the descriptive form of rationality can be salvaged. It is clear enough that the normative theory of rationality, linking action to desires and beliefs, does not even get off the ground in such cases. According to the principle of methodological individualism,[8] there do not exist collective desires or collective beliefs. A family may, after some discussion, decide on a way of spending its income, but the decision is not based on 'its' goals and 'its' beliefs, since there are no such things. We might hope, nevertheless, that the observed choices made by such larger units have at least the consistency properties required by the descriptive conception of rationality. Unfortunately, since the publication of Arrow's impossibility theorem for social choice we know that this is not in general the case.[9] The simplest example is the Condorcet Paradox: there may exist a majority for x over y, for y over z and for z over x. Arrow

showed that such phenomena are unavoidable. Even if the individuals in a group have consistent preferences, there exists no non-
dictatorial procedure for arriving at group preferences which are
similarly consistent. Many firms and households are no doubt run
on dictatorial lines, but for those which are not, Arrow's result
implies that one always runs the risk of finding inconsistent patterns of behaviour.[10]

This argument may sound excessively strong. The dominant
paradigm in economics, neoclassical theory, does, after all, assume
rational behaviour on the part of households and firms. It is not
obvious, however, that the dominance of neoclassical economics is
due to its having solid micro-foundations in rational-choice theory.
For one thing, many of its predictive successes are largely independent of the precise motivations assigned to the economic agents.[11]
For another, its staying power may be due more to the lack of a
viable alternative than to sustained predictive or explanatory success. I return to this question in section v below.

II   BASIC CONCEPTS

In order to justify and explain behaviour, rational-choice theory
appeals to three distinct elements in the choice situation. The first
element is the feasible set, i.e. the set of all courses of action which
(are rationally believed to) satisfy various logical, physical and
economic constraints. The second is (a set of rational beliefs about)
the causal structure of the situation, which determines what courses
of action will lead to what outcomes. The third is a subjective
ranking of the feasible alternatives, usually derived from a ranking
of the outcomes to which they (are expected to) lead. To act
rationally, then, simply means to choose the highest-ranked element in the feasible set. Consumer theory provides a paradigm
example. The feasible set confronting the consumer is determined
by his income, by the physical availability of goods and by their
prices, as far as they are known to him. He has opinions about what
the effects on him will be of consuming various goods in various
proportions, and a value system that allows him to assess these
effects and, derivatively, to rank the options in the feasible set.

It is important to stress the subjective nature of the choice
situation. The fact that options are objectively available to an agent
cannot enter into the explanation of his behaviour if he has no
rational grounds for believing that they are available, nor can the
fact that certain options will objectively lead to certain outcomes if
he has no reason to think that they will. This point is sometimes

overlooked. Some economists have proposed rational-choice explanations of technical change by assuming that firms select the profit-
maximizing locus on the 'innovation-possibility frontier', without
explaining how entrepreneurs get information about the latter.[12]
Another example is the idea that a rational individual will collect
information up to the point where the expected marginal value of
more innovation equals the expected marginal cost of collecting it.
Again we must ask how the individual could possibly know the
value of information he does not yet have. I return to this important
problem in sections IV and V.

Choice situations can be divided along two main dimensions.
(For a fuller discussion, see Harsanyi's essay.) First, there is a
distinction between perfect and imperfect information about the
outcomes that will follow from the alternative courses of action.
When a farmer chooses between two crop varieties, their expected
yields depend on the state of the weather next year, which cannot
be predicted with certainty. Virtually all actual situations are of this
kind, but some of them approximate very closely to the limiting
case of full certainty. When I buy a standardized well tested consumer product I usually do not have to take account of the negligible probability that it might be flawed, especially since a similarly
small probability of being defective would attach to any alternative
product.

Choice situations with genuinely incomplete information may be
characterized by risk or by uncertainty.[13] Risk is defined as a
situation in which numerical probabilities can be attached to the
various possible outcomes of each course of action, uncertainty as a
situation in which this is not possible. There is considerable disagreement as to whether we ever are in a state of uncertainty in this
sense. I shall return to this question, but first let me say a few words
about risk – which no one would deny to exist.[14]

The normatively proper decision criterion under risk is to choose
the option that maximizes expected utility. The expected utility of
an action is defined as the weighted average of the utilities that it
will yield under different states of the world, the weights being the
probabilities of the states. This is not the place to discuss the
economist's notion of utility, a fairly arcane and subtle topic.[15] One
point ought, however, to be made. Consider a farmer or a peasant
who must choose between two grain varieties, a and b. The size of
the crop next year will depend on the severity of the winter. For
simplicity, assume that the winter will be either mild (state 1) or
severe (state 2). Assume, moreover, that the income of the farmer in
the various cases is given by:

	Crop *a* is chosen	Crop *b* is chosen
State 1 occurs	30	50
State 2 occurs	25	15

We stipulate that the two states have an equal probability of occurring. Clearly, crop *b* has the highest expected yield. It need not, however, have the highest expected utility and hence need not be the one which a rational agent would choose. If an income of 20 is the minimum required for subsistence, the agent would be foolish to prefer a course of action that gave him a 50 per cent chance of starving to death over one that assured survival. This is a special, dramatic case of the more general fact that money has decreasing marginal utility, from which it follows that *the utility of expected income is larger than the expected utility of income.* Applied to the present case the utility of (50 + 15)/2 > (the utility of 50 + the utility of 15)/2. Rationality dictates the choice of the option with the largest expected utility, and this need not be the option with the largest expected income – even when all utility is derived from income. This phenomenon is also referred to as *risk-aversion.*[16]

The existence of choices under uncertainty seems doubtful to many. After all, they argue, we always have some information, however vague and diffuse, which we can use to assess the probabilities of the various outcomes. More specifically, they point to the existence of procedures that will elicit the agent's subjective probabilities in any choice situation that he confronts. Once these probabilities are given, the principle of maximizing expected utility can be applied as before. The question, however, is whether the probabilities thus elicited reflect a stable cognitive state, or are mere artefacts of the procedure of elicitation. Amos Tversky and Daniel Kahneman have argued, I think successfully, that it is often irrational to put one's trust in subjective probabilities.[17] It is difficult to imagine that anyone could deny that we are sometimes in a state of genuine uncertainty, for instance with respect to choices that can be expected to have important consequences far into the future, such as the choice of nuclear energy vs other forms of energy production.[18]

Assuming that we are facing a choice under uncertainty, does rational-choice theory tell us anything about what we ought to do? The answer is: very little. What it tells us is that we cannot rationally take account of any consequences of an option except the best and the worst.[19] This principle may eliminate some options, but usually the hard choices are left unresolved. With respect to radically new medical technology, for instance, we may believe that it offers prospects for great improvements *and* for great dangers, so that the best consequence is better and the worst consequence worse than the status quo. Many people then want to play safe, by adopting the 'maxi-min' criterion of choosing the option whose worst consequence is better than the worst consequences of any other. This, while consistent with rationality, is not dictated by it. The 'maxi-max' principle of choosing the option with the best best consequence is equally consistent, as are intermediate principles that attach some weight both to the best and to the worst that could happen. I say more about this lack of determinacy in section III.

The other main distinction that applies to rational-choice situations is that between parametric and strategic decisions. In a parametric decision the agent faces external constraints that are in some sense given or parametric. First he estimates them as well as he can, and then he decides what to do. A strategic situation is characterized by interdependence of decisions. Before making up his mind, each agent has to anticipate what others are likely to do, which may require an estimate of what they anticipate that he will do. His decision enters as part-determinant of the constraints that shape his decision. For a long time this was thought to involve an infinite regress, until it was shown in this century that it can be short-circuited by the notion of an equilibrium point. This is defined as a set of decisions, one for each of the persons involved in the interaction, with the property that no one can improve his situation by deviating from his equilibrium choice as long as the others stick to theirs. An equilibrium point is a set of choices that are optimal against each other. With some exceptions discussed in section IV, all games have at least one equilibrium point.

Strategic decisions are the topic of game theory. The analysis of a game-theoretic situation involves the following elements. There is a set of agents and, for each of them, a set of possible choices or strategies. When the agents choose one element from their respective strategy sets, they bring about a certain state of the world. Each agent has a preference ranking over the possible states of the world. In the general case, three kinds of interdependencies may obtain in strategic situations. *The reward of each depends on the rewards of all.* If people are moved by envy, altruism and the like, their preferences over states may take account of other people's preferences. Again, this might appear to be an infinite regress; but, again, the appearance is misleading.[20] *The reward of each depends on the choice of all.* This is simply a statement of the fact of social causality. *The choice of each depends on the choice of all.* This is the specifically strategic element added by game theory.

Game theory studies these situations from two perspectives. Non-cooperative game theory considers the decision problem from the point of view of the rational individual. As we shall see, individually rational choices may well lead to outcomes that are worse for all agents than some other outcome which they might have brought about by choosing different strategies. Cooperative game theory assumes that this will not happen. Since this assumption cannot be grounded in individual rational choice, I shall not pursue cooperative game theory any further. In particular, I shall not discuss the important special case of bargaining theory.[21]

Non-cooperative games can be further divided with respect to their structure and their outcome. A first distinction is between constant-sum (also called zero-sum) and variable-sum (or non-zero-sum) games. In a constant-sum game there is a given total to be divided among the agents, so that a gain to one will necessarily mean losses for others. In a variable-sum game the strategies chosen by the agents will also affect the total to be divided. There are not many real-life examples of constant-sum games. The struggle over the division of the total can be more or less costly. Since the costs will have to be weighed against the gains, the sum of *net* benefits is usually variable even when the sum of gross benefits is constant.

Constant-sum games are games of pure conflict. Variable-sum games can be games of pure cooperation or games of mixed conflict and cooperation. Pure cooperation is a feature of coordination games, such as the choice between driving on the left or the right side of the road or the choice between linguistic conventions. It doesn't matter what one does as long as everybody does the same. Games of mixed conflict and cooperation form the central topic of applied game theory. One way in which they can arise is if it is better for all if all make the same choice than if they differ, but some individuals prefer that all should do X and others that all should do Y. If a wife and a husband would both rather eat at the same restaurant than in different places, but the wife prefers Chinese and the husband Greek food, they have both a common interest and a conflict of interest. The game is usually referred to as 'The Battle of the Sexes', although it also occurs in many other contexts.[22]

Other examples of mixed conflict-cooperation games arise in situations where people have the choice between two strategies that can be characterized as cooperation (C) and defection (D). In the case of two persons – easily generalized to any number of persons – this yields four possibilities:

	I choose	The other chooses
X	C	C
Y	C	D
Z	D	C
W	D	D

In the 'Prisoner's Dilemma' (extensively discussed in the essays by Sen, Parfit, Harsanyi and Popkin) the individuals rank these outcomes in the order Z–X–W–Y. The result is mutual defection, with the outcome worse for both. In the game of 'Chicken' – after a ritual of American juvenile culture in which two cars are on a course of head-on collision and the point is not to be the first to 'chicken out' – they are ranked in the order Z–X–Y–W. Here the worst that can happen is not unilateral cooperation (being 'suckered'), as in the Prisoner's Dilemma, but mutual defection.[23] In the 'Assurance Game' the order is X–Z–W–Y. Each is willing to co-operate, but only if the other does.[24] To work out the differences between these structures (including the Battle of the Sexes) it is a useful exercise to consider the conditions under which each of them would represent the structure of disarmament negotiations.

Non-cooperative games may further be distinguished according to the outcome we may expect rational actors to bring about. Is there a unique outcome? If so, what are its properties? The central concept here is that of a non-cooperative *solution*. Intuitively, it is the set of strategies that would be chosen by rational and fully informed agents – not by an explicit (and enforceable) agreement but by tacit convergence based upon the anticipation of what others will do. Obviously, any solution will have to be an equilibrium point. If there is more than one equilibrium point (as in all the games cited above except the Prisoner's Dilemma), there are two ways in which one of them can be singled out as the solution. It will be the solution if it is better for everybody than any other equilibrium point, as universal cooperation in the Assurance Game. Or the solution may be singled out by having a certain perceptual salience. If two agents are told that they will both get a reward if, given the choice between 5 and 4.43, they pick the same number, both will pick 5. T. C. Schelling has extensively discussed the properties of such 'focal points' or, as they have also come to be called, 'Schelling points'.[25] If neither condition obtains, we are dealing with a game without a non-cooperative solution. This class of decision problems is further discussed in section IV.

It is one thing to know that a solution exists, in the abstract sense just defined, another to have reasons for thinking it will be realized. In particular, the assumption that the agents are not only fully rational, but also fully informed about the choice situation, is often unrealistic. If, for instance, each player in an Assurance Game wrongly believes that the other has Prisoner's Dilemma preferences, or wrongly believes that the other wrongly believes that he has such preferences, they will behave as if the game were a Prisoner's Dilemma and choose the defection strategy. Instead of saying that in such cases the solution is not realized, we might construct a different solution concept that takes account of the beliefs of the agents.[26] The first response is useful for the normative purpose of comparing the actual choices with ideally rational behaviour. The second is more useful for explanatory purposes (and for the normative purpose of comparing actual behaviour with 'second-best' rational behaviour).

Up to this point this survey has proceeded as if *time* were irrelevant for rational choice. In reality, it is almost the other way around. Choice situations in which time does not play a crucial role are rare. Most obviously, the consequences of any given action are spread out over time. One alternative might yield quick immediate gains; another might yield larger but delayed benefits. To choose between alternatives whose consequences have different temporal patterns, one must have a rationally justified way of comparing or weighing benefits that accrue at different points in time.

An extreme view would be that temporal considerations have no rational force. A benefit should not count for less simply because it is not instantaneously available. Letting it count for less solely for that reason is a sign of weakness of the will or of the imagination. This view cannot be upheld in this unqualified form. The simple fact that we know that we shall die, but not when, makes it rational to attach less weight to benefits that may be produced when we are no longer there to enjoy them. The view must, accordingly, be restated as the view that it is irrational to prefer the present over the future over and above what is justified by the contemplation of mortality tables and similar evidence. It should also be restated so as to distinguish clearly between time preferences on the one hand, and 'temporal utility externalities' (regret, anticipation and the like) on the other.[27]

Thus restated, is the view a plausible one? Derek Parfit argues that it is not. In his view, the use of temporal discounting can be defended by a reductionist view of personal identity.[28] The person is 'nothing but' a more or less tightly connected sequence of mental and bodily states. The looser the connections, the more similar are our future states to the states of other persons, and the more difficult is it to defend temporal neutrality on the sole ground of rationality. (It can, however, be defended on the grounds of morality.) Many economists arrive at a similar conclusion through different arguments. On the descriptive view of rationality as consistency, there is nothing irrational about discounting *per se*, as long as it does not give rise to choice reversals. Some would argue that even the normative concept of rationality is consistent with time discounting. To argue otherwise, they say, is to use rationality as a guide to the choice of ends, instead of its proper but subordinate place as a guide to the choice of means. Preferring the present over the future is like preferring apples over oranges, and *de gustibus non est disputandum*.

I disagree. Against the economists, I believe that it is irrational if one knowingly does what will make one's life as a whole turn out worse than it could have been. I have no argument against Parfit's view that a person who expected his future states to be weakly connected would not be irrational in discounting the future. I believe, however, that a person who takes his future states as given, rather than something to be created, is fundamentally irrational. Moreover, I believe a person will be better off by striving for connectedness, since only then will he be able to form the long-term plans that are a condition for living a meaningful life, *even in the present*.

These are difficult, controversial issues. A statement that will command more agreement is that inconsistent time preferences are irrational. In a justly famous article R. H. Strotz showed that time preferences will lead to inconsistency (choice reversals) if they have a non-exponential form.[29] That time preferences are exponential means that the present value of the future decays at a constant rate as we go further and further into the future; conversely, non-exponential time preferences imply that some parts of the future lose their value more rapidly than others. Imagine a person who inherits a fortune and decides to use half of it on an enormous spree the first year and then divide the other half evenly over the rest of his life. At the end of the first year he reconsiders his decision, in the light of his (unchanged) time preferences. He now plans to use half of the remaining half on a smaller spree in the second year, and then allocate the last 25 per cent evenly over what will then be the rest of his life. The planning is inconsistent because the value attached to the future declines abruptly after the end of the first year, and then remains constant over all following years. I return to this phenomenon in section III, where it reappears in the guise of weakness of the will.

In strategic situations, the time element can make an important difference for what is considered rational. In a one-shot Prisoner's Dilemma, defection is unambiguously, if perversely, rational. In repeated play between the same individuals, however, cooperation may become the rational choice.[30] Repetition creates the possibility of using implicit threats and promises, so that cooperation is motivated by fear of retaliation, hope of reciprocation or both. Clearly, this will not work if the individuals have a very steep rate of time discounting. For myopic individuals the immediate gain from defection will dominate the future gains from cooperation. Hence we see a connection between individually and collectively self-destructive behaviour: myopia can block cooperation.[31]

III THE STRUCTURE OF RATIONAL-CHOICE EXPLANATION[32]

Rational-choice explanation is a variety of intentional explanation. The latter is characterized by various relations that obtain between, on the one hand, the action to be explained and, on the other hand, the desires and the beliefs of the agent. Rational-choice explanation is defined by these relations and a few additional ones.

An intentional explanation of a piece of behaviour, then, amounts to demonstrating a three-place relation between the behaviour (B), a set of cognitions (C) entertained by the individual and a set of desires (D) that can also be imputed to him.[33] The relation is defined by three conditions. First, the desires and beliefs are *reasons* for the behaviour. By this I mean

(1) Given C, B is the best means to realize D.

The presence of such reasons is not, however, sufficient for the occurrence of the behaviour for which they are reasons. An actor might be asked to shudder as part of the scene, but find himself unable to do so. More importantly, even if he does shudder the presence of reasons for doing so does not automatically provide a rational-choice explanation. The sight of a snake on the set might cause the actor to shudder involuntarily – whether or not he is also able to shudder intentionally. We must add, then, a clause ensuring that his behaviour was actually caused by his reasons:

(2) C and D caused B.

It is not sufficient, however, to require that the reasons be causes of the action which they rationalize. To see why, consider a rifleman who wants to hit a target because he believes that only by hitting it can he achieve some further, very important goal. The belief and the desire provide reasons for pulling the trigger when the rifle is pointed towards the target. They may, on the other hand, cause him to behave quite differently. If he is unnerved by the high stakes, his hand may shake so badly that he pulls the trigger at the wrong moment. If he had cared less about hitting the target, he might have succeeded more easily. Here, the strong desire to hit the target causes the behaviour, but it does not cause it *qua* reason for it. Donald Davidson has pointed out that even when the desire and the belief do cause that action for which they are reasons, they might still not cause it *qua* reasons.[34] Hence in a rational-choice explanation, as opposed to an explanation in terms of causes that also happen to be reasons, the following condition must be satisfied:

(3) C and D caused B *qua* reasons.

To go from intentional explanation to rational-choice explanation, we first add two consistency conditions:

(4) The set of beliefs C is internally consistent.
(5) The set of desires D is internally consistent.

It might be thought that these are required not just for rational-choice explanation, but for intentional explanation generally. If a desire is inconsistent, so that there is no way of realizing it, how could one choose the best means to realize it? The answer is that the agent could believe, mistakenly, that the desire is feasible and that it will best be promoted by a certain action. A simple but representative example of an inconsistent desire is provided by a child who tries to act on the following instruction from a parent: 'Remember that you musn't even *think* about this forbidden topic.' Hegel, Sartre and modern psychiatry have explored a rich variety of such phenomena.[35]

We demand a more stringent form of rationality of desires and beliefs than mere consistency. At the very least, for an action to be rational the beliefs sustaining it must themselves be rational, in the sense of being grounded in the available evidence. This condition in turn divides into three, which closely parallel (1)–(3) above:

(1b) The belief has a maximal degree of inductive plausibility, given the evidence.
(2b) The belief is caused by the available evidence.
(3b) The evidence causes the belief 'in the right way'.

As before, the first condition is an optimality condition; the others ensure that the person entertains the belief *because* it is rational, not by coincidence. Condition (2b) excludes, for instance, beliefs caused by wishful thinking that just happen to be the ones that are justified by the evidence.[36] Condition (3b) excludes such cases as compensating errors in the inference process – two inferential wrongs making a right.[37]

Furthermore, we might want to impose an optimality condition on how much evidence to collect before forming the belief. Every decision to act can be seen as accompanied by a *shadow decision* – the decision about when to stop collecting information. The rationality of the former decision depends on that of the latter, on which it is founded. It is not possible, however, to give general optimality criteria for the gathering of information. One frequently made proposal – to collect information up to the point where expected marginal value of more evidence equals marginal cost of collecting it – fails because it does not respect the subjective character of rational choice (section II). The argument that agents who fail to use objectively optimal criteria will be wiped out by competition is only relevant in limited settings and turns out to fail even there (section v). The only condition one can impose on information-gathering is a rather weak one:

(N) The collected amount of information lies between the upper and lower bounds that are defined by the problem situation, including the desires of the agent.

In any given case it is usually possible to point to some information that it would be irrational not to collect, and some information that it is obviously pointless to collect. For an action to be rational, it must respect this rough constraint on information. The search for a general principle that could eliminate the gap between the upper and lower bounds is, however, chimerical. Summarizing, we have

(6) The relation between C, D and E satisfies (1b), (2b), (3b) and (N).

Could one similarly stipulate that an action, to be rational, must be guided by a rational desire? Most economists, emphasizing the instrumental character of rational choice, would say 'No'. Although I cannot provide a positive answer which is sufficiently robust to be incorporated into the formal definition of rational-choice explanation, some tentative speculations will be reported.[38]

The definition of a rational desire would include, first, an optimality property: that of leading to choices which maximize utility. If people very strongly desire what they cannot get, they will be unhappy; such desires, therefore, are irrational. A rational desire is one which is optimally adjusted to the feasible set. To this clause we would have to add, secondly, a condition on the process whereby this adjustment is achieved. If the adaptation of desires to possibilities is brought about by some unconscious mechanism of dissonance reduction, as exemplified in the fable of the fox and the sour grapes, we would hardly call the result a paradigm of rationality. Our intuitions would rather suggest the opposite conclusion: to be under the sway of opaque psychological forces is a mark of irrationality. To be rational, the adjustment of desires to possibilities would have to be freely and consciously willed. This course was advocated by Buddhism, the Stoa and Spinoza. It amounts to making *autonomy* part of the notion of rationality, and is thus inconsistent with any purely welfarist conception of rational choice.[39] Acting rationally means more than acting in ways that are conducive to welfare: it also implies that the beliefs and desires behind the action have a causal history with which we can identify ourselves.

The final condition to be imposed on rational-choice explanation concerns the relation between desires and behaviour. It is designed to exclude akratic behaviour, or weakness of the will.[40] Akrasia is characterized by the following features. (1) There is a prima facie judgement that X is good; (2) There is a prima facie judgement that Y is good; (3) There is an all-things-considered judgement that X is best; (4) There is the fact that Y is chosen. Taking a drink against one's own better judgement is a familiar example. One frequent form of akrasia can be described in terms of inconsistent time preferences (section II). When comparing, well ahead of the time of choice, a later larger reward X with an earlier smaller reward Y, the agent thinks X is best. This is his calm, reflected judgement of what is best, all things considered. When the time of choice approaches, however, the imminent availability of Y disturbs his judgement, there occurs a preference reversal, and Y is chosen.

Akratic behaviour falls within the scope of intentional explanation. Conditions (1)–(3) above include an implicit existential quantifier: *there exist* a belief and a desire that constitute reasons for the action and that actually, *qua* reasons, cause it. But these reasons need not be all the reasons there are. The agent has a reason for taking a drink: this explains why he takes it. But he also has a reason, which in his judgement is stronger, for abstaining. To exclude such akratic behaviour from being considered rational, we must add the following condition:

(7) Given C, B is the best action with respect to the full set of weighted desires (the weights being assigned by the agent himself).

Ideally, then, a rational-choice explanation of an action would satisfy three sets of requirements. First, there are three optimality conditions. The action is the best way for the agent to satisfy his desire, given his belief; the belief is the best he could form, given the evidence; the amount of evidence collected is itself optimal, given his desire. Next, there is a set of consistency conditions. Both the belief and the desire must be free of internal contradictions. The agent must not act on a desire that, in his own opinion, is less weighty than other desires which are reasons for not performing the action. Finally, there are a set of causal conditions. The action must not only be rationalized by the desire and the belief; it must also be caused by them and, moreover, caused 'in the right way'. Two similar causal conditions are imposed on the relation between belief and evidence.

In rational-choice explanation as actually practised by social scientists, the focus is almost exclusively on the optimality conditions, in part for good reasons. Usually the goal is not to explain individual action, but the behaviour of large numbers of people placed in similar external circumstances. Scrutinizing mental states to ensure satisfaction of the causal conditions is then both impossible and pointless. It is practically impossible to gather the required kind of psychological information about large numbers of people; and it is pointless because it is highly improbable that the coincidences that create the need for conditions (2), (3), (2b) and (3b) could arise on a mass scale. If many similarly placed people do the rational thing, we can assume that with few exceptions they do it because it is rational. The consistency conditions (4) and (5) can usually be taken to be satisfied. The usual neglect of condition (7) in social–scientific uses of rational-choice explanation is more difficult to justify. The self-destructive behaviour which can arise when people act against their better judgement is so widespread in our societies that it ought to be given a much more central place in the analysis of human action.[41]

IV LIMITATIONS AND FAILURES OF RATIONAL-CHOICE THEORY

How useful is rational-choice theory, in its normative and explanatory functions? To assess its power in these two respects, we must distinguish between two kinds of problem that arise in trying to apply it. First, both in its normative and its explanatory role the theory presupposes that the notion of rational choice is well defined, perhaps even uniquely defined. To the extent that we cannot tell, or cannot tell uniquely, what the rational choice would be, the theory fails. Secondly, assuming that we can tell what the rational choice would be, the theory fails in its explanatory role if the observed behaviour differs from the normatively prescribed behaviour. (I shall ignore here that it might also fail because the prescribed behaviour arises by the wrong kind of causal process.) In a word, rational-choice theory can fail because it does not tell us what rationality requires or because people don't behave as rationality requires them to do.

The first problem can arise in two ways: because of the non-existence and non-unicity of rationality. It can arise at each of the three levels for which optimality conditions were formulated: action, belief and evidence. I shall only consider four problems, since the others do not arise in practical decision-making:

	Non-unicity	Non-existence
Action	1	2
Belief		3
Evidence		4

1. Keeping desires and beliefs fixed, could there be more than one action prescribed by rational-choice theory? The most frequent case is when a person is indifferent between two top-ranked alternatives in the feasible set. With one important exception, this fact does not present any difficulties for normative rational-choice theory. If two options are equally and maximally good, we don't need a theory to tell us how to choose between them.[42] (Compare also Sen's discussion in chapter 2 of Buridan's ass.) For explanatory purposes, however, this indeterminacy creates a problem, at least when the top-ranked alternatives are quite different from each other. (Indifference can arise because two options have the same features, like two identical cans of soup, or because they differ in several ways that exactly offset each other in the evaluation of the agent.)

The exception arises in game theory. To explain it, the notion of a mixed strategy must be introduced. Consider again the Battle of the Sexes. The husband and the wife have two pure strategies: the Greek restaurant and the Chinese one. They also, however, have an infinity of mixed strategies. Each of these consists in setting up a lottery so that the Greek restaurant is chosen with probability p and the Chinese with probability $1 - p$, where p could be any fraction between 0 and 1. If each uses a mixed strategy, the outcome is not uniquely determined, but the expected outcome is, hence the principle of maximizing expected utility applies. The notion of mixed strategies is what makes game theory mathematically tractable. In particular, it is only with respect to this extended feasible set that most games have an equilibrium point. (For an ingenious use of the notion of mixed strategies, see Boudon's essay in chapter 7.)

In any equilibrium that consists of mixed strategies, however, the following disturbing fact is true. Given that the other agents stick to their equilibrium strategies, each individual agent is indifferent between all his (pure and mixed) strategies. If he entertains the slightest uncertainty or suspicion about the motivation and information of the other agents, he might as well choose a play-safe strategy, i.e. the maxi-min strategy that has attached to it the highest minimal utility. Moreover, he will know that the same thought will occur to others, so that there are indeed reasons for being suspicious. The equilibrium point unravels. Given the central importance of mixed strategies in game theory, this instability points to a very serious difficulty.[43]

2. Non-existence of rational behaviour arises if the agent is unable to make pair-wise comparisons of all the alternatives. There may be two or more options with the property that no remaining option is judged to be at least as good. The preference ranking is then said to be incomplete or unconnected. (Compare again Sen's essay.) The reason why the agent cannot compare the alternatives could be that they are very different from anything he has ever experienced and also from each other: he simply does not know how he would actually react to them. Another reason could be that a comparison of the alternatives would involve an interpersonal comparison of utilities that he feels unable to perform.[44] Faced with the choice between giving ten dollars to person A and giving them to B, I may well find myself unable to express a preference. I may find, moreover, that I am equally inarticulate when the options are giving eleven dollars to A and ten to B – whereas I would rather give eleven than ten dollars to A. This constellation shows a lack of connectedness in my preferences. True, one might construct a procedure to elicit my preferences, just as one may always elicit subjective probabilities in choices under uncertainty, but in both

cases there is a risk that the outcome reflects properties of the procedure rather than some stable feature of my mental states.

3. Non-existence of rational belief arises in choices under uncertainty. It blocks our ranking of the feasible alternatives, not because we are unable to rank the outcomes (as in case 2), but because uncertainty prevents us from deriving a ranking of the available actions from our ranking of the outcomes. The problem also arises in games which lack a non-cooperative solution – either because they have no equilibrium point[45] or because they have several equilibria none of which can be singled out as the solution. The Battle of the Sexes and Chicken are examples of the latter. The problem in these cases is that we have no grounds for forming a rational expectation about what the other player(s) will do. Some decision problems are subject both to uncertainty and to strategic indeterminacy, as when firms try to decide how much to invest in research and development.[46] In addition to the fact that the outcome of innovative activities is inherently uncertain, the winner-takes-all nature of innovation creates an interaction structure similar to that of Chicken.

4. The non-existence of an optimal amount of evidence arises, as explained in section II, from our inability to assess the expected marginal value of the search for information. Unless the situation is highly stereotyped, as in certain forms of medical diagnosis, we cannot know ahead of time what we are likely to find by collecting more information. In many everyday decisions, not to speak of military, political or business decisions, a number of factors conspire to pull the lower and upper bounds apart from each other. The situation is novel, so that past experience is of little help. It is changing rapidly, so that information runs the risk of becoming obsolete. If the decision is urgent and important one may expect both the benefits and the opportunity costs of information-collecting to be high, but this is not to say that one could estimate the relevant marginal magnitudes. It may be more important to make *some* decision and then stick to it, than to make the best decision. A rational man will make a choice, rather than procrastinate indefinitely, but this is not to say that he makes a rational choice.

Non-existence and non-unicity create difficulties for rational choice, but they do not totally invalidate it. For normative as well as explanatory purposes, it can still help us to eliminate some alternatives from consideration, even if it does not conform to the ideal of eliminating all options but one. Exactly how much the theory can help us will vary from case to case. Edna Margalit has suggested that rational-choice theory is at its most useful in medium-sized decisions, when the alternatives differ somewhat but not greatly.[47] When alternatives differ very little, the agent may be indifferent between them; when they differ very much, he may be unable to compare them. The theory has less power in strategic decisions than in parametric ones, less power in urgent decisions than in less urgent. What kind of car or apartment to buy are problems eminently amenable to rational-choice theory. What kind of education to take or what kind of person to marry are problems less suited to the approach, which is not to say that it cannot help us a good deal even here.

For normative purposes, the limitations of rational-choice theory points to some form of *decisionism*. In the midst of battle, one must simply take a stand, be it one that cannot be justified by argument. For explanatory purposes, rational-choice theory must be supplemented by a causal theory that specifies the mechanism – perceptual salience, habit and the like – by which one of the alternatives that have not been eliminated by rational-choice considerations is singled out for realization. In such cases action must be considered as the outcome of three filters, not two. First, the constraints operate to define the feasible set; secondly, rationality operates to exclude some elements of that set; thirdly, some other mechanism operates to single out one member among the remaining ones.

A second line of criticism of rational-choice theory is more radical. It says that even when people could be rational, they sometimes are not. On the two-filter theory the objection is that in such cases some mechanism other than rational choice is responsible for singling out one member of the feasible set. On the three-filter theory the objection would be that the second filter is bypassed entirely. The explanatory claims of rational-choice theory are falsified, however weak we try to make them.

Violations of rationality can occur at each link in the explanatory chain: in the action itself, in the formation of beliefs and desires, and in the accumulation of evidence. At the level of action, weakness of will is a widespread form of irrationality. Another is a phenomenon much studied in recent years, non-expected utility.[48] In numerous cases of decision-making under risk, people do not conform to the principle of maximizing expected utility. They tend, for example, to overemphasize low probabilities and underemphasize large probabilities, a propensity which could lead to an irrational opposition to projects which have associated with them a very small risk of a very large accident.

A further, intriguing example of irrational action is a form of magical behaviour that has been called 'everyday Calvinism', after the paradox of predestination. In an eighteenth-century Methodist pamphlet, exhorting people to come to a religious meeting, we read that 'The coming soul need not fear that he is not elected, for none but such would be willing to come',[49] as if by going to the meeting one could, magically, bring it about that one had already been elected. There is a considerable philosophical and psychological literature on such behaviour and its rationality or lack of it.[50] Finally, there are self-defeating forms of rational action. Some states – spontaneity, forgetfulness, sleep and the like – are such that an attempt to bring them about through instrumental action is likely to interfere with the goal itself.[51]

At the level of belief-formation, there is evidence that beliefs are influenced by 'hot' as well as by 'cold' irrationality. Hot or motivated irrationality underlies the paradoxes of self-deception and wishful thinking. An example is the widespread tendency among normal subjects to overestimate their own ability. Somewhat depressingly, it turns out that clinically depressed subjects have a more realistic understanding of what they can do.[52] Although these phenomena are still poorly understood, it is hard to deny their reality.[53] Cold irrationality in belief-formation has been widely demonstrated by cognitive psychologists over the last decades.[54] It can take the form of generalizing from small samples, of ignoring the statistical tendency of regression towards the mean, of treating the probability of compound events as if it was the sum rather than the product of the probabilities of the component events, and so on.

Although there is little agreement on what constitutes a rational desire, it may be somewhat easier to agree on examples of irrationality in the formation and modification of desires. A person with 'counteradaptive preferences', always preferring most what he does not have and ceasing to want it when he gets it, will not derive much happiness from life, beyond pleasures of anticipation.[55] People with a strong preference for novel experiences may even be led to 'improve themselves to death', if exposed to a suitable sequence of pair-wise choices. In each choice, one alternative is the status quo and the other an option which offers more of some good of which the status quo offers little, but less of other goods. A novelty-loving person will take the second option, which then becomes the status quo in the next choice. After a few choices, the person may have less of all goods than when he started.[56]

At the level of evidence-collection, finally, there is scope for wishful thinking over and above that which operates at the level of belief-formation. A fairly common procedure is to stop collecting evidence when the belief that is rationally justified by the evidence collected so far is also the one that one wants to be true. If the amount collected is below the lower bound of information that ought to be collected, this behaviour is certainly irrational; similarly if one goes on collecting evidence beyond the upper bound in the hope that eventually one will have reasons for holding the belief which one would like to be true.

V ALTERNATIVES TO RATIONAL-CHOICE THEORY

There is no alternative to rational-choice theory as a set of normative prescriptions. It just tells us to do what will best promote our aims, whatever they are. The only part of the theory that is somewhat controversial from the normative viewpoint is that which deals with rational desires. Note, however, that it is hard to think of any other theory of what we ought to desire that is excluded by the idea that desires ought to be rational, in the sense of being satisfiable. If we tell people, for instance, that they ought to desire the morally good, the generally accepted view that 'ought implies can' already embodies the notion of a rational desire. Yet rational-choice theory often needs to be supplemented by other forms of normative advice, when by itself it does not yield a unique prescription. In particular, it is often advisable to make *some* decision, with as little delay as possible, when we cannot think of *which* decision to make.

There are, however, several alternatives to rational-choice theory, in its claim to provide *the* correct explanation of human behaviour. These are intended partly to supplement rational-choice theory when it yields indeterminate predictions, partly to replace it when it yields determinate and incorrect predictions; and partly to pre-empt it by eliminating all scope for choice – be it rational or irrational.

Pre-emption of rational choice amounts to denying that anything but the first filter matters. This 'structuralist' theory asserts that the constraints narrow the feasible set down to a single point in the space of alternatives, so that nothing is left for choice. Although I do not know of anyone who has defended this view in the form just stated, something like it seems to be presupposed by some of the French structuralists[57] as well as by many writers of Marxist persuasion.[58] Although there may well be some cases to which it applies, it is quite implausible as a general theory. Were one to argue, for instance, that the ruling class manipulates the subjects by restricting their feasible set, this presupposes that the ruling class itself has some scope for deliberate action and choice. Also, a rational ruling class would only reduce the feasible set to the degree that the alternative preferred within it by the subjects is also the one preferred within the unrestricted set by the ruling class.

Another, more interesting alternative is the view that human action must be understood in terms of *social norms* rather than individual rationality. In this view rationality as means–end efficacy is itself a particular social norm, specific to modern Western societies. In other societies which attach less importance to instrumental efficacy actions are valued for themselves, not because of the outcome they produce. Moreover, even in societies which profess instrumental rationality as the supreme value, much behaviour cannot be explained as the choice of the best means to a given end. Many actions are performed out of habit, tradition, custom or duty – either as a deliberate act to meet the expectations of other people and to conform to one's own self-image, or as the unthinking acting-out of what one is. Social norms are prior to individuals in the explanatory order, and cannot simply be reduced to subjective feelings about what to do.[59]

Let us disregard the challenge to methodological individualism raised by the last statement, and focus on the challenge to the theory of rational choice. If we try to restate the theory of social norms in the framework of filters, it can be understood either as a statement that such norms enter into the constraints that define the first filter or as the view that they substitute for rational choice in the second. The second view seems the more natural. Although norms often feel constraining, they differ from ordinary constraints in that they can also be violated. The operational content of the norms theory thus understood is that behaviour is unaffected by an expansion of the feasible set. Rational-choice theory predicts that if new elements are added to the choice set, behaviour will change if one of them is seen as better than the formerly top-ranked alternative. The theory of social norms, in its most abstract and general form, denies that this will happen.

Thus starkly stated, the theory of social norms cannot be correct. For one thing, it is incomplete, since it does not tell us what will happen if the feasible set contracts so that the formerly chosen behaviour becomes impossible. For another, there are innumerable examples of traditional behaviour being discarded when new opportunities become available – not because they are better embodiments of the value inherent in customary behaviour, but because the individual finds that they serve his goal better. (For further discussion of the flaws of norm-explanations, see the essays by Boudon and Popkin in chapters 7 and 8.) The theory is nevertheless correct in pointing out that behaviour does not immediately and automatically adjust to opportunities. The response of a rational-choice theorist to this observation would be that because adjustment is not costless, it may be rational to postpone it until one knows for certain that the change is a durable one. I believe, however, that there are cases where norms exercise an independent power, not reducible to adjustment costs. In the presence of norms of cooperation, for instance, newly created possibilities for free-rider behaviour are not always taken up. Voting did not fall to zero as a result of the introduction of the secret ballot.

Indeed, voting behaviour provides one of the strongest cases against the omnipotence of rational-choice explanation.[60] Voting does seem to be a case in which the action itself, rather than the outcome it can be expected to produce, is what matters. As a hunch, which is probably not capable of rigorous demonstration, I would say that even for a rational utilitarian it would be objectively pointless to vote on purely instrumental grounds. In any case, the following thought experiment may be helpful. When faced with the choice between voting himself and helping two other people to vote for his candidate, at the expense of his own voting, a person would prefer the former if what matters to him is that he do *his* duty, not that the best outcome be produced.

Another instance in which norms can explain what rationality fails to explain, is the following.[61] I would not mow my neighbour's lawn for 20 dollars, but neither would I pay my neighbour's son more than 8 dollars to mow my own, identical lawn. For an economist, this failure to treat opportunity costs (that is, income forgone) on a par with out-of-pocket expenses is a violation of rationality. The behaviour can be explained, however, by assuming that the norms of the community, internalized in my self-image, prevent me from mowing other people's lawns for money. Given my self-image, it would be a demeaning thing to do.

There can be little doubt that the appeal to norms sometimes enables us to explain where rational choice fails. The appeal tends, however, to be *ad hoc* and *ex post facto*. There does not exist a robust, well confirmed theory specifying the conditions under which, and the limits within which, norms override rationality. In particular, we do not know what determines when norms remain strong and stable and when they yield to the pressure of self-interest. We cannot answer the question simply by finding how much people must be paid to violate their norms, although this is often a relevant consideration.[62] More important is the process whereby the operation of norms becomes undermined, so that people find themselves able to violate them without any psychic costs for which they need compensation. For instance, norms often cease to have motivational force as a result of 'framing', as defined in Tversky and Kahneman's essay. I may accept mowing my neighbour's lawn if he tells me he will give 20 dollars to charity in return, since 'mowing for charity' does not offend my self-image as mowing for money does. Having mown his lawn, I may feel that I can abstain from making a 20-dollar contribution to charity that I would otherwise have made. In material terms this is equivalent to mowing for money, but because of the framing effect it does not appear as a norm violation.

Another alternative that also has a somewhat 'sociological' flavour is the theory of satisficing or bounded rationality, first developed by Herbert Simon and represented here by James March's essay. It asserts that people do not seek the best alternative in the feasible set, but limit themselves to what seems to be 'good enough' or satisfactory. Consider technical choice and technical change.[63] Firms do not engage in constant, relentless efforts to improve their performance. As long as profits remain high enough to keep shareholders satisfied, a firm does not engage in any search for new techniques. It is only when profits drop below the critical level that it starts looking for a superior method. 'Necessity is the mother of invention.' More generally, the internal decision-making process of the firm is not characterized by constant calculation with a view to maximizing profits. Rather, the firm employs some rough rules of thumb, not because it has found them to be optimal but because they work. The rules are not replaced when superior ones become available, but when they no longer work reasonably well.

Neoclassical economists typically employ two strategies in trying to rebut Simon's theory. The first line of argument is that satisficing is simply a form of maximizing behaviour which takes account of some costs and constraints not usually considered in standard models. Given the omnipresence of costs of decision-making, including the costs of collecting and processing information, it is often optimal to employ some rough-and-ready rule of thumb rather than trying to find the decision that would have been best if found costlessly.[64] The answer to this argument was given in section II. To maximize subject to the constraint of information cost one would have to know the expected value of information, but this is not in general possible. Although it is true, as argued by Becker in chapter 4, that one should rationally spend more time acquiring information when entering into marriage than when purchasing a sofa, this does not answer the unanswerable question of *how much* information one should collect before proposing marriage.

The next, fall-back argument is that firms employ optimal rules of thumb because otherwise they would have been wiped out by competition. The argument rests on an economic analogy of the biological theory of chance variation and natural selection.[65] It does not provide a rational-*choice* explanation of firm behaviour, since the objectively optimal behaviour is not conceived as the outcome of a subjetive process of optimization. The argument satisfies the optimality conditions of rational-choice explanation, not the causal conditions. The optimality conditions are not, however, satisfied accidentally. The natural-selection model says that the optimal behaviour occurs *because* it is optimal. If successful, it provides a rationality explanation, but not a rational-choice explanation.

I do not think it succeeds, however, because the analogy between biological and economic evolution breaks down at a crucial point. The process of biological adaptation is a bit like trying to hit a moving target, since the environment to which organisms adapt is constantly changing. Human beings facing this predicament can aim at where the target will be by the time their arrow reaches it, but evolution is constrained to aim in the direction of the target's location at any given time. Adaptation is successful, nevertheless, because adaptation occurs much faster than changes of the environment. In economic evolution, the environment changes much more rapidly, relative to the speed with which inefficient firms are eliminated by competition. With a different economic environment, different rules of thumb become optimal, and the process of adaptation has to start all over again. It is unlikely that an equilibrium will be reached or even approximated. At any given time we are likely to observe efficient and inefficient firms coexisting in the economy.[66]

If both neoclassical responses to the satisficing theory fail, why has it not replaced neoclassical economics as the dominant paradigm? The answer lies in a disturbing element of *ad-hoc*-ness in the notion of satisficing. The theory does not offer an answer to the crucial question of why people have the aspiration or satisfaction levels they have. (Why do some people spend five minutes looking for a good place to pick mushrooms, while others spend two hours before they begin picking?) These levels must simply be taken as given, which means that the theory offers little more than 'thick description'. Neoclassical economics will be dethroned if and when satisficing theory and psychology join forces to produce a simple and robust explanation of aspiration levels, or sociological theory comes up with a simple and robust theory of the relation between social norms and instrumental rationality. Until this happens, the continued dominance of neoclassical theory is ensured by the fact that one can't beat something with nothing.

VI CONCLUSION

There are strong *a priori* grounds for assuming that people, by and large, behave rationally. We all want to be rational. We take no pride in our occasional or frequent irrationality. At best we accept it as an inevitable byproduct of other, desirable dispositions, which means that it is in some broader sense rational. (See Parfit's discussion in chapter 1 of individually self-defeating theories.) In our dealings with other people, we are compelled to treat them as, by and large, rational. Communication and discussion rest on the tacit premise that each interlocutor believes in the rationality of the others, since otherwise there would be no point to the exchange.[67] To understand other people, we must assume that, by and large, they have consistent desires and beliefs and act consistently upon them. The alternative to this assumption is not irrationality, which can only be predicated on a broad background of rationality, but chaos.[68]

These general considerations create a very strong presumption for rationality, and a strong case for not imputing irrationality lightly. They justify the efforts of economists to show that apparently or allegedly irrational behaviour can, on closer inspection, be derived from the assumption that the agents maximize expected utility. One may remain unpersuaded by arguments purporting to show that murder, addiction, marriage, church-going, joining a revolutionary movement or writing *Paradise Lost* are all to be understood in terms of rational choice under constraints. Yet some such efforts, which initially appeared quite absurd, were crowned with success; others, which still look absurd, may achieve success in the future. And even if they fail, they will have failed honourably. Moreover, it is only by close consideration of the reasons for failure that it will be possible to construct a more general account of human behaviour in which the concept of rationality will have a privileged, but not exclusive role.

NOTES

1 By this I am not suggesting that moral advice must take the form of the categorical imperative. Moral injunctions may tell us to act in a certain way if and only if other people behave similarly; see, for instance, R. Sugden, 'Reciprocity: the supply of public goods through voluntary contributions', *Economic Journal*, 94 (1984), pp. 772–87 and J. Elster, 'Weakness of will and the free-rider problem', in *Economics and Philosophy*, 1 (1985). There is a difference between action being conditional upon the aim one wants to achieve and action being conditional upon what other people do.

2 D. Davidson, 'Rational animals', *Dialectica*, 36 (1982), pp. 317–27.

3 See for instance B. Beck, *Animal Tool Behaviour* (Garland, New York, 1980); cp. also the discussion in J. Elster, *Explaining Technical Change* (Cambridge University Press, Cambridge, 1983), chapter 6.

4 J. Elster, *Ulysses and the Sirens* (rev. edn) (Cambridge University Press, Cambridge, 1984), chapter 1 has a further discussion of the relation between rationality and the ability to relate to states of affairs not immediately given to the senses.

5 J. H. Kagel et al., 'Consumer demand theory applied to choice behavior of rats', in J. E. R. Staddon (ed.), *The Limits to Action: The Allocation of Individual Behavior* (Academic Press, New York, 1980) 237–68; R. C. Battalio et al., 'Commodity-choice behavior with pigeons as subject', *Journal of Political Economy*, 89 (1981), pp. 67–91. A valuable general discussion is H. Rachlin, 'Economics and behavioral psychology', in Staddon, *The Limits to Action*.

6 M. H. Rachlin and L. Green, 'Commitment, choice and self-control', *Journal of the Experimental Analysis of Behavior*, 17 (1972), 15–22; G. Ainslie, 'Specious reward', *Psychological Bulletin*, 82 (1975), pp. 463–96.

7 Elster, *Ulysses and the Sirens*, chapter 1; J. E. R. Staddon, *Adaptive Behavior and Learning* (Cambridge University Press, Cambridge, 1983).

8 For a clear statement of this principle see G. Homans, *The Nature of Social Science* (Harcourt Brace, New York, 1967). Further discussions are found in the essays by Brodbeck, Gellner and Watkins in M. Brodbeck (ed.), *Readings in the Philosophy of the Social Sciences* (Macmillan, London, 1968).

9 For surveys see K. Arrow, *Social Choice and Individual Values*, 2nd edn (Wiley, New York, 1963) and A. Sen, *Collective Choice and Social Welfare* (Holden Day, San Francisco, 1970).

10 Even dictatorially organized groups face the difficulty of implementing decisions. Groups as such do not carry out actions, any more than they entertain beliefs and desires. To realize his desires, the dictator must act through his underlings, which means that he is constrained by their self-interested desires. For this 'principal-agent problem', see North's essay in chapter 9.

11 G. Becker, 'Irrational behaviour in economic theory,' *Journal of Political Economy*, 70 (1962), pp. 1–13; reprinted in G. Becker, *The Economic Approach to Human Behaviour* (Chicago University Press, Chicago, 1976).

12 This explanation is proposed by C. Kennedy, 'Induced bias in innovations and the theory of distribution', *Economic Journal*, 74 (1964), pp. 541–7. For a criticism along the present lines see W. Nordhaus, 'Some sceptical thoughts on the theory of induced innovations', *Quarterly Journal of Economics*, 87 (1973), pp. 208–19.

13 The terms are used here in a technical sense (defined in the text) which was introduced by Frank Knight.

14 Extensive discussions are found in the readings in P. Diamond and M. Rothschild, *Uncertainty in Economics* (Academic Press, New York, 1978). Despite the title, the book is exclusively concerned with risk (as that term is used here). A useful reader with a broader, sociological perspective is J. Dowie and P. Lefrere (eds), *Risk and Change* (Open University Press, Milton Keynes, 1980).

15 A superb introduction to utility theory – and, indeed, to rational-choice theory quite generally – is R. D. Luce and H. Raiffa, *Games and Decisions* (Wiley, New York, 1957).

16 Here, risk-aversion is assumed to be a consequence of decreasing marginal utility. It could also, however, derive from a cautious, conservative attitude towards risk-taking. If the numbers in the example are interpreted as utility rather than money, a cautious individual might still prefer crop *a* if he finds that the prospect of only getting 15 units of utility generates too much anxiety in him. This intuitively plausible statement is, however, meaningless within the standard economic theory of utility, for reasons that have to do with the way in which the notion of utility is constructed (Luce and Raiffa, *Games and Decisions*, p. 32). Moreover, no one has succeeded so far in constructing an operationally precise theory of utility in which that intuition can be meaningfully stated.

17 A. Tversky and D. Kahneman, 'Judgment under uncertainty', *Science*, 185 (1974), pp.1124–30, reprinted in Diamond and Rothschild, 1978. Further arguments are found in R. Nisbett and L. Ross, *Human Inference: Strategies and Shortcomings of Social Judgement* (Prentice-Hall, Englewood Cliffs, N.J., 1980) and in D. Kahneman, P. Slovic and A. Tversky (eds), *Judgment under Uncertainty* (Cambridge University Press, Cambridge, 1982).

18 For further discussion see J. Elster, 'Risk, uncertainty and nuclear power', *Social Science Information*, 18 (1979), pp. 378–400, reprinted as Appendix 1 in Elster, *Explaining Technical Change*.

19 K. Arrow and L. Hurwicz, 'An optimality criterion for decision-making under uncertainty', in C. F. Carter and J. L. Ford (eds), *Uncertainty and Expectation in Economics* (Kelley, Clifton, N.J., 1971), pp. 1–11. See also Luce and Raffia, *Games and Decisions*, chapter 13.

20 For a discussion of mutually interdependent utility functions, see Becker, *The Economic Approach to Human Behavior*.

21 A good survey of bargaining theory is E. Kalai, 'Solutions to the bargaining problem', in L. Hurwicz, D. Schmeidler and H. Sonnenstein (eds), *Social Goals and Social Organization* (Cambridge University Press, Cambridge, 1985).

22 For a discussion this game see Luce and Raiffa, *Games and Decisions*, p. 90 ff. Another example could be the choice of a cartel price in an industry where firms have different cost structures.

23 For discussion of the two-person variety of Chicken see A. Rapoport, *Two-Person Game Theory* (University of Michigan Press, Ann Arbor, 1966), p. 137 ff. For extension to the *n*-person case, see M. Taylor and H. Ward, 'Chickens, whales and lumpy goods: alternative models of public goods provision', *Political Studies*, 30 (1982), pp. 350–70.

24 For the Assurance Game see A. Sen, 'Isolation, assurance and the social rate of discount', *Quarterly Journal of Economics*, 80 (1967), pp. 112–24.

25 T. C. Schelling, *The Strategy of Conflict* (Harvard University Press, Cambridge, Mass., 1963). This solution concept is not only applicable to games of coordination. It may also find application in mixed conflict–cooperation games; see J. Elster, 'Weakness of will and the free-rider problem', *Economics and Philosophy*, 1 (1985), pp. 231–65.

26 J. Harsanyi, 'Games with incomplete information played by "Bayesian" players', *Management Science*, 14 (1968), pp. 159–82, 320–34 and 486–502.

27 I. Steedman and U. Krause, 'Goethe's *Faust*, Arrow's impossibility theorem and the individual decision taker', in J. Elster (ed.), *The Multiple Self*, (Cambridge University Press, Cambridge, 1985); Elster, 'Weakness of will'.

28 D. Parfit, *Reasons and Persons* (Oxford University Press, Oxford, 1984).

29 R. H. Strotz, 'Myopia and inconsistency in dynamic utility maximization', *Reviews of Economic Studies*, 23 (1955–56), pp. 165–80.

30 M. Taylor, *Anarchy and Cooperation* (Wiley, Chichester, 1976) and R. Axelrod, *The Evolution of Cooperation* (Basic Books, New York, 1984) have extensive discussions of cooperation in iterated Prisoner's Dilemmas.

31 This connection is explored in detail in Elster, 'Weakness of will'.

32 This section draws heavily on J. Elster, 'The nature and scope of rational-choice explanation', in B. MacLaughlin and E. LePore (eds), *A Companion to Actions and Events* (Basil Blackwell, Oxford, 1985).

33 The following account is heavily indebted to the essays in D. Davidson, *Essays on Actions and Events* (Oxford University Press, Oxford, 1980).

34 'A climber might want to rid himself of the weight and danger of holding another man on a rope, and he might know that by loosening his hold on the rope, he could rid himself of the weight and the danger. This belief and want might so unnerve him as to cause him to loosen his hold, and yet it might be the case that he never *chose* to loosen his hold, nor did he do so intentionally.' (Ibid., p. 79)

35 For a survey, see J. Elster, *Logic and Society* (Wiley, Chichester, 1978), chapter 4.

36 This possibility is contested by M. D. Pears, *Motivated Irrationality* (Oxford University Press, Oxford, 1984), ch. 5. He argues that wishful thinking only comes into play after the person has considered and rejected the rationally justified belief. There is no superfluous hot irrationality. For some objections to this view, see J. Elster, 'Review of Pears', *Times Literary Supplement*, 1984.

37 For examples, see R. Nisbett and L. Ross, *Human Inference: Strategies and Shortcomings of Social Judgment* (Prentice-Hall, Englewood Cliffs, N.J., 1980), pp. 267–8.

38 The following draws heavily on J. Elster, *Sour Grapes* (Cambridge University Press, Cambridge, 1983), chapters I.3 and III.3. See also the discussion in J. Elster, 'Sadder but wiser? Rationality and the emotions', *Social Science Information*, 24 (1985), pp. 375–406, of the rationality of emotions.

39 For the notion of welfarism, see A. Sen, 'Welfarism and utilitarianism', *Journal of Philosophy*, 76 (1979), pp. 463–88.

40 The following draws heavily on Davidson, *Essays on Actions and Events*, Chapter 2.

41 See notably G. Ainslie, 'Specious Reward', *Psychological Bulletin*, 82 (1975), pp. 463–96 and 'A behavioral approach to the defence mechanism,' *Social Science Information*, 21 (1982), pp. 735–9, for penetrating analyses.

42 A rich discussion of such cases is E. Margalit and S. Morgenbesser, 'Picking and Choosing', *Social Research*, 44 (1977), pp. 757–85.

43 J. Harsanyi (*Rational Behavior and Bargaining Equilibrium in Games and Social Situations* (Cambridge University Press, Cambridge, 1977)) proposes to admit only mixed strategies that assign equal probability to each of the pure strategies being chosen. This goes together with an argument that a mixed strategy is not the result of a deliberate choice, but the outcome of an unconscious chance mechanism. It is not clear to me that this really resolves the problem of instability.

44 A. Sen and B. Williams, Editorial Introduction to *Utilitarianism and Beyond* (Cambridge University Press, Cambridge, 1982).

45 A game without an equilibrium can be generated by asking each of a number of persons to write down a number, and telling them that the winner will be the one who has written down the largest number. Hyperinflation may be a real-life example of this phenomenon. By and large, however, games without equilibria form a small and not very important subset of games without a solution.

46 For more about this problem see Elster, *Explaining Technical Change*, chapter 4.

47 E. Margalit, 'Opting: the case of "big" decisions' (unpublished ms, 1985), cp. also Margalit and Morgenbesser, 'Picking and Choosing'.

48 For lucid expositions see M. Machina, 'Generalized expected utility analysis and the nature of observed violations of the independence

axiom', in B. Stigum and F. Wenstøp (eds), *Foundations of Utility and Risk Theory with Applications* (Reidel, Dordrecht, 1983) and *The Economic Theory of Individual Behavior Toward Risk: Theory, Evidence and New Directions,* Technical Report no. 433, Institute for Mathematical Studies in the Social Sciences, Stanford University.

49 Cited after E. P. Thompson, *The Making of the English Working Class* (Penguin, Harmondsworth, 1968).

50 See, for instance, R. Nozick, 'Newcomb's problem and two principles of choice', in N. Rescher (ed.), *Essays in Honor of Carl Hempel* (Reidel, Dordrecht, 1969), pp. 114–46.

51 See Elster, *Sour Grapes,* chapter II for such 'states that are essentially byproducts'.

52 See, notably, L. Alloy and L. Abrahamson, 'Judgment of contingency in depressed and nondepressed students: Sadder but wiser?' *Journal of Experimental Psychology: General,* 41 (1979), pp. 1129–40.

53 A recent, sophisticated survey is Pears, *Motivated Irrationality.*

54 Nisbett and Ross, *Human Inference*; Kahneman, Stovic and Tversky, *Judgment under Uncertainty.*

55 For counteradaptive preferences, see Elster, *Sour Grapes,* chapter III. 2. For the pleasures of anticipation and their relation to the pleasures of consumption, see Elster, 'Sadder but wiser'.

56 See C. C. von Weizsäcker, 'Notes on endogenous change of tastes', *Journal of Economic Theory,* 3 (1971), pp. 345–72 for the demonstration of this possibility. It is illustrated in the well-known folk tale of the man who went off to the market in the morning to sell his cow, and came back in the evening with some insignificant object which was the end result of a series of pair-wise exchanges.

57 See for example P. Bourdieu, J.-C. Passeron and J.-C. Chamboredon, *Le Métier de Sociologue* (Mouton, The Hague, 1968).

58 See J. Elster, *Making Sense of Marx* (Cambridge University Press, Cambridge, 1985).

59 This statement of the theory of social norms is a composite picture, drawing among others on P. Bourdieu, *Outline of a Theory of Practice* (Cambridge University Press, Cambridge, 1977), T. Parsons, *The Social System* (The Free Press, Glencoe, Ill., 1951) and C. Taylor, 'Interpretation and the sciences of man', *Review of Metaphysics,* 25 (1971), pp. 3–51.

60 B. Barry, *Economists, Sociologists and Democracy* (2nd edn) (Chicago University Press, Chicago, 1979) has a useful survey of rationality-oriented vs norms-oriented theories of voting, although the latter are not, perhaps, presented in their best versions.

61 The example draws on R. Thaler, 'Towards a positive theory of consumer choice', *Journal of Economic Behavior and Organisation* (1980), pp. 39–60, and on discussions with Amos Tversky.

62 For this approach, see D. North, *Structure and Change in Economic History* (Norton, New York, 1981), chapter 5 as well as Becker's essay in chapter 4.

63 A superb application of satisficing theory to technical change is R. Nelson and S. Winter, *An Evolutionary Theory of Economic Change* (Harvard University Press, Cambridge, Mass., 1982).

64 For this reply, see for instance W. Riker and P. C. Ordeshook, *An Introduction to Positive Political Theory* (Prentice-Hall, Englewood Cliffs, N.J., 1973).

65 A. Alchian, 'Uncertainty, evolution and economic theory', *Journal of Political Economy*, 58 (1950), pp. 211–22 is the origin of this line of argument. For more sophisticated versions, with more emphasis on the disanalogies between biological and economic selection processes, see S. Winter, 'Economic "natural selection" and the theory of the firm', *Yale Economics Essays*, 4 (1964), pp. 225–72 and 'Optimization and evolution in the theory of the firm', in R. H. Day and T. Groves (eds), *Adaptive Economic Models* (Academic Press, New York, 1975), pp. 73–118.

66 This argument owes much to Nelson and Winter, *An Evolutionary Theory*.

67 J. Habermas, *Zur Theorie des Kommunikativen Handelns* (Suhrkamp, Frankfurt-am-Main, 1982). See also K. Midgaard, 'On the significance of language and a richer concept of rationality', in L. Lewin and E. Vedierg (eds), *Politics as Rational Action* (Reidel, Dordrecht, 1980).

68 D. Davidson, *Essays on Actions and Events*.

1

Prudence, Morality, and the Prisoner's Dilemma

DEREK PARFIT

There are many theories about what we have reason to do. Some of these theories are, in certain cases, directly self-defeating. What does this show?

I

Consider first *the Prisoner's Dilemma*. You and I are questioned separately about some joint crime. The outcomes would be these:

	You confess	You keep silent
I confess	Each gets 10 years	I go free, you get 12 years
I keep silent	I get 12 years, you go free	Each gets 2 years

It will be better for each if he[1] confesses. This is so whatever the other does. But if both confess that will be worse for each than if both keep silent.

Let us simplify. It will be worse for each if each rather than neither does what will be better for himself. One case occurs when

> *Positive Condition*: each could either (1) give himself some benefit or (2) give the other some greater benefit,

and

> *Negative Condition*: neither's choice would be in other ways better or worse for either.

This essay is reproduced by permission of the British Academy, 1978 Philosophical Lecture, *Proceedings of the British Academy*, 65. Published by Oxford University Press.

When the Positive Condition holds, the outcomes would be these:

	You do (1)	do (2)
I do (1)	Each gets the lesser benefit	I get both benefits, you get neither
do (2)	I get neither benefit, you get both	Each gets the greater benefit

If we add the Negative Condition, the diagram becomes:

	You do (1)	do (2)
I do (1)	Third-best for both	Best for me, worst for you
do (2)	Worst for me, best for you	Second-best for both

Part of the Negative Condition cannot be shown in this diagram. There must be *no reciprocity*: it must be true that neither's choice would cause the other to make the same choice. It will then be better for each if he does (1) rather than (2). This is so whatever the other does. But if both do (1) that will be worse for each than if both do (2).

When could there be no reciprocity? Only when each must make a final choice before learning what the other chose. This is not common. Nor would it ensure the Negative Condition. There might, for instance, be delayed reciprocity. Either's choice might affect whether he is later benefited by the other. We can therefore seldom know that we face a Two-Person Prisoner's Dilemma.

We can often know that we face a Many-Person version. One can be called *the Samaritan's Dilemma*. Each of us could sometimes help a stranger at some lesser cost to himself. Each could about as often be similarly helped. In small communities, the cost of helping might be indirectly met. If I help, this may cause me to be later helped in return. But in large communities this is unlikely. It may here be better for each if he never helps. But it would be worse for each if no one ever helps. Each might gain from never helping, but he would lose, and lose more, from never being helped.

Another case occurs when

> *Positive Condition*: each of us could, at some cost to himself, give to the others a greater total sum of benefits,[2]

and

> *Negative Condition*: there would be no indirect effects cancelling out these direct effects.

The Positive Condition often holds. If we are numerous, so does the Negative Condition. What each does would here be unlikely to affect what the others do.

The commonest examples are *Contributor's Dilemmas*. These involve *public goods*: outcomes which benefit even those who do not help to produce them. It can be true of each person that, if he helps, he will add to the sum of benefits. But his share of what he adds may be very small. It may not repay his contribution. It may thus be better for each if he does not help. This can be so whatever others do. But it would be worse for each if fewer others help. And if none help that would be worse for each than if all do.

Some public goods need financial contributions. This is true of roads, the police, or national defence. Others need cooperative efforts. When in large firms wages depend on profits, it can be better for each if others work harder, worse for each if he does. The same can be true for peasants on collective farms. A third kind of public good is the avoidance of an evil. This often needs self-restraint. Such cases may involve

> *Commuters*: Each goes faster if he drives, but if all drive each goes slower than if all take buses.
> *Soldiers*: Each will be safer if he turns and runs, but if all do more will be killed than if none do.
> *Fishermen*: When the sea is overfished, it can be better for each if he tries to catch more, worse for each if all do.
> *Peasants*: When the land is overcrowded, it can be better for each if he has more children, worse for each if all do.

There are many other cases. It can be better for each if he adds to pollution, uses more energy, jumps queues, and breaks agreements; but if all do these things that can be worse for each than if none do. It is very often true that, if each rather than none does what will be better for himself, that will be worse for everyone.

II

Each may be disposed to do what will be better for himself. There is then a practical problem. Unless something changes, the actual outcome will be worse for everyone.

Let us use labels. Each has two alternatives: S (self-benefiting), A (altruistic). If all do S that will be worse for each than if all do A. But, whatever others do, it will be better for each if he does S. The problem is that, for this reason, each is now disposed to do S.

The problem will be partly solved if most do A, wholly solved if all do. Figure 1.1 shows how a solution may be reached in one or more ways.

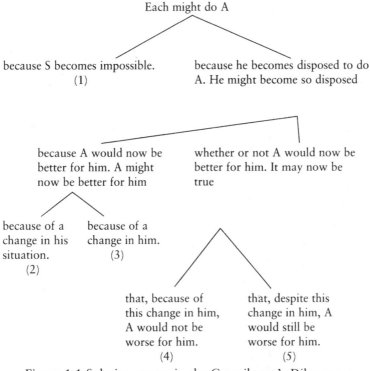

Each might do A

because S becomes impossible.
(1)

because he becomes disposed to do A. He might become so disposed

because A would now be better for him. A might now be better for him

whether or not A would now be better for him. It may now be true

because of a change in his situation.
(2)

because of a change in him.
(3)

that, because of this change in him, A would not be worse for him.
(4)

that, despite this change in him, A would still be worse for him.
(5)

Figure 1.1 Solution routes in the Contributor's Dilemma

(1) to (4) abolish the Dilemma. The altruistic choice ceases to be worse for each. These are often good solutions. But they are sometimes inefficient, or unattainable. We then need (5). This

solves the practical problem. But it does not abolish the Dilemma. A theoretical problem remains.

In solution (1), the self-benefiting choice is made impossible. This is sometimes best. In many Contributor's Dilemmas, there should be inescapable taxation. But (1) would often be a poor solution. Fishing nets could be destroyed, soldiers chained to their posts. Both have disadvantages.

(2) is a less direct solution. S remains possible, but A is made better for each. There might be a system of rewards. But if this works all must be rewarded. It may be better if the sole reward is to escape some penalty. If this works, no one pays. If all deserters would be shot, there may be no deserters.

(1) and (2) are political solutions. What is changed is our situation. (3) to (5) are psychological. It is we who change. This change may be specific, solving only one Dilemma. The fishermen might grow lazy, the soldiers might come to prefer death to dishonour. Here are four changes of a more general kind:

We might become *trustworthy*. Each might then agree to do A on condition that the others join in this agreement.

We might become *reluctant to be 'free-riders'*. If each believes that many others will do A, he may then prefer to do his share.

We might become *Kantians*. Each would then do only what he could rationally will everyone to do. None could rationally will that all do S. Each would therefore do A.

We might become *more altruistic*. Given sufficient altruism, each would do A.

These are moral solutions. Because they might solve any Dilemma, they are the most important psychological solutions.

They are often better than the political solutions. This is in part because they do not need to be enforced. Take the Samaritan's Dilemma. It cannot be made impossible not to help strangers. Bad Samaritans cannot easily be caught and fined. Good Samaritans can be rewarded. But for this to be ensured the law might have to intervene. Given the administrative costs, this solution may not be worth while. It would be much better if we became directly disposed to help strangers.

It is not enough to know which solution would be best. Any solution must be introduced. This is often easier with the political solutions. Situations can be changed more easily than people. But we often face another Contributor's Dilemma. Few political solutions can be introduced by a single person. Most require co-operation by many people. But a solution is a public good, benefiting each whether or not he does his share in bringing it about. In most large groups, it will not be better for each if he does his share. His own contribution will not make enough difference.

This problem may be small in well-organized democracies. It may be sufficient here to get the original problem widely understood. This may be difficult. But we may then vote for a political solution. With a responsive government, there may even be no need to hold a vote.

The problem is greater when there is no government. This is what worried Hobbes. One example is the spread of nuclear weapons. Without world government, it may be hard to achieve a solution.

The problem is greatest when its solution is opposed by some ruling group. This is *the Dilemma of the Oppressed.*

Such Contributor's Dilemmas often need moral solutions. We often need some people who are directly disposed to do their share. If these can change the situation, so as to achieve a political solution, this may be self-sustaining. But without such people it may never be achieved.

The moral solutions are, then, often best; and they are often the only attainable solutions. We therefore need the moral motives. How could these be introduced? Fortunately, that is not our problem. They exist. That is how we solve many Prisoner's Dilemmas. Our need is to make these motives stronger, and more widely spread.

With this task, theory helps. Prisoner's Dilemmas need to be explained. So do their moral solutions. Both have been too little understood.

One solution is, we saw, a conditional agreement. For this to be possible, it must first be true that we can all communicate. If we are self-interested, this would seldom make a difference. In most large groups, it would be pointless to agree that we will make the altruistic choice, since it would be better for each if he breaks this agreement. But suppose that we are trustworthy. Each could now promise to do A, on condition that everyone else makes the same promise. If we know that we are all trustworthy, each will have a motive to join this conditional agreement. Each will know that, unless he joins, the agreement will not take effect. Once we have all made this promise, we will all do A.

In cases that involve only a few people, such a joint conditional agreement may be a good solution. But in cases that involve large numbers it is of little use. It will take some effort both to enable all to communicate and then to reach a joint agreement. But the agreement is a public good, benefiting each whether or not he helps to produce it. In most large groups, it will not be better for each if he helps. To this Contributor's Dilemma, trustworthiness provides no solution.

If we are reluctant to be free-riders, this problem is reduced. There is now no need for an actual agreement. All that is needed is an assurance that there will be many who do A. Each would then prefer to do his share. But a reluctance to free-ride cannot by itself create this assurance. So there are many cases where it provides no solution.

The Kantian Test could always provide a solution. This Test has its own problems. Could I rationally will either that none practise medicine, or that all do? If we refine the Test, we may solve such problems. But in Prisoner's Dilemmas they do not arise. These are the cases where we naturally say, 'What if everyone did that?'

The fourth solution is sufficient altruism. This has been the least understood. Each altruistic choice benefits others. But in Contributor's Dilemmas the benefit to each of the others may be very small. It may even not be perceptible. Some believe that such benefits make no moral difference. If that were so, rational altruists would not contribute.

It cannot be so. Consider *the Donor's Paradox*. Many wounded men lie out in the desert. Each of us has one pint of water, which he could carry to some wounded man. But if our pints are carried separately, much of the water would evaporate. If instead we pour our pints into a water-cart, there would be no evaporation. For rational altruists, this would be a better way of giving. Each wounded man would receive more water. But the pint that each of us contributes would now be shared between all these many men. It would give to each man only a single drop. Even to a wounded man, each drop of water is a very tiny benefit. If we ignore such benefits, we shall be forced to conclude that each of our contributions is now wasted.[3]

Let us next subdivide the moral solutions. When some moral motive leads someone to do A, what he does may either be, or not be, worse for him. This distinction raises deep questions. But I shall simply state what my arguments assume. What is in our interests partly depends on what our motives are. If we have moral motives, it may therefore not be true that doing A is worse for us. But this might be true. Even if we know it is, we might still do A.

I am here dismissing four claims. Some say that no one does what he believes to be worse for him. This has been often refuted. Others say that what each does is, by definition, best for him. In the economist's phrase, it will 'maximize his utility'. Since this is merely a definition, it cannot be false. But it is here irrelevant. It is simply not about what is in a person's long-term self-interest. Others say that virtue is always rewarded. Unless there is an after-life, this has also been refuted. Others say that virtue is its own reward. This is too obscure to be easily dismissed – or discussed here.

To return to my own claims. Many Prisoner's Dilemmas need moral solutions. We must become directly disposed to make the altruistic choice. These solutions are of two kinds. Some abolish the Dilemma. In such cases, because of this change in us, it is no longer true that it will be worse for each if he does A. But in other cases this is still true. Even in such cases, we might do A. Each might do, for moral reasons, what he knows to be worse for him.

We often need moral solutions of this second kind. Call them *self-denying*. They solve the practical problem. The outcome is better for everyone. But they do not abolish the Dilemma. A theoretical problem remains.

III

It is this. We may have moral reasons to do A. But it will be better for each if he does S. Morality conflicts with self-interest. When these conflict, what is it rational to do?

On one view, it is the self-benefiting choice which is rational. This view lacks a good name. Call it *prudence*. If we accept this view, we will be ambivalent about self-denying moral solutions. We will believe that, to achieve such solutions, we must all act irrationally.

Many writers resist this conclusion. Some claim that moral reasons are no weaker than prudential reasons. Others claim, more boldly, that they are stronger. On their view, it is the altruistic choice which is rational.

This debate may seem unresolvable. How can these two kinds of reason be weighed against each other? Moral reasons are, of course, morally supreme. But prudential reasons are prudentially supreme. Where can we find a neutral scale?

Some believe we do not need a neutral scale. They claim that, in Prisoner's Dilemmas, prudence is *self-defeating*. Even in prudential terms, morality wins.

Is this so? Call prudence

individually self-defeating when it would be worse for someone if he is prudent,

and

collectively self-defeating when it would be worse for each if all rather than none are prudent.

Prudence might be individually self-defeating. Either of these might be true:

1 It might be worse for someone if he acted prudently. When there is uncertainty, the prudent act may not be the one which turns out best.
2 It might be worse for someone if he was disposed to act prudently. This might be worse for him even if he always did what would be best for him. One example is the 'paradox of hedonism': happiness, if aimed at, may be harder to achieve.

In Prisoner's Dilemmas, neither of these is true. The bad effects are here produced by acts, not dispositions. And there is no uncertainty. It will be better for each if he acts prudently. It is the self-benefiting choice which is prudent; and, whatever others do, it will be better for each if he makes this choice. So prudence is not here individually self-defeating. But it is collectively self-defeating. If all act prudently, that will be worse for each than if none do.

Does this show that, if we all act prudently, we are irrational? We can start with a smaller question. Do our own assumptions show us this? Is our prudence failing even in its own terms?

We might answer: 'No. The prudence of each is better for him. It succeeds. Why is our prudence here collectively self-defeating? Only because the prudence of each is worse for others. That does not make it unsuccessful. It is not benevolence.' If we are prudent, we will of course deplore Prisoner's Dilemmas. These are not the cases loved by classical economists, where each gains from universal prudence. We might say: 'In those cases, prudence both works and approves the situation. In Prisoner's Dilemmas, prudence still works. Each still gains from his own prudence. But since each loses even more from the prudence of others, prudence here condemns the situation.'

This may seem an evasion. When it is worse for each if we are all prudent, it may seem that our prudence should condemn itself. Suppose that in some other group, facing the same Dilemmas, all make the altruistic choice. They might say to us: 'You think us irrational. But we are better off than you. We do better even in prudential terms.'

We could answer: 'That is just a play on words. You "do better" only in the sense that you are better off. Each of you is *doing* worse in prudential terms. He is doing what is worse for him.' We might add: 'What is worse for each of us is that, in our group, there are no fools. Each of you has better luck. His own irrationality is worse for him, but he gains even more from the irrationality of others.'

They might answer: 'You are partly right. Each of us *is* doing worse in prudential terms. But, though *each* is doing worse, *we* are doing better. That is not a play on words. Each of us is better off because of what we *do*.'

This suggestion looks more promising. Return to the simpler Two-Person Case. Each could either benefit himself (S) or give to the other some greater benefit (A). The outcomes would be these:

		You	
		do S	do A
I	do S	Third-best for each	Best for me, worst for you
	do A	Worst for me, best for you	Second-best for each

To ensure that neither's choice can affect the other's, suppose that we cannot communicate. If I do A rather than S, that will then be worse for me. This is so whatever you do. And the same holds for you. If we both do A rather than S, each is therefore doing worse in prudential terms. The suggestion is that *we* are doing better.

What makes this promising is that it contrasts 'each' with 'we'. In some claims, these are equivalent. It cannot be true that each is old but we are young. But in other claims they are not equivalent. It might be true that each is weak but we are strong. We *together* might be strong. Our suggestion is of this second kind. It might be true that, though each is doing worse in prudential terms, we together are doing better.

Is this true? Let us use this test. Our prudence gives to each a certain aim. Each does better, in prudential terms, if he more effectively achieves this aim. *We* do better, in the same terms, if we more effectively achieve the aim of each. This test seems fair. It might show that, if each does the best he can, we together could not do better.

What is the aim that our prudence gives to each? We might say, 'to act prudently'. This is true, but misleading. Some aims are fundamental. Others are derived from these. Call the former *goals*. When we are measuring success, only goals count. Suppose that we are trying to scratch our own backs. The goal of each might be that he cease to itch. We would then do better if we scratched each other's backs. But we might be contortionists: the goal of each might be that his back be scratched *by himself*. If we scratched each other's backs, we would then do worse.

If we are prudent, what is the goal of each? Is it that his interests be advanced, or that his interests be advanced *by himself*? If it was the second, we would not be prudent. Perhaps we are Nietzscheans, whose ideal is 'the fiercest self-reliance'. If we both do A rather than S, we would be doing worse in these terms. The interests of each would be better advanced. But neither's would be advanced by himself. Neither's goal would be achieved.

This Nietzschean ideal is not prudence. Both give each the aim of self-advancement. But only for Nietzscheans is this the goal. For the prudent, any act is a mere means. The goal is always the effect – whether this be pleasure, or some other benefit. (Nietzsche's 'blond beasts' were, it is said, lions. But, for them too, acting is a means. They prefer to eat what others kill.)

The goal of each person's prudence is the best possible outcome for himself. If we both do A rather than S, we make the outcome better for each. We cause the goal of each to be better achieved. We are therefore doing better in prudential terms. This confirms the suggestion made above. The prudent act is S. If we both act prudently, we are doing worse than we could even in prudential terms.

Does this show that our prudence here condemns itself? It may seem so. And it is tempting to contrast prudence with morality. We might say: 'Prudence breeds conflict, telling each to work against others. That is how universal prudence can be bad for all. Where prudence divides, morality unites. It tells us to work together – to do the best *we* can. Even on the scale provided by self-interest, morality therefore wins. This is what we learn from Prisoner's Dilemmas. If we exchange prudence for morality, we do better even in prudential terms.'

This is too swift. *We* do better, but *each* does worse. If we both do A rather than S, *we* make the outcome better for each, but *each* makes the outcome worse for himself. Whatever the other does, it woud be better for each if he did S. In Prisoner's Dilemmas, the problem is this. Should *each* do the best he can for himself? Or should *we* do the best we can for each? If *each* does what is best for himself, *we* do worse than we could for each. But *we* do better for each only if *each* does worse than he could for himself.

This is just a special case of a wider problem. Consider any theory about what we have reason to do. There might be cases where, if each does better in this theory's terms, we do worse, and vice versa. Call such cases *Each–We Dilemmas*.

Some theories cannot produce such Dilemmas. We shall later see why, for certain theories, this is so. If a theory does produce Each–We Dilemmas, it is not obvious what this shows. Reconsider prudence. This tells each to do the best he can for himself. We are discussing cases where, if we all act prudently, we are doing what is worse for each. Prudence is here collectively self-defeating. But it is not obvious that this is a fault. Why should a theory be collectively successful? Why is it not enough that, at the individual level, it works?

We might say: 'But a theory cannot apply only to a single individual. If it is rational for me to act prudently, it must be rational for everyone to do so. Any acceptable theory therefore must be successful at the collective level.'

This involves a confusion. Call a theory *universal* if it applies to everyone, *collective* if it claims success at the collective level. Some theories have both features. One example is a Kantian morality. This tells each to do only what he could rationally will everyone to do. The plans or policies of each must be tested at the collective level. For a Kantian, the essence of morality is the move from *each* to *we*.

At the collective level – as an answer to the question, 'How should we all act? – prudence *would* condemn itself. Suppose that we are choosing what code of conduct will be publicly encouraged, or taught in schools. It would here be prudent to vote against prudence. If we are choosing a collective code, the prudent choice would be morality.

Prudence is a universal theory, applying to everyone. But it is not a collective code. It is a theory of individual rationality. This answers the smaller question that we asked above. In Prisoner's Dilemmas, where it is only collectively self-defeating, prudence does not condemn itself.

IV

Many bad theories do not condemn themselves. So the larger question remains open. In such cases, what is it rational to do?

It may help to introduce another common theory. This tells each to do what will best achieve his present aims. Call this *the instrumental theory*. Suppose that, in some Prisoner's Dilemma, my aim is the outcome which is best for me. On the instrumental theory, it is then the prudent choice which is rational. If my aim is to benefit others, or to apply the Kantian Test, it is the altruistic choice which is rational. If my aim is to do what others do – perhaps because I do not wish to be a free-rider – it is uncertain which choice is rational. This depends on my beliefs about what others do.

As these remarks show, the instrumental theory may conflict with prudence. What will best achieve my present aims may be against my own long-term self-interest. Since the two theories may conflict, those who believe in prudence must reject the instrumental theory.

They might point out that, even at the individual level, it can be self-defeating. It can produce intertemporal Dilemmas. These will be most common if I care less about my further future. Suppose that, at different times, I have conflicting aims. At each time I could either (1) do what will best achieve my present aims or (2) do what will best achieve, or enable me to achieve, all of my aims over time. On the instrumental theory, I should always do (1) rather than (2). Only so will I at each time do the best I can in instrumental terms. But over time I may then do worse, in these same terms. Over time, I may be less successful in achieving my aims at each time. (Here is a trivial example. At each time I will best achieve my present aims if I then waste no energy on being tidy. But if I am never tidy this may cause me at each later time to achieve less.)

Those who believe in prudence may appeal to such cases. They might say: 'The instrumental theory is here self-defeating. Even in this theory's terms, prudence is superior. The prudent act is (2). If you always do (2) rather than (1), you will more effectively achieve your aims at each time. If you are prudent, you do better even in instrumental terms.'

This is again too swift. I do better *over time*. But *at each time* I do worse. If I always do (2), I am at each time doing what will less effectively achieve the aims that I then have. (1) is what will best achieve these. Remember the interpersonal Dilemma. For the word 'we' substitute 'I over time', and for the word 'each' substitute 'I at each time'. In the interpersonal Dilemma, we do better only if each does worse than he could. In the intertemporal Dilemma, I do better over time only if at each time I do worse than I then could.

We must again distinguish two levels. The instrumental theory is here *intertemporally* self-defeating. But it does not claim to be successful at the intertemporal level. So it does not condemn itself. It is not a failure in its own terms.

Those who believe in prudence must claim that, none the less, it should be rejected. They might say: 'Any acceptable theory must be intertemporally successful. It is no defence that the instrumental theory does not claim such success. That merely shows it to be structurally flawed. If a theory is intertemporally self-defeating, this is enough to show that it should be rejected.'

This is a dangerous argument. If it refutes the instrumental theory that it is intertemporally self-defeating, why does it not refute prudence that it is collectively self-defeating? And if it is a good reply that prudence does not claim to be collectively successful, why can the instrumental theorist not make a similar reply?

As this shows, prudence can be challenged from two directions. This makes it harder to defend. Answers to either challenge may undermine answers to the other.

One challenge comes from moral theories. The other challenge need not come from the instrumental theory. It can come from theories which are more plausible. The instrumental theory has two features. It is *time-relative*: appealing to the agent's aims at the time of acting. And it is *purely instrumental*: it discusses only means, taking the agent's aims as given. According to this theory, no aim is irrational. Any aim can provide reasons for acting.

Other theories are time-relative, but not purely instrumental. One example is *the deliberative theory*. This appeals, not to the agent's actual aims at the time of acting, but to the aims he would then have, if he knew the facts and was thinking clearly. According to this theory, if an aim would not survive such deliberation, it does not provide good reasons for acting. A deliberative theorist may add further claims. He may say that, even if they would survive this test, certain kinds of aim are intrinsically irrational.

Since it is time-relative, the deliberative theory may conflict with prudence. Someone may be thinking clearly, yet have aims which he knows to be against his own long-term self-interest. And we may deny that all such aims are thereby shown to be irrational. We may believe that there are many aims which are not less rational than the pursuit of self-interest. Some examples might be: benefiting others, discovering truths, or creating beauty. On a time-relative theory, what it is rational for me to do now depends on which among these many aims are the ones that I have now.

Those who believe in prudence must reject such theories. They must claim that reasons for acting cannot be time-relative. They might say: 'The force of a reason extends over time. Since I *will* have reason to promote my future aims, I have reason to do so *now*.' This claim is at the heart of prudence.

Many moral theorists make a second claim. They believe that certain reasons are not agent-relative. They might say: 'The force of a reason may extend, not only over time, but over different lives.

Thus, if *you* have reason to relieve your pain, this is a reason for me too. *I* have a reason to relieve *your* pain.'

Prudence makes the first claim, but rejects the second. It may be hard to defend both halves of this position. In reply to the moralist, the prudent man may ask, 'Why should *I* give weight to aims which are not *mine*?' But he can then be asked, 'Why should I give weight *now* to aims which are not mine *now*?' He may answer by appealing to the intertemporal Dilemmas, where time-relative theories are intertemporally self-defeating. But he can then be challenged with the interpersonal Dilemmas, where his own theory is collectively self-defeating. The moralist might say: 'The argument for prudence carries us beyond prudence. Properly understood, it is an argument for morality.'

This is a tempting line of thought. But something else should be discussed first. At the interpersonal level, the contrast is *not* between prudence and morality.

v

It will help to draw some more distinctions. We have been considering different theories about rationality. We can describe such theories by saying what they tell us to try to achieve. According to all these theories, we should try to act rationally. Call this our *formal* aim. We can ignore this here. By 'aims' we can mean *substantive* aims. We can describe moral theories in the same way. According to all these theories, we should try to act morally. Different moral theories give us different substantive aims.

We can next distinguish two ways in which a theory might be substantively self-defeating. Call this theory *T*, and the aims it gives us *our T-given aims*. Say that we *successfully follow T* when each succeeds in doing what, of the acts available, best achieves his T-given aims. Call T

> *indirectly self-defeating* when we will best achieve our T-given aims only if we do not try to do so,

and

> *directly self-defeating* when we will best achieve our T-given aims only if we do not successfully follow T.

Consider first a moral theory: Act Consequentialism, or AC. This gives to all one common aim: the best possible outcome. If we try to achieve this aim, we may often fail. Even when we succeed, the fact that we are disposed to try might make the outcome worse. AC might thus be indirectly self-defeating. What does this show? A consequentialist might say: 'It shows that AC should be only one part of our moral theory. It should be the part that covers successful acts. When we are certain to succeed, we should aim for the best possible outcome. Our wider theory should be this: we should have the aims and dispositions having which would make the outcome best. This wider theory would not be self-defeating. So the objection has been met.'

Could AC be *directly* self-defeating? Could it be true that we will make the outcome best only if we do not successfully follow AC? This is not possible. We successfully follow AC when each does what, of the acts available, makes the outcome best. This does not ensure that our acts jointly produce the best possible outcome. But, if they do, we must be successfully following AC. So AC cannot be directly self-defeating.

We can widen this conclusion. When any theory T gives to all agents *common* aims, it cannot be directly self-defeating. If we cause these common aims to be best achieved, we must be successfully following T. So it cannot be true that we will best achieve our T-given aims only if we do not successfully follow T.

What if T gives to *different* agents *different* aims? There may then be no way in which we can *best* achieve the T-given aims *of each*. So we must change our definition. And we need our earlier distinction. Call T

> *directly individually self-defeating* when it is certain that, if someone successfully follows T, he will thereby cause his T-given aims to be worse achieved,

and

> *directly collectively self-defeating* when it is certain that, if all rather than none successfully follow T, we will thereby cause the T-given aims of each to be worse achieved.

Suppose that T gives to you and me different aims. And suppose that each could either (1) promote his own T-given aim or (2) more effectively promote the other's. The outcomes would be these:

		You	
		do (1)	do (2)
I	do (1)	The T-given aim of each is third-best achieved	Mine is best achieved, yours worst
	do (2)	Mine is worst achieved, yours best	The T-given aim of each is second-best achieved

Suppose finally that neither's choice will affect the other's. It will then be true of each that, if he does (1) rather than (2), he will thereby cause his T-given aim to be better achieved. This is so whatever the other does. So we both successfully follow T only if we both do (1) rather than (2). Only then is each doing what, of the acts available, best achieves his T-given aim. But it is certain that if both rather than neither successfully follow T – if both do (1) rather than (2) – we will thereby cause the T-given aim of each to be worse achieved. Theory T is here directly collectively self-defeating.

If for 'T' we substitute 'prudence', we have just described a Prisoner's Dilemma. As this shows, nothing depends on the content of prudence. Such cases may occur when

(a) theory T is *agent-relative*, giving to different agents different aims,

(b) the achievement of each person's aim partly depends on what others do,

and

(c) what each does will not affect what these others do.

These conditions may hold if for 'T' we substitute 'common-sense morality'.

VI

Most of us believe that there are certain people to whom we have special obligations. These are the people to whom we stand in certain relations – such as our children, parents, pupils, patients, members of our own trade union, or those whom we represent. We believe we ought to help these people in certain ways. We should try to protect them from certain kinds of harm, and should try to give them certain kinds of benefit. Common-sense morality largely consists in such obligations.

Carrying out these obligations has priority over helping strangers. This priority is not absolute. We may not believe that I ought to save my child from some minor harm rather than saving a stranger's life. But I ought to protect my child rather than saving strangers from *somewhat* greater harms. My duty to my child is not overridden whenever I could do somewhat greater good elsewhere.

When I try to protect my child, what should my aim be? Should it simply be that he is not harmed? Or should it rather be that he is saved from harm by me? If you would have a better chance of saving him from harm, I would be wrong to insist that the attempt be made by me. This suggests that my aim should take the simpler form. Let us assume that this is so.

Consider *the Parent's Dilemma*. We cannot communicate. But each could either (1) save his own child from some harm or (2) save the other's child from another somewhat greater harm. The outcomes would be these:

| | | You | |
		do(1)	do (2)
I	do (1)	Both our children suffer the greater harm	Mine suffers neither harm, yours both
	do (2)	Mine suffers both, yours neither	Both suffer the lesser harm

Since we cannot communicate, neither's choice will affect the other's. If the aim of each should be that his child not be harmed, each should here do (1) rather than (2). Each would thus ensure that his child is harmed less. This is so whatever the other does. But if both do (1) rather than (2) both our children will be harmed more. This is *Case One*.

Consider next those benefits which I ought to try to give my child. What should my aim here be? Should I insist that it be *I* who benefits my child, if I knew that this would be worse for him? Some would answer, 'No'. But this answer may be too sweeping. It treats parental care as a mere means. We may think it more than that. We may agree that, with some kinds of benefit, my aim should take the simpler form. It should simply be that the outcome be better for my child. But there may be other kinds of benefit, which my child should receive *from me*.

With both kinds of benefit, we can face Parent's Dilemmas. Consider *Case Two*. We cannot communicate. But each could either (1) benefit his own child or (2) benefit the other's child somewhat more. The outcomes would be these:

		You	
		do (1)	do (2)
I	do (1)	Third-best both our children	Best for mine, worst for yours
	do (2)	Worst for mine, best for yours	Second-best for both

If my aim should here be that the outcome be better for my child, I should again do (1) rather than (2). And the same holds for you. But if both do (1) rather than (2) that will be worse for both our children. Compare *Case Three*. We cannot communicate. But I could either (1) enable myself to give my child some benefit or (2) enable you to benefit yours somewhat more. You have the same alternatives with respect to me. The outcomes would be these:

		You	
		do (1)	do (2)
I	do (1)	Each can give his child some benefit	I can benefit mine most, you can benefit yours least
	do (2)	I can benefit mine least, you can benefit yours most	Each can benefit his child more

If my aim should here be that I benefit my child, I should again do (1) rather than (2). And the same holds for you. But if both do (1) rather than (2) each can benefit his child less. Note the difference between these two examples. In Case Two we are concerned with what happens. The aim of each is that the outcome be better for his child. This is an aim that the other can directly cause to be achieved. In Case Three we are concerned with what we *do*. Since my aim is that *I* benefit my child, you cannot, on my behalf, do so. But you might enable me to do so. You might thus indirectly help my aim to be achieved.

Two-Person Parent's Dilemmas are unlikely to occur. But we often face many-person versions. It is often true that, if all rather than none give priority to our own children, that will either be worse for all our children, or will enable each to benefit his children less. Thus there are many outcomes which would benefit our children whether or not we help to produce them. It can be true of each parent that, if he does not help, that will be better for his own children. He can spend what he saves – whether in money, time, or energy – directly on them. But if none help, that will be worse for all our children than if all do. In another common case, each could either (1) add to his own earnings or (2) (by self-restraint) add more to the earnings of others. It will here be true of each that, if he does (1) rather than (2), he can benefit his children more. This is so whatever others do. But if all do (1) rather than (2) each can benefit his children less. These are only two of the ways in which such cases can occur. There are many others.

Similar remarks apply to all similar obligations – such as those to pupils, patients, clients or constituents. With all such obligations, there are countless many-person versions of my three examples. They are as common, and as varied, as prudential Each–We Dilemmas. As we have just seen, they will often have the same cause. Here is another way in which this might be true. Suppose that, in the original case, it is our lawyers who must choose. This is the *Prisoner's Lawyer's Dilemma*. If both lawyers give priority to their own clients, that will be worse for both clients than if neither does. Any prudential Dilemma may thus yield a moral Dilemma. If one group face the former, another may in consequence face the latter. This can be so if we believe that each member of the second group ought to give priority to some members of the first. The problem comes from the giving of priority. It makes no difference whether this is given to oneself or certain others.

My examples all involve harms or benefits. But the problem can arise for other parts of common-sense morality. It can arise whenever this morality gives to different people different duties. Suppose that each could either (1) carry out some of his own duties or (2) enable others to carry out more of theirs. If all rather than none give priority to our own duties, each may be able to carry out fewer. Deontologists can face Each–We Dilemmas. But I shall not discuss these here.

VII

What do such cases show? Common-sense morality is the moral theory most of us accept. According to this theory, there are certain things that each of us ought to try to achieve. These are what I call our 'moral aims'. We successfully follow this moral theory when each does what, of the acts available, best achieves his moral aims. In my cases it is certain that, if all rather than none successfully follow this theory, we will thereby cause the moral aims of each to be worse achieved. Our moral theory is here directly collectively self-defeating. Is this an objection?

Let us start with a smaller question. Could we revise our theory, so that it would not be self-defeating? If there is no such revision, ours may be the best possible theory. Since we believe our theory, we should ask what is the smallest such revision. So we should first identify the part of our theory which is self-defeating.

It will help to bring together two distinctions. One part of a moral theory may cover *successful acts*, on the assumption of *full compliance*. Call this part *ideal act theory*. This says what we should all try to do, simply on the assumptions that we all try, and all succeed. Call this *what we should all ideally do*.

Note next that, in my examples, what is true is this. If *all* of us *successfully* follow our moral theory, it will be self-defeating. It is our ideal act theory which is self-defeating. If we ought to revise our theory, this is the part that must certainly be revised.

The revision would be this. Call our theory *M*. In such cases we should all ideally do what will cause the M-given aims of each to be better achieved. Thus in my Parent's Dilemmas we should all ideally do (2) rather than (1). That will make the outcome better for all our children, and will enable each to benefit his children more.

Call this revision *R*. Note first that R applies only to those cases where M is self-defeating. If we decide to adopt R, we will need to consider how such cases can be recognized. I believe that they are very common. But I have no space to show this here.

Note next that R is restricted to our ideal act theory. It does not say what we ought to do when there are some others who do not follow R. Nor does it say what our aims should be when our attempts may fail. Nor does it say what dispositions we should have. Since these are the questions with most practical importance, it may seem that adopting R would make little difference. But this is not likely. If we revise this part of our theory, we shall probably revise the rest. Take the case of a public good which would benefit our children. One such good is the conservation of a scarce resource. Suppose that we are fishermen, trying to feed our children. We are faced with declining stocks. It is true of each that, if he does not restrict his catch, that will be better for his own children. This is so whatever others do. But if none restrict their catches that will be worse for all our children than if all do. According to R, we should all ideally restrict our catches. If some fail to do so, R ceases to apply. But it would be natural to make this further claim: each should restrict his catch provided that enough others do so too. We would need to decide what counts as enough. But, whatever we decide, adopting R would have made a difference. Failure to restrict our catches would now be at most a defensive second-best. Consider next the relation between acts and dispositions. Suppose that each could either (1) save his own child from some lesser harm or (2) save another's child from some greater harm. According to R, we should all ideally do (2). Should we be *disposed* to do (2)? If the lesser harms would themselves be great, such a disposition might be incompatible with love for our own children. This may lead us to decide that we should remain disposed to do (1). This would mean that, in such cases, our children would be harmed more; but, if we are to love them, this is the price they must pay. Such remarks cannot be made whenever M is self-defeating. It would be possible to love one's children and contribute to most public goods. Nor could such remarks cover all similar obligations – such as those to pupils, patients, clients or constituents. It is therefore likely that, if we adopt R, we will be led to change our view about some dispositions.

We can now return to the main question. Ought we to adopt R? Is it an objection to our moral theory that, in certain cases, it is self-defeating? If it is, R is the obvious remedy. R revises M only where M is self-defeating. And the only difference is that R is not.

Remember first that, in these cases, M is *directly* self-defeating. The problem is not that, in our attempts to follow M, we are somehow failing. That might be no objection. The problem is that we all *successfully* follow M. Each succeeds in doing what, of the acts available, best achieves his M-given aims. This is what makes M self-defeating. And this does seem an objection. If there is any assumption on which a moral theory should *not* be self-defeating, it is surely the assumption that it is universally successful followed.

Remember next that by 'aims' I mean substantive aims. I have ignored our formal aim: the avoidance of wrongdoing. This may seem to remove the objection. Take those cases where, if we follow M, either the outcome will be worse for all our children, or each can benefit his children less. We might say: 'These results are, of course, unfortunate. But how could we avoid them? Only by failing to give priority to our own children. That would be wrong. So these cases cast no doubt on our moral theory. Even to achieve our other moral aims, we should never act wrongly.'

These remarks are confused. It is true that, in these cases, M is not formally self-defeating. If we follow M, we are not doing what we believe to be wrong. On the contrary we think it wrong *not* to follow M. But M is substantively self-defeating. Unless we all do what we now think wrong, we will cause our M-given aims to be worse achieved. The question is: Might this show that we are mistaken? Ought we perhaps to do what we *now think* wrong? We cannot answer, 'No – we should never act wrongly.' If we are mistaken, we would *not* be acting wrongly. Nor can we simply say, 'But, even in these cases, we *ought* to give priority to our own children.' This just assumes that we are not mistaken. To defend our theory, we must claim more than this. We must claim that it is no objection to our theory that, in such cases, it is substantively self-defeating.

This would be no objection if it simply did not matter whether our M-given aims will be achieved. But this does matter. The sense in which it matters may be unclear. If we have not acted wrongly, it may not matter morally. But it matters in a way which has moral implications. Why should we try to achieve our M-given aims? Part of the reason is that, in this other sense, their achievement matters.

Someone might say: 'You call M *self*-defeating. So your objection must appeal *to* M. You should not appeal to some rival theory. This is what you have now done. When you claim that it matters whether our M-given aims will be achieved, you are merely claiming that, if they are not, the outcome would be worse. This assumes consequentialism. So you beg the question.'

This is not so. When our aims are held in common, call them *agent-neutral*. Other aims are agent-relative. Any aim may be concerned either with what happens or with what is done. So there are four kinds of aim. Here are some examples:

| | Concerned with ||
	what happens	what is done
agent-neutral	that children do not starve	that children are cared for by their own parents
agent-relative	that my children do not starve	that I care for my children

When I claim that it matters whether our M-given aims will be achieved, I am not assuming consequentialism. Some of these aims are concerned with what we *do*. Thus parental care may not be for us a mere means. More important, I am not assuming agent-neutralism. Since our moral theory is, for the most part, agent-relative, this would beg the question. But it need not be begged.

There are here two points. First, I am not assuming that what matters is the achievement of *M-given aims*. Suppose that I could either (1) promote my own M-given aims or (2) more effectively promote yours. According to M, I should here do (1) rather than (2). I would thereby cause M-given aims to be, on the whole, worse achieved. But this does not make M self-defeating. I would cause *my* M-given aims to be *better* achieved. In my examples the point is not that, if we all do (1) rather than (2), we cause M-given aims to be worse achieved. The point is that we cause *each of our own* M-given aims to be worse achieved. We do worse not just in agent-neutral but in agent-relative terms.

The second point is that this can matter in an agent-relative way. It will help to remember prudence, or P. In Prisoner's Dilemmas, P is directly self-defeating. If all rather than none successfully follow P, we will thereby cause the P-given aim of each to be worse achieved. We will make the outcome worse for everyone. If we believe in prudence, will we think this matters? Or does it only matter whether each achieves his formal aim: the avoidance of irrationality? The answer is clear. According to prudence, acting rationally is a mere means. All that matters is the achievement of our substantive P-given aims. What concerns us here is this. The achievement of these aims matters in an agent-relative way. To think it an objection that our prudence is self-defeating, we need not appeal to its agent-neutral form: Utilitarianism. Prudence is not a moral theory. But the comparison shows that, in discussing common-sense morality, we need not beg the question. If it matters whether our M-given aims will be achieved, this, too, can matter in an agent-relative way.

Does this matter? Note that I am not asking whether this is all that matters. I am not suggesting that the achievement of our formal aim – the avoidance of wrongdoing – is a mere means. Though assumed by consequentialists, this is not what most of us believe. We may even think that the achievement of our formal aim always matters most. But this is here irrelevant. We are asking whether it casts doubt on M that it is substantively self-defeating. Might this show that, in such cases, M is incorrect? It may be true that what matters most is that we avoid wrongdoing. But this truth cannot show M to be correct. It cannot help us to decide what *is* wrong.

Can we claim that our formal aim is all that matters? If that were so, my examples would show nothing. We could say, 'To be substantively self-defeating is, in the case of common-sense morality, *not* to be self-defeating.' Can we defend our moral theory in this way? In the case of some M-given aims, perhaps we can. Consider trivial promises. We might believe both that we should try to keep such promises, and that it would not matter if, through no fault of ours, we failed. But we do not have such beliefs about all of our M-given aims. If our children suffer harm, or we can benefit them less, this matters.

Remember finally that, in my examples, M is collectively *but not individually* self-defeating. Could this provide a defence?

This is the central question I have raised. It is because M is individually successful that, at the collective level, it is here *directly* self-defeating. Why is it true that, if we all do (1) rather than (2), we *successfully* follow M? Because *each* is doing what, of the acts available, *best* achieves his M-given aims. Is it perhaps no objection that *we* thereby cause the M-given aims of each to be *worse* achieved?

It will again help to remember prudence. In Prisoner's Dilemmas, prudence is collectively self-defeating. If we were choosing a collective code, something that we will all follow, prudence would here tell us to reject itself. It would be prudent to vote against prudence. But those who believe in prudence may think this irrelevant. They can say: 'Prudence does not claim to be a collective code. To be collectively self-defeating is, in the case of prudence, *not* to be self-defeating.'

Can we defend our moral theory in this way? This depends on our view about the nature of morality. On most views, the answer is 'No'. But I must here leave this question open.[4]

NOTES

1 'He' means 'he or she' throughout.
2 Or *expected* benefits (possible benefits multiplied by the chances that his act will produce them). In many of my later claims, 'benefit' could mean 'expected benefit'.
3 I follow J. Glover, 'It makes no difference whether or not I do it', *Proceedings of the Aristotelian Society, Suppl.* 49 (1975). A similar argument could show that, when our acts may benefit or harm large numbers of people, we should not ignore very tiny chances.

4 Many other questions need to be discussed. I discuss some of these, and expand this lecture, in my book *Reasons and Persons* (Oxford University Press, 1984). In preparing this lecture I have been greatly helped by R. M. Adams, R. M. Dworkin, J. L., Mackie, D. Regan and J. J. Thomson; also by B. Barry, S. Blackburn, D. Braybrooke, P. Bricker, L. J. Cohen, N. E. Davis, D. Dennett, M. G. J. Evans, P. Foot, J. P. Griffin, G. Harman, M. Hollis, S. Kagan, R. Lindley, P. Maddy, T. Nagel, R. Nozick, C. Peacocke, J. Raz, J. Sartorelli, T. Scanlon, F. Schick, A. K. Sen, J. H. Sobel, H. Steiner and L. Temkin. My sections III and IV owe a great deal to T. Nagel, *The Possibility of Altruism* (Oxford, 1970). My section V owes much to D. Regan, *Utilitarianism and Cooperation* (Oxford, 1980), D. Lyons, *Forms and Limits of Utilitarianism* (Oxford, 1965), and R. M. Adams, 'Motive Utilitarianism', *Journal of Philosophy*, 12 August 1976. My section II owes much to E. Ullman-Margalit, *The Emergence of Norms* (Oxford, 1977), D. Braybrooke, 'The insoluble problem of the social contract', *Dialogue*, March 1976, and F. Miller and R. Sartorius, 'Population policy and public goods', *Philosophy and Public Affairs*, Winter 1979. The other publications to which I owe most are: K. Baier, 'Rationality and morality', *Erkenntnis*, 1977; B. Barry, *Sociologists, Economists and Democracy* (London, 1970); J. M. Buchanan, *The Demand and Supply of Public Goods* (Chicago, 1969); D. Gauthier, 'Morality and advantage', *The Philosophical Review*, 1967, and 'Reason and maximization', *Canadian Journal of Philosophy*, March 1975; G. Hardin, 'The tragedy of the commons', *Science*, 13 December 1968; R. M. Hare, 'Ethical theory and utilitarianism', in H. D. Lewis (ed.), *Contemporary British Philosophy* (London, 1976); M. Olson Jr., *The Logic of Collective Action* (Cambridge, Mass., 1965); A. Rapoport, *Fights, Games and Debates* (Ann Arbor, 1960); T. Schelling, 'Hockey helmets, concealed weapons, and daylight saving', *The Journal of Conflict Resolution*, September 1973; A. K. Sen, 'Choice, Orderings, and Morality', in S. Körner (ed.), *Practical Reason* (New Haven, 1974); J. H. Sobel, 'The need for coercion', in J. Pennock and H. Chapman (eds), *Coercion* (Chicago, 1972); and J. Watkin, 'Imperfect rationality', in R. Borger and F. Cioffi (eds), *Explanation in the Behavioural Sciences* (Cambridge, 1970).

2

Behaviour and the Concept of Preference

AMARTYA SEN

I

Thirty-five years have passed since Paul Samuelson published in the house journal of the London School of Economics his pioneering contribution to the theory of 'revealed preference'.[1] The term was perhaps not altogether a fortunate one. Revelation conveys something rather dramatic, and the biblical association induced the late Sir Dennis Robertson to wonder whether 'to some latter-day saint, in some new Patmos off the coast of Massachusetts, the final solution to all these mysteries had been revealed in a new apocalypse'.[2] While the appropriateness of the terminology may be debatable, the approach of revealed preference has gradually taken hold of choice theory in general and of demand theory in particular.

My intention in this lecture is to examine the philosophy behind the approach of revealed preference and to raise some queries about its use, and then to go on to discuss the implications of these issues for normative economics. The crux of the question lies in the interpretation of underlying preference from observations of behaviour.

'The individual guinea-pig', wrote Paul Samuelson, 'by his market behaviour, reveals his preference pattern – if there is such a consistent pattern.'[3] If a collection of goods y could have been bought by a certain individual within his budget when he in fact was observed to buy another collection x, it is to be presumed that he has revealed a preference for x over y. The outside observer notices that this person *chose* x when y was available and infers that he *preferred* x to y. From the point of view of introspection of the person in question, the process runs from his preference to his choice, but from the point of view of the scientific observer the

This essay was first published in *Economica*, 40 (August 1973), 241–59.

arrow runs in the opposite direction: choices are observed first and preferences are then presumed from these observations.

The consistency condition that Samuelson based his theory on, which has come to be known as the Weak Axiom of Revealed Preference, says that if a person reveals a preference – in the sense just defined – for x over y, then he must not also reveal a preference for y over x. That is, if he chooses x when y is available, then he will not choose y in a situation in which x is also obtainable. Armed with this innocuous-looking axiom, Samuelson proceeded to obtain analytically the standard results of the theory of consumer's behaviour with remarkable economy.[4] It also opened up the way for empirical studies of preferences based on observed market behaviour.[5]

The approach of revealed preference need not be confined to market choices only, and indeed it has been used in studying preferences revealed by non-market behaviour such as government decisions, choices of public bodies and political acts like voting. The exact mathematical structure of the problem differs substantially from case to case, and the formulation in the context of preferences revealed by political or bureaucratic decisions will differ from that in the context of consumer's choices. But there are common methodological elements, and I shall be concerned with them in this lecture.

II

Before I proceed to examine the status of the preference revealed by choice, I would like to comment on one very elementary issue that seems to me to have certainly clouded the interpretation of revealed preference theory. This concerns the somewhat surprising claim that has been frequently made that the theory of revealed preference 'frees' demand theory from the concept of preference and *a fortiori* from the concept of utility on which traditional demand theory was based.

In his pioneering paper, Samuelson argued that his object was 'to develop the theory of consumer's behaviour freed from any vestigial traces of the utility concept'.[6] The exact content of the statement was not altogether clear, and in pushing forward the revealed preference approach in a classic paper, Little argued that one of his main aims was to demonstrate 'that a theory of consumer's demand can be based solely on consistent behaviour',[7] adding that 'the new formulation is scientifically more respectable [since] if an individual's behaviour is consistent, then it must be possible to explain that behaviour without reference to anything other than behaviour.'[8] In a similar vein, Hicks stated that 'the econometric theory of demand does study human beings, but only as entities having certain patterns of market behaviour; it makes no claim, no pretence, to be able to see inside their heads.'[9]

On this interpretation the use of the word 'preference' in revealed preference would appear to represent an elaborate pun. In saying that x is revealed preferred to y, it would not be asserted that x is preferred to y in the usual sense of the word 'preferred'. A redefinition of the expression 'preference' is, of course, possible, but it is then legitimate to ask what does 'consistency' of behaviour stand for and on what basis are the required consistency conditions chosen. The alleged inconsistency between (1) choosing x when y is available and (2) choosing y when x is available, would seem to have something to do with the surmise about the person's preference underlying his choices.

Preferring x to y is inconsistent with preferring y to x, but if it is asserted that choice has nothing to do with preference, then choosing x rather than y in one case and y rather than x in another need not necessarily be at all inconsistent. What makes them look inconsistent is precisely the peep into the head of the consumer, the avoidance of which is alleged to be the aim of the revealed preference approach.

It could, however, be argued that what was at issue was not really whether the axiom of revealed preference represented a requirement of consistency, but whether as a hypothesis it was empirically verified. This line would not take one very far either. Consider the simplest situation of one consumer facing two divisible commodities – the case that figures on blackboards in every Economics Department in the world, and would have, I imagine, adorned the magnificent glass doors of the St Clement's Building but for the greater deference shown by our architects to the even more classic demand-and-supply intersection. Even in this rudimentary case, the set of possible choice situations for any individual is infinite – indeed uncountable. To check whether the Weak Axiom holds for the entire field of all market choices, we have to observe the person's choices under infinitely many price–income configurations. In contrast, the number of actual choices that can be studied is extremely limited. Not only is the ratio of observations to potential choices equal to zero, but moreover the absolute number of cases investigated is also fairly small. Comparisons have to be made within a fairly short time to avoid taste change, but the time elapsed must also be sufficiently long so that the mutton purchased last time is not still in the larder, making the choices non-comparable. With durable goods the problem is quite vicious. The actual number of tests carried out has, not surprisingly, been very small. Faith in the axioms of revealed preference arises, therefore, not from empirical verification, but from the intuitive reasonableness of these axioms interpreted precisely in terms of preference. In fact, the concept of taste change is itself a preference-based notion, and the whole framework of revealed preference analysis of behaviour is steeped with implicit ideas about preference and psychology.

I would, therefore, argue that the claim of explaining 'behaviour without reference to anything other than behaviour'[10] is pure rhetoric, and if the theory of revealed preference makes sense it does so not because no psychological assumptions are used but because the psychological assumptions used are sensibly chosen. The use of the word preference in revealed preference must indeed be taken to be more than a pun.

Indeed, the psychological assumptions involved have been discussed explicitly or by implication in all the major contributions to revealed preference theory. There have also been discussions about 'the transition to welfare economics' from revealed preference theory, and even Ian Little has argued that among the possible routes for this transition is the view 'that a person is, on the whole, likely to be happier the more he is able to have what he would choose.'[11] Samuelson had in any case put less emphasis on sticking exclusively to observed behaviour, and his statement, which I quoted earlier, that 'the individual guinea-pig, by his market behaviour, reveals his preference pattern,'[12] makes the fundamental assumption of revealed preference theory explicit. The rationale of the revealed preference approach lies in the assumption of revelation and not in doing away with the notion of underlying preferences, despite occasional noises to the contrary. So we would be justified in examining the philosophical foundations of the revealed preference approach precisely in terms of the assumptions of revelation. This is what I shall now go on to do.

III

I shall take up a relatively minor question first. The Weak Axiom of Revealed Preference is a condition of consistency of two choices only. If x is revealed preferred to y, then y should not be revealed preferred to x. Perhaps because of this concentration on the consistency between any *two* choices and no more, the Weak Axiom has appeared to many to be a condition of what Hicks calls 'two-term consistency'. And it has appeared as if the other well-known requirement of consistency, viz., transitivity, lay outside its scope. Transitivity is a simple condition to state: if x is regarded as at least as good as y, and y as at least as good as z, then x should be regarded as at least as good as z. In the case of preference, it implies that if x is preferred to y and y preferred to z, then it should also be the case that x is preferred to z. Since this condition involves at least three choices and since the Weak Axiom involves a requirement of consistency only over *pairs* of choices, it might look as if the Weak Axiom could not possibly imply transitivity. This has indeed been taken to be so in much of the literature on the subject, and additional conditions for transitivity have been sought. In a very limited sense this point about transitivity is indeed correct. But it can be shown that the limited sense in which this is true ignores precisely the methodological point concerning the *interpretation* of revealed preference theory which I discussed a few minutes ago.

The philosophical issue involved is, therefore, worth discussing in the light of the logical problems raised by revealed preference theory. Consider a case in which we find a consumer choosing x and rejecting y, and another in which he is found to choose y and reject z. So he has revealed a preference for x over y and also for y over z. Of course, even under the assumption of transitivity of the underlying preference, the person is not obliged to *reveal* a preference for x over z since such a choice may not in fact arise in his uneventful life. But suppose we could offer this person choices over *any* combination of alternatives and could thus ensure that he had to choose between x and z. Then clearly it would be required by transitivity that he must choose x and reject z. Is this guaranteed by the Weak Axiom? The answer is: clearly yes.

To understand why this is so, imagine the contrary and suppose that he did choose z instead of x. We could then offer him the choice over the set of three alternatives, x, y and z. What could this man now choose? If he chose x, which would involve rejecting z, this would violate the Weak Axiom since he had earlier rejected x and chosen z. If he chose y, which would imply that he would be rejecting x, this would also violate the Weak Axiom since he had rejected y and chosen x earlier. Finally, if he chose z, which would imply a rejection of y, he would again be running counter to the Weak Axiom since earlier he had chosen y rejecting z. So no matter what he chose out of this set of three alternatives (x, y, z), he must violate the Weak Axiom. He is in this impasse only because he chose z and rejected x after having revealed a preference for x over y and for y over z. To be able to choose in a manner consistent with the Weak Axiom of Revealed Preference, he would have to choose *x* faced with a choice between the two.

Further, if he chose *both* *x* and *z* in a choice between the two, there must be inconsistency also. In a choice over (*x*, *y*, *z*), he could not choose *z* since he had chosen *y* rejecting *z* in a choice between the two. For the same reason he could not choose *y* since he had revealed a preference for *x* over *y*. So he would have to choose only *x* in the choice over *x*, *y*, *z*, rejecting *z*. But then he could not choose *z* in the presence of *x* in the choice over that pair in view of the Weak Axiom of Revealed Preference and this is a contradiction.

The Weak Axiom not only guarantees two-term consistency, it also prevents the violation of transitivity. The fact that the Axiom applies to two choices at a time does not rule out its repeated use to get the result of transitivity.

Why is it then that people have looked for stronger conditions than the Weak Axiom to get transitivity or similar properties? For example, Houthakker has proposed a condition, the so-called Strong Axiom of Revealed Preference, which demands more than the Weak Axiom of Samuelson to get us towards transitivity.[13] Similar conditions have been proposed by Ville, von Neumann and Morgenstern, and others.[14] Hicks, who noted that the Weak Axiom did make things fine for transitivity in a world of two goods only, proceeded to argue that 'three-term inconsistency is only ruled out in the two-goods case by the special properties of that case.'[15] But the simple argument we examined a few minutes ago assumed nothing about there being only two goods. What explains this mystery?

The clue lies in the fact that in the revealed preference literature it has been customary to assume, usually implicitly, that the Weak Axiom holds only for those choices that can be observed in the market and not necessarily for other choices.[16] And given divisible commodities, the market can never offer the man under observation the choice, say, between *x*, *y* and *z* only. If these three baskets of goods were available then so should be an infinite number of other baskets that would cost no more at given market prices. This is how in the theory of consumer's behaviour, the man can get away with satisfying the Weak Axiom over all the cases in which his behaviour can be observed in the market and nevertheless harbour an intransitive preference relation.

The moment this is recognized the question arises: why this distinction between those choices in which the person's behaviour can be observed in the market and other choices in which it cannot be? Presumably, the argument lies in the fact that if market choices are the only observable choices, then the Weak Axiom can be verified only for those choices and not for others that cannot be observed in the market. But as we saw earlier, the Weak Axiom cannot be verified anyway even for market choices and the case for its use lies not in verification but in its intuitive plausibility given the preference-based interpretation of choice. And there is no reason whatsoever to expect that the Weak Axiom is more plausible for 'budget triangles' thrown up by market choice situations than for other choices that cannot be observed in the market; at any rate I have not seen any argument that has been put forward justifying such a dichotomy. The distinction lies only in the verification question and that, as we have seen, is really a red herring.

Treated as an *axiom* in the light of which consumer's choices are analysed and interpreted, rather than as a *hypothesis* which is up for verification, there is no case for restricting the scope of the Weak Axiom arbitrarily to budget sets only, and in the absence of this invidious distinction, transitivity follows directly from the Weak Axiom of Revealed Preference. If a consumer has chosen x rejecting y in one case, chosen y rejecting z in another, and chosen z rejecting x in a third case, then he has not only violated transitivity, he must violate the Weak Axiom of Revealed Preference as well. No matter what he chooses given the choice over x, y and z, he must run counter to the Weak Axiom, as demonstrated. The fact that he cannot be observed in a choice over (x, y, z) makes no real difference since *no matter what he chooses* he must logically violate the Weak Axiom.

In this sense, an observed violation of the Strong Axiom will logically imply a violation of the Weak Axiom as well. A number of other distinct axioms that have been proposed in the literature can also be shown to be equivalent once the arbitrary restrictions are removed.[17] (If the domain of the choice function includes all pairs and triples, then these apparently different axioms turn out to be logically equivalent.)

IV

I would now like to turn to the fundamental assumption of the revealed preference approach, viz., that people do reveal their underlying preferences through their actual choices. Is this a reasonable presumption? If a person chose x when y was available, it would seem reasonable to argue that he did not really regard y to be better than x. There is, of course, the problem that a person's choices may not be made after much thinking or after systematic comparisons of alternatives. I am inclined to believe that the chair on which you are currently sitting in this room was not chosen entirely thoughtlessly, but I am not totally persuaded that you in fact did choose the particular chair you have chosen through a careful calculation of the pros and cons of sitting in each possible chair that was vacant when you came in. Even some important decisions in life seem to be taken on the basis of incomplete thinking about the possible courses of action, and the hypothesis of revealed preference, as psychological generalization, may not be altogether convincing. These questions are well known as also are the difficulties arising from open or hidden persuasion involved in advertisements and propaganda, which frequently mess up not only one's attitude towards the alternatives available but also towards the act of choice itself. These problems are important, but I shall not go into them any further, partly because they have been much discussed elsewhere, but also because I have no competence whatever to throw light on the psychological issues underlying these problems. Instead I shall try to discuss one and a half other issues which seem to me to be also important. The half issue should perhaps come first.

The logical property of connectedness (or completeness as it is sometimes called) of binary relations is an important characteristic to examine in the context of evaluating the fundamental assumption of revealed preference. Connectedness of preference requires that between any two alternatives x and y, the person in question either prefers x to y, or prefers y to x, or is indifferent between x and y. The approach of revealed preference makes considerable use of connectedness. If a person chooses x rather than y, it is presumed that he regards x to be at least as good as y, and not that maybe he has no clue about what to choose and has chosen x because he had to choose something.

The point can be illustrated with a variation of the classic story of Buridan's ass. This ass, as we all know, could not make up its mind between two haystacks; it liked both very much but could not decide which one was better. Being unable to choose, this dithering animal died ultimately of starvation. The dilemma of the ass is easy to understand, but it is possible that the animal would have agreed that it would have been better off by choosing either of the haystacks rather than nothing at all. Not choosing anything is also a choice, and in this case this really meant the choice of starvation. On the other hand, had it chosen either of the haystacks, it would have been presumed that the ass regarded that haystack to be at least as good as the other, which in this version of the story was not

the case. The ass was in a real dilemma *vis-à-vis* the revealed
preference approach.

The traditional interpretation of the story is that the ass was
indifferent between the two haystacks. That indifference may be a
cause for dithering has often been stated. For example, Ian Little
prefaced his closely reasoned attack on the concept of indifference
by posing the rather thoughtful question: 'How long must a person
dither before he is pronounced indifferent?'[18] But in fact there is
hardly any real cause for dithering if one is *really* indifferent, since
the loss from choosing one alternative rather than another is
exactly zero. The person can choose either alternative and regret
nothing in either case. This, however, is not the case if the preference relation is unconnected over this pair, i.e. if the chooser can
neither say that he prefers x to y, nor y to x, nor that he is
indifferent between the two.

If Buridan's ass was indifferent, choosing either haystack would
have been quite legitimate and would not have misled the observer
armed with revealed preference theory provided the observer chose
a version of the theory that permitted indifference.[19] The real
dilemma would arise if the ass had an unconnected preference.
Choosing either haystack would have appeared to reveal a view
that that haystack was no worse than the other, but this view the
ass was unable to subscribe to since it could not decide what its
preference should be. By choosing either haystack it would have
given a wrong signal to the revealed preference theorist since this
would have implied that he regarded the chosen haystack to be at
least as good as the other. There is very little doubt that Buridan's
ass died for the cause of revealed preference, though – alas – he was
not entirely successful since non-choice leading to starvation would
have looked like the chosen alternative, at any rate from the point
of view of mechanical use of the fundamental assumption of
revealed preference. There was no way the ass could have rescued
that assumption given its unconnected preference.

But what if all these problems are ruled out? That is, if the person
has a connected preference relation, takes his decisions deliberately
after considering all alternatives, and is not swayed to and fro by
the lure of advertisements. Obviously none of the problems discussed in the last few minutes will then arise. Will the life of the
revealed preference theorist, then, be uncomplicated? I fear that it
will not, and there is, it seems to me, a difficulty in some sense more
fundamental than all the ones discussed so far. This problem I
would like to go into now.

The difficulty is seen most easily in terms of a well-known game, viz., 'the Prisoner's Dilemma[20],' which has cropped up frequently in economics in other contexts. The story goes something like this. Two prisoners are known to be guilty of a very serious crime, but there is not enough evidence to convict them. There is, however, sufficient evidence to convict them of a minor crime. The District Attorney – it is an American story – separates the two and tells each that they will be given the option to confess if they wish to. If both of them do confess, they will be convicted of the major crime on each other's evidence, but in view of the good behaviour shown in squealing, the District Attorney will ask for a penalty of 10 years each rather than the full penalty of 20 years. If neither confesses, each will be convicted only of the minor crime and get 2 years. If one confesses and the other does not, then the one who does confess will go free and the other will go to prison for 20 years.

What should the prisoners do? It is not doubted by the game theorist that any self-respecting prisoner will begin by drawing a pay-off matrix to facilitate rational choice. The table of pay-offs will look something like that shown below. (The first number in each slot is the sentence of prisoner 1 and the second of prisoner 2. The numbers are negative to remind us that the prisoners dislike going to prison.)

		Prisoner 2	
		Confess	Not Confess
Prisoner 1	Confess	$-10, -10$	$0-, -20$
	Not Confess	$-20, \quad 0$	$-2, \quad -2$

Each prisoner sees that it is definitely in his interest to confess no matter what the other does. If the other confesses, then by confessing himself this prisoner reduces his own sentence from twenty years to ten. If the other does not confess, then by confessing he himself goes free rather than getting a two year sentence. So each prisoner feels that no matter what the other does it is always better for him to confess. So both of them do confess guided by rational self-interest, and each goes to prison for ten years. If, however, neither had confessed, both would have been in prison only for two years each. Rational choice would seem to cost each person eight additional years in prison.

This game has been much discussed in the literature of resource allocation as an illustration of the failure of individualistic decision taking and as a justification of a collective contract. It has an obvious bearing on the theory of optimum savings, on taxation theory, on allocation decisions involving externalities and public goods, and on a number of related issues.[21] Through a collective contract the group of individuals can do better than they will do under individualistic action. The distinction has something to do with Rousseau's contrast between 'the general will' and 'the will of all,' and with the necessity of a 'social contract' to achieve what the general will wills.[22] In the particular story of the Prisoner's Dilemma, the general will can be interpreted to be the rule of non-confession which is beneficial for both, and the vehicle for achieving this will be a mutual non-confession treaty. If such a social contract can be accepted and enforced, both prisoners will be better off. So far so good. But what if no such contract can be arrived at? Are the prisoners doomed to suffer a heavy penalty constrained by their own rational choice calculus?

It is possible to argue that this is precisely the type of situation in which moral rules of behaviour have traditionally played an important part. Situations of the type of the Prisoner's Dilemma occur in many ways in our lives and some of the traditional rules of good behaviour take the form of demanding suspension of calculations geared to individual rationality. In different periods of history in different social situations in response to different types of problems particular rules of behaviour have been proposed which have in common the analytical property of trying to generate the results of a social contract without there being any such formal contract. Behavioural rules to handle problems of interdependence, arising in specific social and economic formations, can be seen in such diverse approaches as Christian or Buddhist ethics on the one hand and the philosophy of the Chinese 'cultural revolution' on the other. I shall have a bit more to say on this presently, but the implication of all this for the theory of revealed preference should be first spelt out.

Suppose each prisoner in the dilemma acts not on the basis of the rational calculations outlined earlier but proceeds to follow the dictum of not letting the other person down irrespective of the consequences for himself. Then neither person will confess and they will both get off lightly. Now, consider the job of the observer trying to guess the preferences that have been revealed by the choice of non-confession. There is, of course, an element of uncertainty in the exercise of choice that the prisoners face, for neither of them knows what the other is up to. It should be clear, however, that if there is anything in the assumption of revealed preference as it stands, it must be presumed that each prisoner prefers at least one of the possible outcomes resulting from his non-confession to what would have happened had he confessed, given other things. That is, either he prefers the consequence of his not confessing given the other prisoner's non-confession, or the consequence of his not confessing given the other prisoner's confession. But in fact neither happens to be true. The prisoner does not prefer to go to prison for twenty years rather than for ten; nor does he prefer a sentence of two years to being free. His choice has not revealed his preference in the manner postulated.

At this stage a couple of warnings may be worth stating since the point that is being made can be easily misunderstood. The prisoners' non-confession will be quite easy to put within the framework of revealed preference if it were the case that they had so much concern for the sufferings of each other that they would choose non-confession on grounds of joint welfare of the two. There is indeed nothing extraordinary in assuming that a person may prefer that both should go to prison for two years each rather than that the other should suffer twenty years while he himself goes free. The problem arises precisely because that is *not* being assumed. Each is assumed to be self-centred and interested basically only in his own prison term, and the choice of non-confession follows *not* from calculations based on this welfare function, but from following a moral code of behaviour suspending the rational calculus. The preference is no different in this case from that in the earlier example, but behaviour is. And it is this difference that is inimical to the revealed preference approach to the study of human behaviour.

A second point to note is that the entire problem under discussion can be easily translated into the case in which each person does worry about the other's welfare as well and is not concerned only with his own welfare. The numbers in the pay-off matrix can be interpreted simply as welfare indices of the two persons and each person's welfare index can incorporate concern for the other. The prisoner's dilemma type of problem can arise even where there is concern for each other.

Third, no special importance should be attached to the specific story of the prisoners in terms of which this particular analytical problem is expounded. The interest in the Prisoner's Dilemma lies not in the fiction which gives the problem its colour, but in the existence of a strictly dominant strategy for each person which together produce a strictly inferior outcome for all. One feature of the Prisoner's Dilemma is, in fact, particularly misleading. This concerns the complete symmetry of the positions of the two players. Some suggestions for the resolution of the dilemma within the framework of rational choice make considerable use of this particular feature,[23] but even with asymmetrical prison sentences, as long as the orderings of the penalties are the same we can get exactly the same dilemma and the same implications for revealed preference theory.

V

The concentration on the contractual side of the Prisoner's Dilemma has perhaps tended to obscure the important implications of this type of situation for the relation between choice and preference. If the prisoners agree to a non-confession treaty and if that treaty can be enforced the prisoners will indeed get off the hook, but such a contract may be difficult to devise and conceivably impossible to enforce under certain circumstances. When it comes to the use of this type of model in economics in interpreting problems of resource allocation, one can distinguish between those situations in which a contract may be easy to operate and those cases in which it will be far from easy to do so.

I am concerned here with cases in which a contractual solution is not possible. This corresponds to the case in which the prisoners are not bound by any contract but nevertheless decide not to confess. The essence of the problem is that if both prisoners behave *as if* they are maximizing a different welfare function from the one that they actually have, they will both end up being better off even in terms of their *actual* welfare function. To take the extreme case, if both prisoners try to maximize the welfare of the other, neither will confess in the case outlined since non-confession will be a superior strategy no matter what is assumed about the other person's action. The result of each trying to maximize the welfare of the other will, therefore, lead to a better situation for each in terms of his own welfare as well. It is not necessary that the prisoners in fact have this much concern – or indeed any concern – for the other, but if they behave *as if* they have this concern, they will end up being better off in terms of their real preference. This is where the revealed preference approach goes off the rails altogether. The behaviour pattern that will make each better off in terms of their real preferences is not at all the behaviour pattern that will *reveal* those real preferences. Choices that reveal individual preferences may be quite inefficient for achieving welfare of the group.

I would argue that the philosophy of the revealed preference approach essentially underestimates the fact that man is a social animal and his choices are not rigidly bound to his own preferences only. I do not find it difficult to believe that birds and bees and dogs and cats do reveal their preferences by their choice; it is with human beings that the proposition is not particularly persuasive. An act of choice for this social animal is, in a fundamental sense, always a social act. He may be only dimly aware of the immense problems of interdependence that characterize a society, of which the problem under discussion is only one. But his behaviour is something more than a mere translation of his personal preferences.

VI

In economic analysis individual preferences seem to enter in two different roles: preferences come in as determinants of behaviour and they also come in as the basis of welfare judgements. For example, in the theory of general equilibrium the behaviour of individuals is assumed to be determined by their respective preference orderings, and problems of existence, uniqueness and stability of an equilibrium are studied in the context of such a framework. At the same time, the optimality of an equilibrium, i.e., whether the market can lead to a position which yields maximal social welfare in some sense, is also examined in terms of preference with the convention that a preferred position involves a higher level of welfare of that individual.[24] This dual link between choice and preference on the one hand and preference and welfare on the other is crucial to the normative aspects of general equilibrium theory. All the important results in this field depend on this relationship between behaviour and welfare through the intermediary of preference.

The question that is relevant in this context is whether such heavy weight can be put on the slender shoulders of the concept of preference. Certainly, there is no remarkable difficulty in simply defining preference as the underlying relation in terms of which individual choices can be explained; provided choices satisfy certain elementary axioms, the underlying relation will be binary, and with some additional assumptions it will be an ordering with the property of transitivity.[25] In this mathematical operation preference will simply be the binary representation of individual choice. The difficulty arises in interpreting preference thus defined as preference in the usual sense with the property that if a person prefers x to y then he must regard himself to be better off with x than with

y. As illustrated with the example of the Prisoner's Dilemma, the behaviour of human beings may involve a great deal more than maximizing gains in terms of one's preferences and the complex interrelationships in a society may generate mores and rules of behaviour that will drive a wedge between behaviour and welfare. People's behaviour may still correspond to some consistent *as if* preference but a numerical presentation of the *as if* preference cannot be interpreted as individual welfare. In particular, basing normative criteria, for example, Pareto optimality, on these *as if* preferences poses immense difficulties.

To look at the positive side of the issue, the possibilities of affecting human behaviour through means other than economic incentives may be a great deal more substantial than is typically assumed in the economic literature. The rigid correspondence between choice, preference and welfare assumed in traditional economic theory makes the analysis simpler but also rules out important avenues of social and economic change. An example may make the point clearer.

Suppose it is the case that there are strong environmental reasons for using glass bottles for distributing soft drinks (rather than single-use steel cans) and for persuading the customers to return the bottles to the shops from where they buy these drinks (rather than disposing of them in the dustbin). For a relatively rich country the financial incentives offered for returning the bottles may not be adequate if the consumers neither worry about the environment nor are thrilled by receiving back small change. The environment affects the life of all, true enough, but from the point of view of any one individual the harm that he can do to the environment by adding his bottles to those of others will be exceedingly tiny. Being generally interested in the environment but also being lazy about returning bottles, this person may be best off if the others return bottles but not he, next best if all return bottles, next best if none does, and worst of all if he alone returns bottles while others do not. If others feel in a symmetrical way we shall then be in a prisoner's dilemma type situation in which people will not return bottles but at the same time all would have preferred that all of them should return bottles rather than none. To tackle this problem, suppose now that people are persuaded that non-return is a highly irresponsible behaviour, and while the individuals in question continue to have exactly the same view of their welfare, they fall prey to ethical persuasion, political propaganda, or moral rhetoric. The welfare functions and the preference relations are still exactly the same and all that changes is behaviour. The result is good for the environment but sad for the theory of revealed preference.

I am not, of course, arguing that a change in the sense of responsibility is the *only* way of solving this problem. Penalizing non-return and highly rewarding return of bottles are other methods of doing this, as indeed will occur to any economist. In this particular case, these methods can also be used quite easily (since the problem of checking is not serious with the return of bottles), even though any system of payments and rewards also involves other issues like income distribution. The real difficulty arises when the checking of people's actions is not easy. Examples of these cases vary from such simple acts as littering the streets to such complex behaviour as paying one's taxes.

VII

To avoid a possible misunderstanding, I would like to distinguish clearly between four possible cases all of which involve the same choice (e.g., the use and re-use of glass bottles) but the underlying preferences have different interpretations:

1 The person simply prefers using glass bottles rather than steel cans from a purely self-regarding point of view, for example, because he likes glass, or (perhaps somewhat incredibly) he believes the impact on the environment of his using single-use steel cans (*given* the choices of others) will hurt him significantly.

2 The person is worried about the welfare of others as well, and his own welfare function includes concern for other people's welfare,[26] and he refuses glass bottles because he takes the hurt on others as hurt on himself.

3 The person's concern for other people's welfare reflected in his notion of his own welfare would not be sufficient to prevent him from using single-use steel cans if he could do it on the sly, but he is afraid of the social stigma of being seen to do the 'wrong' thing, or afraid of others emulating him in doing the 'wrong' thing and thereby his getting hit indirectly.

4 The person can do the 'wrong' thing on the sly without being noticed and he feels that if he did that he personally would be better off (even after taking note of whatever weight he might wish to put on the welfare of the others), but he feels that he would be acting socially irresponsibly if he did proceed to do it, and therefore does not do so.

I am primarily concerned with case 4, even though case 3 would also pose some problem for revealed preference theory (and the normative aspects of general equilibrium) since preferences are not usually defined on the space of stigmas and such things, and identical commodity choices will involve quite different welfare levels depending on the reaction of others. But case 3 can be, in principle, taken care of through a suitable redefinition of the domain of choice. Case 4 poses a more serious difficulty and it is with this case that I am concerned.

It is, of course, perfectly possible to argue that actions based on considerations of social responsibility as opposed to one's own welfare do reflect one's 'ultimate' preferences, and in a certain sense this is undoubtedly so. The question is whether the identification of welfare with preference (in the sense of the former being a numerical representation of the latter) will survive under this interpretation. The problem arises from the dual link-up between choice and preference on the one hand and preference and welfare on the other. Preference can be quite reasonably defined in such a way as to maintain one or the other, but the issue is whether *both* can be maintained through some definition of preference, and it is this dual role that I am trying to question here.[27]

With what frequency do problems of the kind of case 4 arise? I do not know the answer to this question. It seems clear, however, that they arise often enough for us to be worried about their implications for traditional economic analysis. Moral considerations involving the question 'if I do not do it, how can I morally want others to do it?' do affect the behaviour of people. The 'others' involved may be members of narrowly defined groups or classes, or widely defined societies, but such considerations do have a role in influencing choice.[28]

What harm would there be, it might be asked, in identifying welfare with what is revealed by a person's choices, even if that is not what he would claim to be his welfare as he himself sees it? Apart from the danger of being misled by the confusing use of words, like 'preference' or 'welfare', which have some specific meanings as used in normal communication, there are also some difficulties for normative economics in basing optimality criteria (for example, Pareto optimality) on *as if* preferences. There is a distinction from the point of view of social judgement between the relevance of a choice made under a moral sense of social responsibility and that made under a straightforward pursuit of one's welfare (including any pleasure one takes in the happiness of others). The identification of welfare with *as if* preferences blurs this distinction and withholds relevant information from the analysis of social welfare and collective choice.

VIII

An interesting illustration of the problem of the relation between preference, choice and social responsibility can be seen in the recent Chinese debates on the use of financial incentives in the allocation of labour in communal agriculture. During the so-called Great Leap Forward in 1958–60 the Chinese tried to reduce drastically the use of work rewards and raised very substantially the proportion of income distributed in the communes on other criteria such as the size of the family. In the absence of what the Chinese called 'socialist consciousness', a system of this kind produces precisely the prisoner's dilemma type of problem. Each may prefer that others should work hard, but given the actions of others may prefer to take it easy oneself, even though given the choice between all working hard and none doing so people may prefer the former. A social contract of sincere efforts by all is easy to think of but difficult to enforce, given the difficulties of supervision of the intensity of work.

At the end of the Leap Forward period this experiment was abandoned, or drastically cut, and it was generally thought that the experiment was premature. The use of financial incentives was again expanded. How much of the difficulties of the Leap Forward period arose from this attempt at dissociating work from material incentives is not known clearly, but it certainly did not make things any easier.

After the end of the Leap Forward period there have been several further attempts to move away from material incentives. Meanwhile the Chinese also tried out a programme of reorientation of behaviour patterns. The well-known 'cultural revolution' put particular emphasis (as the so-called 'Sixteen Points' explained) on 'an education to develop morally, intellectually and physically and to become labourers with socialist consciousness.'[29] The relation of all this to the problem of work motivation is, of course, very close, and I have tried to discuss it elsewhere.[30] Briefly, this can take one of two forms, viz., either (1) a reorientation of the individual welfare functions of the people involved, or (2) a different basis of behaviour emphasizing social responsibility whether or not individual welfare functions are themselves revised. In practice it was probably a mixture of both.

How successful the Chinese experimentation has been in the reorientation of behaviour patterns, it is difficult to assess fully at this stage. What is, anyway, important for our purposes is to note the relevance of this experiment on work motivation in China to the problem of the relation between choice, preference and welfare.

IX

I should perhaps end with a critical observation on what tends to count as hard information in economics. Much of the empirical work on preference patterns seems to be based on the conviction that behaviour is the only source of information on a person's preferences. That behaviour is a major source of information on preference can hardly be doubted, but the belief that it is the only basis of surmising about people's preferences seems extremely questionable. While this makes a great deal of sense for studying preferences of animals, since direct communication is ruled out (unless one is Dr Dolittle), for human beings surely information need not be restricted to distant observations of choices made. There is, of course, something of a problem in interpreting answers to questions as correct and in taking the stated preference to be the actual preference, and there are well-known limitations of the questionnaire method. But then there are problems, as we have seen, with the interpretation of behaviour as well. The idea that behaviour is the one real source of information is extremely limiting for empirical work and is not easy to justify in terms of the methodological requirements of our discipline.

There is an old story about one behaviourist meeting another, and the first behaviourist asks the second: 'I see you are very well. How am I?' The thrust of the revealed preference approach has been to undermine thinking as a method of self-knowledge and talking as a method of knowing about others. In this, I think, we have been prone, on the one hand, to overstate the difficulties of introspection and communication, and on the other, to underestimate the problems of studying preferences revealed by observed behaviour.

X

Perhaps I should now gather together the main themes that I have tried to develop in this lecture. First, I have tried to argue that the interest of revealed preference theory lies in the skilful use of the assumption that behaviour reveals preference and not, despite claims to the contrary, in explaining 'behaviour without reference to anything other than behaviour'.

Second, if revealed preference is interpreted in this light, some of the additional axioms of revealed preference theory can be seen to be redundant for the purpose for which they are used. For example, the Weak Axiom of Revealed Preference can be seen to be quite strong and certainly sufficient for transitivity without requiring a stronger axiom.

Third, the fundamental assumption about the revelation of preference can be critized from many points of view, including the possibility that behaviour may not be based on systematic comparison of alternatives. More interestingly, the person in question may not have a connected preference pattern and in terms of observation it is difficult to distinguish such incompleteness from indifference.

Fourth, even if all these problems are ruled out, there remains a fundamental question of the relation between preference and behaviour arising from a problem of interdependence of different people's choices which discredits individualistic rational calculus. The problem was illustrated in terms of the game of the prisoner's dilemma. The usual analysis of the prisoner's dilemma has tended to concentrate on the possibility of a collective contract, but in many problems such a contract cannot be devised or enforced. Even in the absence of a contract, the parties involved will be better off following rules of behaviour that require abstention from the rational calculus which is precisely the basis of the revealed preference theory. People may be induced by social codes of behaviour to act *as if* they have different preferences from what they really have. This type of departure may also be stable for those codes since such behaviour will justify itself in terms of results from the point of view of the group as a whole.

Finally, this problem has an important bearing on normative problems of resource allocation formulated in terms of the dual link between choice and preference and between preference and welfare. The type of behaviour in question drives a wedge between choice and welfare, and this is of relevance to general equilibrium theory as well as to other aspects of normative economics. Preference can be defined in such a way as to preserve its correspondence with choice, or defined so as to keep it in line with welfare as seen by the person in question, but it is not in general possible to guarantee both simultaneously. Something has to give at one place or the other.

NOTES

1 P. A. Samuelson, 'A note on the pure theory of consumer's behaviour', *Economica*, 5 (1938). Also 'A note on the pure theory of consumer's behaviour: an addendum', *Economica*, 5 (1938).
2 D. H. Robertson, *Utility and All That* (London, 1952), p. 19.
3 P. A. Samuelson, 'Consumption theory in terms of revealed preference', *Economica*, 15 (1948).
4 See Samuelson's articles (Notes 1 and 3) and also his *Foundations of Economic Analysis* (Cambridge, Mass., 1947).
5 For a recent survey of the analytical literature in this branch of economics, see A. Brown and A. Deaton, 'Models of consumer behaviour: a survey', *Economic Journal*, 82 (1972).
6 Samuelson, 'A note on the pure theory . . .', p. 71.
7 I. M. D. Little, 'A reformulation of the theory of consumer's behaviour', *Oxford Economic Papers*, 1 (1949), p. 90.
8 Ibid., p. 97.
9 J. R. Hicks, *A Revision of Demand Theory* (Oxford, 1956), p. 6. Hicks did not, however, fully subscribe to the revealed preference approach himself. See especially 'The measurement of income', *Oxford Economic Papers*, N.S., 10 (1958). [See also the Introduction to his *Wealth and Welfare: Collected Essays on Economic Theory* (Oxford: Basil Blackwell, 1981), pp. xii–xiv.]
10 Little, 'A reformulation of the theory', p. 97.
11 Ibid., p. 98.
12 Samuelson, 'Consumption theory', p. 243.
13 H. S. Houthakker, 'Revealed preference and the utility function', *Economica*, 17 (1950). The Strong Axiom guarantees a property that Houthakker called semi-transitivity.
14 J. Ville, 'Sur les conditions d'existence d'une ophélimité totale et d'un indice du niveau des prix', *Annales de l'Université de Lyons*, 9 (1946); J. von Neumann and O. Morgenstern, *Theory of Games and Economic Behaviour* (Princeton, 1944).
15 Hicks, *A Revision of Demand Theory*, p. 110.
16 Cf. D. Gale, 'A note on revealed preference', *Economica*, 27 (1960).
17 See K. J. Arrow, 'Rational choice functions and orderings', *Economica*, 26 (1959); and A. K. Sen, 'Choice functions and revealed preference', *Review of Economic Studies*, 38 (1971).
18 Little, 'A reformulation of the theory', p. 92.
19 See Arrow, 'Rational choice functions and orderings'; Sen, 'Choice functions and revealed preference'; H. Herzberger, 'Ordinal choice v. rationality', *Econometrica*, 41 (1973); C. R. Plott, 'Path independence, rationality and social choice', *Econometrica*, 41 (1973).
20 See R. D. Luce and H. Raiffa, *Games and Decisions* (New York, 1958); also A. Rapoport, *Two-Person Game Theory* (Michigan, 1966).
21 See W. J. Baumol, *Welfare Economics and the Theory of the State* (Cambridge, Mass., 1952); A. K. Sen, 'On optimizing the rate of

saving', *Economic Journal,* 71 (1961); S. A. Marglin, 'The social rate of discount and the optimal rate of investment', *Quarterly Journal of Economics,* 77 (1963); A. K. Sen, 'A game theoretic analysis of theories of collectivism in allocation', in T. Majumdar (ed.), *Growth and Choice* (Bombay, 1969).

22 W. G. Runciman and A. K. Sen, 'Games, justice and the general will', *Mind,* 74 (1965); J. Rawls, *A Theory of Justice* (Cambridge, Mass., 1971).

23 See Rapoport, *Two-Person Game Theory*; and J. W. N. Watkins, 'Self-interest and morality in the light of the Prisoner's Dilemma', paper read at the Bristol Conference on 'Practical Reason', September 1972, published in S. Körner (ed.), *Practical Reason* (Oxford, 1974).

24 See J. R. Hicks, *Value and Capital* (Oxford, 1939); P. A. Samuelson, *Foundations of Economic Analysis* (1947); G. Debreu, *Theory of Value* (New York, 1959); K. J. Arrow and F. H. Hahn, *General Competitive Analysis* (San Francisco and Edinburgh, 1971).

25 The respective conditions for binariness, transitivity of strict preference and full transitivity are presented in Sen, 'Choice function and revealed preference'. For the conditions that guarantee a numerical representation of the individual welfare function based on their preference relation, see Debreu, *Theory of Value*; M. K. Richter, 'Revealed preference theory', *Econometrica,* 34 (1966); Arrow and Hahn, *General Competitive Analysis*.

26 Cf. A. K. Sen, 'Labour allocation in a cooperative enterprise', *Review of Economic Studies,* 33 (1966).

27 The problem discussed here should not be confused with the important but different problem of strategic reasons for 'not revealing preference' (see, for example, T. Majumdar, *The Measurement of Utility* (London, 1958); R. Farquharson, *Theory of Voting* (Oxford, 1970)). The latter is a problem of establishing correspondence between rankings of the outcome space and those of the strategy space. Our problem arises in the ranking of the outcome space itself.

28 I have tried to argue elsewhere that there are advantages in viewing moral judgements not as one other ordering of actions or outcomes but as an ordering (or a quasi-ordering) of orderings of actions or outcomes. 'Choice, orderings and morality', paper read at the Bristol Conference on 'Practical Reason', September 1972, published in S. Körner (ed.), *Practical Reason* (Oxford, 1974).

29 For a penetrating analysis of work motivation in China, see C. Riskin, 'Maoism and motivation: a discussion of work motivation in China', *Bulletin of Concerned Asian Scholars,* 1973.

30 A. K. Sen, *On Economic Inequality* (Oxford, 1973), chapter 4.

3

Advances in Understanding Rational Behavior

JOHN C. HARSANYI

I INTRODUCTION

The concept of rational behavior (or of practical rationality) is of considerable philosophical interest.[1] It plays an important role in moral and political philosophy, while the related concept of theoretical rationality is connected with many deep problems in logic, epistemology, and the philosophy of science. Both practical and theoretical rationality are important concepts in psychology and in the study of artificial intelligence. Furthermore, rational-behavior models are widely used in economics and, to an increasing extent, also in other social sciences. This fact is all the more remarkable since rationality is a normative concept and, therefore, it has been claimed (incorrectly, as I shall argue) that it is out of place in non-normative, empirically oriented studies of social behaviour.

Given the important role that the concept of rationality plays in philosophy and in a number of other disciplines, I have thought it may be of some interest to this interdisciplinary audience if I report on some work in decision theory and in game theory that holds out the prospect of replacing our common-sense notion of rational behavior by a much more general, much more precise, and conceptually very much richer notion of rationality. I feel that successful development of an analytically clear, informative, and intuitively satisfactory concept of rationality would have significant philosophical implications.

I shall first discuss the common-sense notion of rational behavior. Then, I shall briefly describe the rationality concepts of classical economic theory and of Bayesian decision theory. Finally, I shall report on some, mostly very recent, results in game theory, which, I believe, are practically unknown to non-specialists. Of

This essay was first published in R. E. Butts and J. Hintikka (eds), *Foundational Problems in the Special Sciences* (Dordrecht, 1977), pp. 315–43, copyright © 1977 by D. Reidel Publishing Company, Dordrecht, Holland.

course, within the space available, I cannot do more than draw a sketchy and very incomplete picture of the relevant work – a picture no doubt strongly colored by my own theoretical views.

II THE MEANS-ENDS CONCEPT OF RATIONAL BEHAVIOR

In everyday life, when we speak of 'rational behavior', in most cases we are thinking of behavior involving a choice of the best *means* available for achieving a given *end*. This implies that, already at a common-sense level, rationality is a *normative* concept: it points to what we *should* do in order to attain a given end or objective. But, even at a common-sense level, this concept of rationality does have important *positive* (non-normative) applications: it is used for *explanation*, for *prediction*, and even for mere *description* of human behavior.

Indeed, the assumption that a given person has acted or will act rationally, often has very considerable explanatory and predictive power, because it may imply that we can explain or predict a large number of possibly very complicated facts about his behavior in terms of a small number of rather simple hypotheses about his goals or objectives.

For example, suppose a given historian comes to the conclusion that Napoleon acted fairly rationally in a certain period. This will have the implication that Napoleon's actions admit of explanation in terms of his political and military objectives – possibly in terms of a rather limited number of such objectives – and that other, often less easily accessible, psychological variables need not be used to any major extent to account for his behavior. On the other hand, if our historian finds that Napoleon's behavior was not very rational, then this will imply that no set of reasonably well-defined policy objectives could be found that would explain Napoleon's behavior, and that any explanation of it must make use of some 'deeper' motivational factors and, ultimately, of some much more specific assumptions about the psychological mechanisms underlying human behavior.

Yet, we do make use of the notion of rationality also in cases where we are not interested in an explanation or prediction of human behavior, but are merely interested in providing an adequate *description* of it. For instance, any historical narrative of Napoleon's political and military decisions will be seriously incomplete, even at a descriptive level, if it contains no discussion of the rationality or irrationality of these decisions. Thus, it will not be enough to report that, in a particular battle, Napoleon attacked the enemy's right wing. Rather, we also want to know whether, under the existing conditions, this attack was a sensible (or perhaps even a brilliant) tactical move or not.

Philosophers, and social scientists outside the economics profession, have often expressed puzzlement about the successful use of the normative concept of rational behavior in positive economics – and, more recently, also in other social sciences[2] – for explanation and prediction, and even for mere description, of human behavior. But there is really nothing surprising about this. All it means is that human behavior is mostly *goal-directed*, often in a fairly consistent manner, in many important classes of social situations. For example, suppose that people are *mainly* after money in business life (even if they do also have a number of other objectives), or are mainly after election or re-election to public office in democratic politics, or are mainly after social status in many social activities, or are mainly after national self-interest in international affairs – at least that these statements are true as a matter of reasonable first approximation. Then, of course, it is in no way surprising if we can explain and sometimes even predict, and can also meaningfully describe, their behavior in terms of the assumption that they are after money, or after public office, or after social status, or after national self-interest.

Even if the subject matter of our investigation were not human behavior, but rather the behavior of goal-pursuing robots, a model of 'rational' (that is, goal-pursuing) robot behavior would be a very valuable analytical tool. Of course, just as in the case of human beings, such a rationalistic model would only work with highly 'rational' (that is, with very well-functioning) robots. To explain the behavior of a robot with a faulty steering mechanism, we would need a more complicated model, based on fairly detailed assumptions about the robot's internal structure and operation.

To be sure, while we could at least conceive of a perfectly well-constructed goal-pursuing robot, completely consistent and completely single-minded in working for his pre-established goal, human beings are seldom that consistent. In some situations, they will be deflected from their objectives by Freudian-type emotional factors, while in others they will fail to pursue any well-defined objectives altogether. Moreover, even if they do aim at well-defined objectives, their limitations in computing (information-processing) ability may prevent them from discovering the most effective strategies (or any reasonably effective strategies) for achieving these objectives. (Of course, any robot of less than infinite structural complexity will be subject to similar computational limitations. But he may not be subject to anything resembling emotional problems.)

Obviously, this means that in *some* situations models of rational behavior will not be very useful in analyzing human behavior – except perhaps after substantial modification (for example along the lines suggested by Simon's[3] theory of limited rationality). Clearly, it is an empirical question what types of social situations lend themselves, and to what extent, to analysis in terms of rational-behavior models. But recent work in political science, in international relations, and in sociology, has shown that a much wider range of social situations seems to admit of rationalistic analysis than most observers would have thought even ten years ago.[4]

III THE RATIONAL-BEHAVIOR MODEL OF ECONOMIC THEORY

Even at a common-sense level, the means-ends model is not the only model of rational behaviour we use. Another, though perhaps less important, model envisages rational behavior as choosing an object (or a person) satisfying certain stipulated formal (possibly non-causal) *criteria*. For instance, if my aim is to climb the highest mountain in California, then it will be rational for me to climb Mount Whitney, and it will be irrational for me to climb any other mountain. But we would not normally say that climbing Mount Whitney is a *means* to climbing the highest mountain in California, because my climbing of Mount Whitney does not causally *lead* to a climbing of the highest mountain. Rather, it already *is* a climbing of the highest mountain. It is a rational action in the sense of being an action (and, indeed, the only action) satisfying the stipulated criterion.[5]

Thus, it would be rather artificial to subsume criterion-satisfying behavior under the means-ends model of rationality. It is more natural to do the converse, and argue that looking for a means to a given end is a special case of looking for an object satisfying a particular criterion, viz. the criterion of being causally effective in attaining a given end.

This implies that the means-ends concept of rational behavior is too narrow because it fails to cover criterion-satisfying behavior. An even more important limitation of this concept lies in the fact that it restricts rational behavior to a choice among alternative *means* to a given end, and fails to include a rational choice among alternative *ends*. Therefore, it cannot explain why a given person may shift from one end to another.

To overcome this limitation, nineteenth and early twentieth century economists introduced a broader concept of rationality which defines rational behavior as a choice among alternative ends, on the basis of a given set of *preferences* and a given set of *opportunities* (i.e. a given set of available alternatives). If I am choosing a given end (or a given set of mutually compatible ends, which can be described as a unique composite end), then typically I have to give up many alternative ends. Giving up these alternative ends is the *opportunity cost* of pursuing this particular end. Thus, under this model, rational behavior consists in choosing one specific end, after careful consideration and in full awareness of the opportunity costs of this choice.

This model will often enable us to explain why a given individual has changed over from pursuing one objective to pursuing another, even if his basic preferences have remained the same. The explanation will lie in the fact that the opportunity costs of various possible objectives (that is, the advantages and the disadvantages associated with them) have changed, or at least the information he has about these opportunity costs has done so.

For example, a given person may seek admission to a particular university, but then may change his mind and fail to attend. He may do so because the tuition fees or other monetary costs have increased; or because the studies he would have to undertake have turned out to be harder or less interesting than he thought they would be; or because he has received unfavorable information about the hoped-for economic advantages of a university degree, etc. All these explanations are compatible with the assumption that, during the whole period, his basic preferences remained the same, and that only the situation (that is, his opportunity costs), or his information about the situation, have changed.[6]

It is easy to verify that the preferences-opportunities model includes both the means-ends model and the criterion-satisfaction model as special cases.

An important result of economic theory has been to show that, if a given person's preferences satisfy certain consistency and continuity axioms, then these preferences will admit of representation by a well-defined (and, indeed, continuous) utility function.[7] Accordingly, for such a person, rational behavior – as defined by the preferences-opportunities model – will be equivalent to *utility-maximization* (utility-maximization theorem).

IV   BAYESIAN DECISION THEORY

Classical economic theory was largely restricted to analyzing human behavior under *certainty*, i.e. under conditions where the decision maker can uniquely predict the outcome of any action he may take (or where one can assume this to be the case at least as a matter of first approximation). It has been left to modern decision theory to extend this analysis to human behavior under risk and under uncertainty.

Both risk and uncertainty refer to situations where the decision maker cannot always uniquely predict the outcomes of his action. But, in the case of *risk*, he will know at least the objective probabilities associated with all possible outcomes. In contrast, in the case of *uncertainty*, even some or all of these objective probabilities will be unknown to him (or may even be undefined altogether).

The utility-maximization model provides a satisfactory characterization of rational behavior under certainty, but fails to do so under risk and under uncertainty. This is so because it is not sufficient to assume that any given lottery (whether it is a 'risky' lottery involving known probabilities, or is an 'uncertain' lottery involving unknown probabilities) will have a well-defined numerical utility to the decision maker. Rather, we need a theory specifying *what value* this utility will have, and how it will depend on the utilities associated with the various prizes. This is exactly what decision theory is trying to specify.

The main conclusion of decision theory is this. If the decision maker's behavior satisfies certain consistency and continuity axioms (a larger number of axioms than we needed to establish the utility-maximization theorem in the case of certainty), then his behaviour will be equivalent to *maximizing his expected utility*, that is, to maximizing the mathematical expectation of his cardinal utility function. In the case of *risk*, this expected utility can be defined in terms of the relevant objective probabilities (which, by assumption, will be known to the decision maker). On the other hand, in the case of *uncertainty*, this expected utility must be defined in terms of the decision maker's own subjective probabilities whenever the relevant objective probabilities are unknown to him (expected-utility maximization theorem).[8]

This result leads to the *Bayesian* approach to decision theory, which proposes to define rational behavior under risk and under uncertainty as expected-utility maximization.[9]

Besides the axioms used already in the case of certainty, we need one additional consistency axiom to establish the expected-utility maximization theorem in the cases of risk and of uncertainty. This axiom is the *sure-thing principle*, which can be stated as follows. 'Let X be a bet[10] that would yield a given prize x to the decision maker if a specified event E took place (for example, if a particular horse won the next race). Let Y be a bet that would yield him another prize *y*, which he *prefers* over *x*, if this event *E* took place. There are no other differences between the two bets. Then, the decision maker will consider bet *Y* to be *at least as desirable* as bet *X*.' (Actually, unless he assigns zero probability to event *E*, he will no doubt positively *prefer* bet *Y*, which would yield the more attractive prize *y*, if event *E* took place. But we do not need this slightly stronger assumption.)

In my opinion, it is hard to envisage any rational decision maker who would knowingly violate the sure-thing principle (or who would violate the − somewhat more technical − continuity axiom we need to prove the expected-utility maximization theorem). This fact is, of course, a strong argument in favor of the Bayesian definition of rational behavior. Another important argument lies in the fact that all alternative definitions of rational behavior (and, in particular, all definitions based on the once fashionable maxi-min principle and on various other related principles) can be shown to lead to highly irrational decisions in many practically important situations.[11]

In the case of risk, acceptance of Bayesian theory is now virtually unanimous. In the case of uncertainty, the Bayesian approach is still somewhat controversial, though the last two decades have produced a clear trend toward its growing acceptance by expert opinion. Admittedly, support for Bayesian theory is weaker among scholars working in other fields than it is among decision theorists and game theorists. (I must add that some of the criticism directed against the Bayesian approach has been rather uninformed, and has shown a clear lack of familiarity with the relevant literature.)

V A GENERAL THEORY OF RATIONAL BEHAVIOR

Whatever the merits of the rationality concept of Bayesian decision theory may be, it is still in need of further generalization, because it does not adequately cover rational behavior in *game situations*, that is, in situations where the outcome depends on the behavior of two or more rational individuals who may have partly or wholly divergent interests. Game situations may be considered to represent a special case of uncertainty, since in general none of the players will be able to predict the outcome, or even the probabilities associated with different possible outcomes. This is so because he will not be able to predict the strategies of the other players, or even the probabilities associated with their various possible strategies. (To be sure, as we shall argue, at least in principle, game-theoretical analysis does enable each player to discover the solution of the game and, therefore, to predict the strategies of the other players, provided that the latter will act in a rational manner. But the point is that, prior to such a game-theoretical analysis, he will be unable to make such predictions.)

Game theory defines rational behavior in game situations by defining solution concepts for various classes of games.

Since the term 'decision theory' is usually restricted to the theory of rational behavior under risk and under uncertainty, I shall use the term *utility theory* to describe the broader theory which includes both decision theory and the theory of rational behavior under certainty (as established by classical economic theory).

Besides utility theory and game theory, I propose to consider *ethics*, also, as a branch of the general theory of rational behavior, since ethical theory can be based on axioms which represent specializations of some of the axioms used in decision theory.[12]

Thus, under the approach here proposed, the *general theory of rational behavior* consists of three branches:

1 *Utility theory*, which is the theory of *individual* rational behavior under certainty, under risk, and under uncertainty. Its main result is that, in these three cases, rational behavior consists in *utility maximization* or *expected-utility maximization*.

2 *Game theory*, which is the theory of rational behavior by *two or more* interacting rational individuals, each of them determined to maximize his own interests, whether selfish or unselfish, as specified by his own utility function (payoff function). (Though some or all players may very well assign high utilities to clearly altruistic objectives, this need not prevent a conflict of interest between them since they may possibly assign high utilities to quite *different*, and perhaps strongly conflicting, altruistic objectives.)

3 *Ethics*, which is the theory of rational moral value judgments, i.e. of rational judgments of preference based on impartial and impersonal criteria. I have tried to show that rational moral value judgments will involve *maximizing* the *average utility level* of all individuals in society.[13]

Whereas game theory is a theory of possibly conflicting (but not necessarily selfish) *individual* interests, ethics can be regarded as a theory of the *common* interests (or of the general welfare) of society as a whole.

John C. Harsanyi

We speak of a game with *complete information* if the players have full information about all *parameters* defining the game, that is, about all variables fully determined *before* the beginning of the game. These variables include the players' payoff functions (utility functions), the strategical possibilities available to each player, and the amount of information each player has about all of these variables. We speak of a game with *incomplete information* if some or all of the players have less than full information about these parameters defining the game.

This distinction must not be confused with another, somewhat similar distinction. We speak of a game with *perfect information* if the players always have full information about the *moves* already made in the game, including the *personal* moves made by the individual players and the *chance moves* decided by chance. Thus, perfect information means full information about all game events that took place *after* the beginning of the game. We speak of a game with *imperfect information* if some or all players have less than full information about the moves already made in the game.

It was a major limitation of classical game theory that it could not handle games with *incomplete* information (though it did deal both with games involving perfect and imperfect information). For, many of the most important real-life game situations are games with incomplete information: the players may have only limited knowledge of each other's payoff functions (that is, of each other's real objectives within the game), and may also know very little about the strategies as well as the information available to the other players.

In the last few years we have discovered how to overcome this limitation. How this is done can be best shown in an example. Suppose we want to analyze arms control negotiations between the United States and the Soviet Union. The difficulty is that neither side really knows the other side's true intentions and technological capabilities. (They may have reasonably good intelligence estimates about each other's weapon systems in actual use, but may know very little about any new military inventions not yet used in actual weapon production.) Now we can employ the following model. The American player, called A, and the Russian player, called R, both can occur in the form of a number of different possible 'types'. For instance, the Russian player could be really R_1, a fellow with very peaceful intentions but with access to very formidable new weapon technologies; and with the expectation that the American player will also have peaceful intentions, yet a ready access to important new technologies. Or, the Russian player could be R_2, who is exactly like R_1, except that he expects the American player to have rather aggressive intentions. Or, the Russian player could be R_3, who shows still another possible combination of all these variables, etc.

Likewise, the American player could be of type A_1 or A_2 or A_3, etc., each of them having a different combination of policy objectives, of access to new technologies, and of expectations about Russian policy objectives and about Russian access to new technologies. (We could, of course, easily add still further variables to this list.)

The game is played as follows. At the beginning of the game, nature conducts a lottery to decide which particular types of the American player and of the Russian player (one type of each) will actually participate in the game. Each possible combination (A_i, R_j) of an American player type and of a Russian player type have a pre-assigned probability p_{ij} of being selected. When a particular pair (A_i, R_j) has been chosen, they will actually play the game. Each player will know his own type but will be ignorant of his opponent's actual type. But, for any given type of his opponent, he will be able to assign a numerical probability to the possibility that his opponent is of this particular type, because each player will know the probability matrix $P = (p_{ij})$.

What this model does is to reduce the original game with *incomplete* information, G, to an artificially constructed game with *complete* information. G^*. The *incomplete* information the players had in G about the basic parameters of the game is represented in the new game G^* as *imperfect* information about a certain chance move at the beginning of the game (viz. the one which determines the types of the players). As the resulting new game G^* is a game with complete (even if with imperfect) information, it is fully accessible to the usual methods of game-theoretical analysis.

The model just described is not the most general model we use in the analysis of games with incomplete information. It makes the assumption that all players' expectations about each other's basic characteristics (or, technically speaking, all players' subjective probability distributions over all possible types of all other players) are sufficiently consistent to be expressible in terms of one basic probability matrix $P = (p_{ij})$. We call this the assumption of *mutually consistent expectations*. In many applications, this is a natural assumption to make and, whenever this is the case, it greatly simplifies the analysis of the game.[14]

There are, however, cases where this assumption seems to be inappropriate. As Reinhard Selten has pointed out (in private communication) even in such cases, the game will admit of analysis in terms of an appropriate probabilistic model, though a more complicated one than would be needed on the assumption of consistent expectations.[15]

VII   NON-COOPERATIVE GAMES AND EQUILIBRIUM POINTS: THE PRISONER'S DILEMMA PROBLEM

We have to distinguish between *cooperative* games, where the players can make fully binding and enforceable commitments (fully binding promises, agreements, and threats, which absolutely *have* to be implemented if the stipulated conditions arise), and *non-cooperative* games, where this is not the case. In real life, what makes commitments fully binding is usually a law-enforcing authority. But in some cases prestige considerations (a fear of losing face) may have similar effects.

Nash,[16] who first proposed this distinction, defined cooperative games as games with enforceable commitments *and* with free communication between the players. He defined non-cooperative games as games without enforceable commitments *and* without communication. These were somewhat misleading definitions. Presence or absence of free communication is only of secondary importance. The crucial issue is the possibility or impossibility of binding and enforceable agreements. (For example, in the prisoner's dilemma case, as I shall argue below, the cooperative solution will be unavailable to the players if no enforceable agreements can be made. This will be true regardless of whether the players can talk to each other or not.)

In a cooperative game, the players can agree on any possible combination of strategies since they can be sure that any such agreement would be kept. In contrast, in a non-cooperative game, only self-enforcing agreements are worth making because only self-enforcing agreements have any real chance of implementation.

A self-enforcing agreement is called an equilibrium point. A more exact definition can be stated as follows. A given strategy of a certain player is called a *best reply* to the other players' strategies if it maximizes this player's payoff so long as the other players' strategies are kept constant. A given combination of strategies (containing exactly one strategy for each player) is called an *equilibrium point* if every player's strategy is a best reply to all other players' strategies. The concept of an equilibrium point, also, is due to Nash.[17]

For example, suppose that the following two-person game is played as a non-cooperative game, so that no enforceable agreements can be made:

	B_1	B_2
A_1	2, 2	0, 3
A_2	3, 0	1, 1

This type of game is called a prisoner's dilemma.[18]

In this game, the strategy pair (A_2, B_2) is an equilibrium point, because player 1's best reply to B_2 is A_2, whereas player 2's best reply to A_2 is B_2. Indeed, the game has no other equilibrium point. If the two players use their equilibrium strategies A_2 and B_2, then they will obtain the payoffs (1, 1).

Obviously, both players would be better off if they could use the strategies A_1 and B_1, which would yield them the payoffs (2, 2). But these two strategies do not form an equilibrium point. Even if the two players explicitly *agreed* to use A_1 and B_1, they would not do so, and would *know* they would not do so. Even if we assumed for a moment that the two players did expect the strategy pair (A_1, B_1) to be the outcome of the game, *this very expectation would make them use another strategy pair* (A_2, B_2) *instead*. For instance, if player 1 expected player 2 to use strategy B_1, he himself would not use A_1 but would rather use A_2, since A_2 would be his best reply to player 2's expected strategy B_1. Likewise, if player 2 expected player 1 to use A_1, he himself would not use B_1 but would rather use B_2, since B_2 would be his best reply to player 1's expected strategy A_1.

Of course, if the game were played as a cooperative game, then agreements would be fully enforceable, and the two players would have no difficulty in agreeing to use strategies A_1 and B_1 so as to obtain the higher payoffs (2, 2). Once they agreed on this, they could be absolutely sure that this agreement would be fully observed.

Thus, we must conclude that, if the game is played as a non-cooperative game, then the outcome will be the equilibrium point (A_2, B_2), which is often called the *non-cooperative solution*. On the other hand, if the game is played as a cooperative game, then the outcome will be the non-equilibrium point strategy pair (A_1, B_1), which is called the *cooperative solution*.

More generally, the solution of a non-cooperative game must always be an equilibrium point. In other words, each player's solution strategy must be a best reply to the other players' solution strategies. This is so because the solution, by definition, must be a strategy combination that the players can rationally *use*, and that they can also rationally *expect* one another to use. But, if any given player's solution strategy were *not* his best reply to the other players' solution strategies, then the very expectation that the other players would use their solution strategies would make it rational for this player *not* to use his solution strategy (but rather to use a strategy that was a best reply to the solution strategies he expected the other players to use). Hence, the alleged 'solution' would not satisfy our definition of a solution.

This argument does not apply to a cooperative game, where each player can irrevocably commit himself to using a given strategy even if the latter is *not* a best reply to the other players' strategies. But it does apply to any non-cooperative game, where such a commitment would have no force.

This conclusion is accepted by almost all game theorists. It is, however, rejected by some distinguished scholars from other disciplines, because it seems to justify certain forms of socially undesirable non-cooperative behavior in real-life conflict situations. Their sentiments underlying this theoretical position are easy to understand and deserve our respect, but I cannot say the same thing about their logic. I find it rather hard to comprehend how anybody can deny that there is a fundamental difference between social situations where agreements are strictly enforceable and social situations where this is not the case; or how anybody can deny that, in situations where agreements are wholly unenforceable, the participants may often have every reason to distrust each other's willingness (and sometimes even to distrust each other's very ability) to keep agreements, in particular if there are strong incentives to violate these agreements.

To be sure, it is quite possible that, in a situation that *looks like* a prisoner's dilemma game, the players will be able to achieve the cooperative solution. Usually this will happen because the players are decent persons and therefore attach considerable disutility to using a non-cooperative strategy like A_2 or B_2 when the other player uses a cooperative strategy like A_1 or B_1. Of course, if the players take this attitude, then this will change the payoff matrix of the game. For instance, suppose that both players assign a disutility of 2 units to such an outcome. This will reduce the utility payoff that player 1 associates with the outcome (A_2, B_1) to $3 - 2 = 1$.

Likewise, it will also reduce the utility payoff that player 2 associates with the outcome (A_1, B_2) to $3 - 2 = 1$. (If the players assigned a special disutility to violating an agreement, and then actually agreed to use the strategy pair (A_1, B_1), this would have similar effects on the payoff matrix of the game.) Consequently, the game will now have the following payoff matrix:

	B_1	B_2
A_1	2, 2	0, 1
A_2	1, 0	1, 1

This new game, of course, is no longer a prisoner's dilemma since now *both* (A_1, B_1) *and* (A_2, B_2) are equilibrium points. Hence, even if the game remains formally a non-cooperative game without enforceable agreements, the players will now have no difficulty in reaching the outcome (A_1, B_1), which we used to call the cooperative solution, so as to obtain the payoffs (2, 2). This conclusion, of course, is fully consistent with our theory because now (A_1, B_1) *is* an equilibrium point.

This example shows that we must clearly distinguish between two different problems. One is the problem of whether a game that *looks like* a prisoner's dilemma *is* in fact a prisoner's dilemma: does the proposed payoff matrix of the game (which would make the game a prisoner's dilemma) correctly express the players' true payoff functions, in accordance with their real preferences and their real strategy objectives within the game? This is *not* a game-theoretical question, because game theory regards the players' payoff functions as *given*. It is, rather, an empirical question about the players' psychological make-up. The other question *is* a game-theoretical question: it is the question of how to define the solution of the game, once the payoff matrix has been correctly specified. A good deal of confusion can be avoided if these two questions are kept strictly apart.

As a practical matter, social situations not permitting enforceable agreements often have a socially very undesirable incentive structure, and may give rise to many very painful human problems. But these problems cannot be solved by arguing that people should act as if agreements were enforceable, even though they are not; or that people should trust each other, even though they have very good reasons to withhold this trust. The solution, if there is one, can only lie in actually providing effective incentives to keep agreements (or in persuading people to assign high utility to keeping agreements, even in the absence of external incentives). What we have to do, if it can be done, is to *change* non-cooperative games into cooperative games by making agreements enforceable, rather than pretend that we live in a make-believe world, where we can take non-cooperative games as they are, and then analyze them simply as if they were cooperative games, if we so desire.

I have discussed at some length the principle that the solution of a non-cooperative game must be an equilibrium point, because this principle will play an important role in the game-theoretical investigations I am going to report on.

VIII   PERFECT EQUILIBRIUM POINTS

After Nash's discovery of the concept of equilibrium points in 1950, for many years game theorists were convinced that the only rationality requirement in a non-cooperative game was that the players' strategies should form an equilibrium point. But in 1965 Reinhard Selten proposed counter-examples to show that even equilibrium points might involve irrational behavior.[19] He has suggested that only a special class of equilibrium points, which he called *perfect* equilibrium points, represent truly rational behavior in a non-cooperative game.

Since the difference between perfect and imperfect equilibrium points is obscured in the normal-form representation,[20] let us consider the following two-person non-cooperative game, given in extensive form (game-tree form).

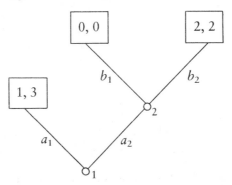

In this game, the first move belongs to player 1. He can choose between moves a_1 and a_2. If he chooses a_1, then the game will end with the payoffs $(1, 3)$ to the two players, without player 2 having any move at all. On the other hand if player 1 chooses move a_2, then player 2 has a choice between moves b_1 and b_2. If he chooses the former, then the game will end with the payoffs $(0, 0)$; while if he chooses the latter, then the game will end with the payoffs $(2, 2)$. The normal form of this game is as follows:

	B_1	B_2
A_1	1, 3	1, 3
A_2	0, 0	2,2

The players' strategies have the following interpretation. Strategy A_1 (or A_2) means that player 1 will choose move a_1 (or a_2) at the beginning of the game. On the other hand, strategy B_1 (or B_2) means that player 2 will choose move b_1 (or b_2) *if player 1 chooses move a_2* (while if player 1 chooses move a_1, then player 2 will do nothing). Player 2's strategies can be described only in terms of these *conditional* statements since he will have a move only if player 1 chooses move a_2.

A look at the normal form will reveal that the game has two pure-strategy equilibrium points, *viz.* $E_1 = (A_1, B_1)$ and $E_2 = (A_2, B_2)$. E_2 is a perfectly reasonable equilibrium point. But, as I propose to show, E_1 is not: it involves irrational behavior, and irrational expectations by the players about each other's behavior.

In fact, player 1 will use strategy A_1 (as E_1 requires him to do) only if he expects player 2 to use strategy B_1. (For if player 2 used B_2, then player 1 would be better off by using A_2.) But it is *irrational* for player 1 to expect player 2 to use strategy B_1, i.e. to expect player 2 to make move b_1 should player 1 himself make move a_2. This is so because move b_1 will yield player 2 only the payoff 0, whereas move b_2 would yield him the payoff 2.

To put it differently, player 2 will obviously prefer the outcome (A_1, B_1), yielding him 3 units of utility, over the outcome (A_2, B_2), yielding him only 2 units. Therefore, player 2 may very well try to induce player 1 to use strategy A_1, i.e. to make move a_1: for instance, he may threaten to use strategy B_1, i.e. to punish player 1 by making move b_1, should player 1 counter his wishes by making move a_2. But the point is that this would *not* be a credible threat because, by making move b_1, player 2 would not only punish player 1 but rather would just as much punish himself. This is so because move b_1 would reduce *both* of their payoffs to 0 (while the alternative move b_2 would give both of them payoffs of 2 units).

To be sure, if player 2 could irrevocably *commit* himself to punish player 1 in this way, and could do this *before* player 1 had made his move, then it would be rational for player 2 to make such a commitment in order to deter player 1 from making move a_2. But, in actual fact, player 2 cannot make such a commitment because this is a non-cooperative game. On the other hand, if player 2 is *not* compelled by such a prior commitment to punish player 1, then he will have no incentive to do so since, once player 1 has made his move, player 2 cannot gain anything by punishing him at the cost of reducing his own payoff at the same time.

To conclude, $E_1 = (A_1, B_1)$ is an irrational equilibrium point because it is based on the unreasonable assumption that player 2 would punish player 1 if the latter made move a_2 – even though this punishing move would reduce not only player 1's payoff but also player 2's own payoff. Following Selten's proposal, we shall call such unreasonable equilibrium points *imperfect* equilibrium points. In contrast, equilibrium points like $E_2 = (A_2, B_2)$, which are not open to such objections, will be called *perfect* equilibrium points.

The question naturally arises how it is possible that an equilibrium point should use a highly irrational strategy like B_1 as an equilibrium strategy at all. The answer lies in the fact that, as long as the two players follow their equilibrium strategies A_1 and B_1, player 2 will never come into a position *where he would have to make the irrational move b_1 prescribed by strategy B_1*. For, strategy B_1 would require him to make move b_1 only if player 1 made move a_2. But this contingency will never arise because player 1 follows strategy A_1 (which requires him to make move a_1 rather than a_2).[21]

In other words, strategy B_1 would require player 2 to make move b_1 only if the game reached the point marked by 2 on our game tree[22] (since this is the point where he had to choose between moves b_1 and b_2). But, so long as the players follow the strategies A_1 and B_1, this point will never be reached by the game.

This fact suggests a mathematical procedure for eliminating imperfect equilibrium points from the game. All we have to do is to assume that, whenever any player tries to make a specific move, he will have a very small but positive probability e of making a 'mistake', which will divert him into making another move than that he wanted to make, so that *every* possible move will occur with some positive probability. The resulting game will be called a *perturbed game*. As a result of the players' assumed 'mistakes', in a perturbed game every point of the game tree will always be reached with a positive probability whenever the game is played. It can be shown that, if the game is perturbed in this way, only the perfect equilibrium points of the original game will remain equilibrium points in the perturbed game, whereas the imperfect equilibrium points will lose the status of equilibrium points. (More exactly, we can find the perfect equilibrium points of the original game if we take the equilibrium points of the perturbed game, and then let the mistake probabilities e go to zero.)

Thus, in our example, suppose that, if player 1 tries to use strategy A_1, then he will be able to implement the intended move a_1 only with probability $(1 - e)$, and will be forced to make the unintended move a_2 with the remaining small probability e. Consequently, it will not be costless any more for player 2 to use strategy B_1 when player 1 uses A_1. This is so because now player 1 will make move a_2 with a positive probability and, therefore, player 2 will have to counter this by making the costly move b_1, likewise with a positive probability. As a result, strategy B_1 will no longer be a best reply to A_1, and (A_1, B_1) will no longer be an equilibrium point.

The difference between perfect and imperfect equilibrium points can be easily recognized in the extensive form of a game but is often hidden in the normal form. This implies that, contrary to a view that used to be the commonly accepted view by game theorists, the normal form of the game in general fails to provide all the information we need for an adequate game-theoretical analysis of the game, and we may have to go back to the extensive form to recover some of the missing information.

On the other hand, if the normal form often contains too little information, the extensive form usually contains far too much, including many unnecessary details about the chance moves and about the time sequence in which individual moves have to be made. For this reason, Reinhard Selten and I have defined an intermediate game form, called the *agent normal form*, which omits the unnecessary details but retains the essential information about the game. (We obtain the agent normal form if we replace each player by as many 'agents' as the number of his information sets in the game, and then construct a normal form with these agents as the players.)[23]

IX   NON-COOPERATIVE BARGAINING MODELS
FOR COOPERATIVE GAMES

Ever since 1944 (the year when von Neumann and Morgenstern first published the *Theory of Games and Economic Behavior*),[24] most research in game theory has been devoted either to a study of the mathematical properties of saddle points in *two-person zero-*

sum games, or to a construction and study of solution concepts for *cooperative* games. Many very interesting cooperative solution concepts were proposed. But this work on cooperative games showed little theoretical unity: taken as a group, the different solution concepts that were suggested shared few common theoretical assumptions, and no clear criteria emerged to decide under what conditions one particular solution concept was to be used and under what conditions another.

Part of the problem is that the authors of the different solution concepts have seldom made it sufficiently clear what institutional arrangements (negotiation rules) each particular solution concept is meant to assume about the bargaining process among the players, through which these players are supposed to reach an agreement about the final outcome of the game. Yet, it is well known that the very same cooperative game may have quite different outcomes, depending on the actual negotiation rules governing this bargaining process in any particular case. The nature of the agreements likely to arise will be often quite sensitive to such factors as who can talk to whom and, in particular, who can talk to whom *first*, ahead of other people; the degree to which negotiations are kept public, or can be conducted in private by smaller groups if the participants so desire; the conditions that decide whether any agreement remains open to repeal and to possible re-negotiation, or is made final and irrevocable; the possibility or impossibility of unilaterally making binding promises and/or threats, etc.

As a simple example, consider the following three-person co-operative game (called a three-person majority game). Each player, acting alone, can only achieve a zero payoff. Any coalition of two players can obtain a joint payoff of $100. The three-person coalition of all three players can likewise obtain a joint payoff of $100. Obviously, in this game, if pairs of players can meet separately, then the two players who manage to meet first are very likely to form a two-person coalition, and to divide the $100 in a ratio 50:50 between them. In contrast, if the negotiation rules disallow pairwise meetings, and if the negotiation time permitted is too short for forming any two-person coalition during the three-person negotiating session, then the likely outcome is a three-person coalition, with payoffs $33\frac{1}{3}:33\frac{1}{3}:33\frac{1}{3}$. Finally, under most other negotiation rules, both two-person and three-person coalitions will arise from time to time, and the probability of either outcome will depend on the extent to which these rules tend to help or hinder two-person agreements.

Another limitation of most cooperative solution concepts is this. Their application is basically restricted to fully cooperative games, and does not extend to that very wide range of real-life game situations which have a status intermediate between fully cooperative games and fully non-cooperative games – such as social situations where some kinds of agreements are enforceable while others are not, or where different agreements may be enforceable to different extents and with different probabilities; or where enforceable agreements are possible among some particular players but are impossible among other players; or where enforceable agreements cannot be concluded at some stages of the game but can be concluded at other stages, etc. In many contexts, it is particularly regrettable that most of these cooperative solution concepts are inapplicable to games possessing a strongly sequential structure, making the emergence of agreements a very gradual process, later agreements being built on earlier agreements and extending the former in various ways.

Yet, John Nash, when he introduced the very concepts of cooperative and of non-cooperative games, also suggested what, in my opinion, is a possible remedy to these deficiencies in the theory of cooperative games.[25] He suggested that an analysis of any cooperative game should start with constructing a precisely defined formal bargaining model (bargaining game) to represent the bargaining process among the players. Of course, this bargaining model must provide a mathematical representation, in the abstract language appropriate to such models, for the negotiation rules we want to assume, whether on empirical or on theoretical grounds, to govern this bargaining process. Then, according to Nash's proposal, this bargaining model should be analyzed as a *non-cooperative* game, by a careful study of its equilibrium points.

Nash's suggestion is based on the assumption that close cooperation among the players in a cooperative game usually requires a prior agreement about the payoffs, which, in most cases, can be achieved only by bargaining among the players. But this bargaining itself must have the nature of a non-cooperative game, unless we want to assume that the players will agree in an even earlier subsidiary bargaining game on how they will act in the main bargaining game – which would be not only a rather implausible assumption but would also lead to an infinite regress.

Nash's proposal, if it can be successfully implemented, will enable us to unify the whole theory of cooperative games, because it provides a uniform method of analysis for all cooperative games.

Of course, even under Nash's proposal, it will remain true that any given cooperative game may have a number of different solutions, depending on the details of the bargaining process assumed to occur among the players. But, as we have argued, this is how it should be, since in real life different bargaining methods do lead to different outcomes. Yet, the game-theoretical analysis of this bargaining process can be based on the same theoretical principles in all cases.[26]

Indeed, Nash's approach will result in a unification of *both* the theory of cooperative games *and* the theory of non-cooperative games, because it essentially reduces the problem of solving a cooperative game to the problem of solving a non-cooperative bargaining game. Moreover, it can be easily extended to games which have any kind of intermediate status between fully cooperative games and fully non-cooperative games (including games of a sequential nature, mentioned before).

X   A BAYESIAN SOLUTION CONCEPT FOR NON-COOPERATIVE GAMES

Nash's proposal, however, runs into a very basic difficulty – the same difficulty, which, up to very recently, also prevented the emergence of any really useful theory of non-cooperative games. This difficulty lies in the fact that almost any interesting non-cooperative game – including almost any interesting non-cooperative bargaining game – will have a great many, and often infinitely many, very different equilibrium points. (This remains true even if we restrict ourselves to perfect equilibrium points.) This means that, if all we can say is that the outcome of the game will be an equilibrium point (or even that it will be a perfect equilibrium point), then we are saying little more than that almost anything can happen in the game.

For instance, consider the very simplest kind of two-person bargaining game, in which the two players have to divide $100. If they cannot agree on how to divide it, then both of them will receive zero payoffs. This game can be analyzed by means of the following formal bargaining model. Both players name a number between 0 and 100. Let the numbers named by players 1 and 2 be x_1 and x_2. (Intuitively, these numbers represent the two players' payoff demands.) If $x_1 + x_2 \leq 100$, then player 1 will obtain $\$x_1$ and player 2 will obtain $\$x_2$. On the other hand if $x_1 + x_2 > 0$, then both players will get $0.

If we assume that money can be divided in any possible fractional amount, then this game has infinitely many equilibrium points, since any pair (x_1, x_2) of payoff demands is an equilibrium point so long as $x_1 + x_2 = 100$. (Of course, by the rules we have assumed for the game, we must also have $0 \leqslant x_1 \leqslant 100$ for $i = 1, 2$.) But even if we assumed that money can be divided only in amounts corresponding to whole numbers of dollars, the game will still have 101 equilibrium points. (Of these, 99 equilibrium points will even be perfect equilibrium points. Only the two 'extreme' equilibrium points giving one player \$100 and giving the other player \$0 turn out to be imperfect.) The situation will be even worse if we study more interesting, and therefore inevitably more complicated, bargaining games.

In view of these facts, several years ago Reinhard Selten and I decided to look into the possibility of defining a new solution concept for non-cooperative games, which will always select *one* particular equilibrium point as the solution for the game. This research project proved to be much more difficult than we had anticipated. But in 1974 we did find such a solution concept which seems to satisfy all intuitive and mathematical requirements. Conceptually, it amounts to an extension of the Bayesian approach, so successful in the analysis of one-person decision situations, to an analysis of non-cooperative games. The definition of this solution concept is based on the disturbed agent normal form of the game (see section VIII above).

Let me introduce the following notation. We shall assume that a given player i ($i = 1, 2, \ldots, n$) has K_i different pure strategies. Therefore, a mixed strategy s_i of player i will be a probability vector of the form $s_i = (s_i^1, s_i^2, \ldots, s_i^{K_i})$, where s_i^k ($k = 1, 2, \ldots, K_i$) is the probability that this mixed strategy s_i assigns to the kth pure strategy of player i.

A strategy combination of all n players will be denoted as $s = (s_1, s_2, \ldots, s_n)$. Let $\bar{s}_i$ denote the strategy combination we obtain if we omit player i's strategy s_i from the strategy combination s. Thus, $\bar{s}_i$ is a strategy combination of the $(n - 1)$ players *other* than player i. We can write $\bar{s}_i = (s_1, \ldots, s_{i-1}, s_{i+1}, \ldots, s_n)$.

Our solution is defined in two steps. As a first step, we construct a *prior probability distribution* p_i, over the pure strategies of each player i ($i = 1, 2, \ldots, n$). The second step involves a mathematical procedure which selects one specific equilibrium point $s^* = (s_1^*, s_2^*, \ldots, s_n^*)$ as the solution of the game, on the basis of these n prior probability distributions $p_1, p_2, \ldots, p_n$.

Each prior probability distribution p_i over the pure strategies of a given player i has the form of a probability vector $p_i = (p_i^1, p_i^2, \ldots, p_i^{K_i})$, where each component p_i^k ($k = 1, 2, \ldots, K_i$) is the initial *subjective* probability that every other player j ($j \neq i$) is assumed to assign to the possibility that player i will use his kth pure strategy in the game. Consequently, the prior probability distribution p_i is a probability vector of the same mathematical form as is any mixed strategy s_i of player i. But, of course, p_i has a very different game-theoretical interpretation. Whereas a mixed strategy s_i expresses the *objective* probabilities s_i^k that player i *himself* chooses to associate with his various pure strategies as a matter of his own strategical decision, the prior probability distribution p_i expresses the *subjective* probabilities p_i^k that the *other* players are assumed to associate with player i's various pure strategies, simply because they do not know in advance which particular strategy player i is going to use.

The numerical prior probability p_i^k our theory assigns to a given pure strategy of each player i is meant to express the theoretical probability that a rational individual, placed in player i's position, will actually use this particular pure strategy in the game. More specifically, p_i^k is meant to express the theoretical probability that player i will find himself in a situation where his best reply is to use this particular pure strategy. (This theoretical probability p_i^k, of course, is not directly given, but can only be obtained from a suitable probabilistic model about the players' behavior in the game.)

For convenience, I shall write the n-vector consisting of the n prior probability distributions as $p = (p_1, p_2, \ldots, p_n)$. I shall write the $(n - 1)$-vector consisting of the $(n - 1)$ prior probability distributions associated with the $(n - 1)$ players other than player i as $\bar{p}_i = (p_1, \ldots, p_{i-1}, p_{i+1}, \ldots, p_n)$. Thus, $\bar{p}_i$ is the $(n-1)$-vector we obtain if we omit the ith component p_i from the n-vector p.

The second step in defining our solution involves a mathematical procedure, based on Bayesian ideas, for selecting one particular equilibrium point s^* as solution, when the vector p of all prior probability distributions is given. The simplest Bayesian model would be to assume that each player i would use a strategy s_i that was his best reply to the prior probability distribution vector $\bar{p}_i$ he would associate with the other $(n - 1)$ players' pure strategies, and then to define the solution as the strategy combination $s = (s_1, s_2 \ldots, s_n)$. But this simple-minded approach is unworkable because in general this best-reply strategy combination s will not be an equilibrium point of the game.

Accordingly, our theory uses a mathematical procedure, called the *tracing procedure*, which takes this best-reply strategy combination s as a starting point, but then systematically modifies this strategy combination in a continuous manner, until it is finally transformed into an equilibrium point s^*, which will serve as the solution of the game.

This mathematical procedure is meant to model the psychological process, to be called the *solution process*, by which the players' expectations converge to a specific equilibrium point as the solution of the game. At the beginning, the players' initial expectations about the other players' strategies will correspond to the subjective probability distributions (prior distributions) p_i, and their initial reaction to these expectations will be an inclination to use their best-reply strategies s_i. Then, they will gradually modify their expectations and their tentative strategy choices until in the end *both* their expectations and their strategy choices will converge to the equilibrium strategies s_i^* corresponding to the solution s^*.[27]

Of course, within the confines of this paper, I could do no more than sketch the barest outlines of our solution concept for non-cooperative games and, more generally, could draw only a very incomplete picture of some recent work in game theory. But I feel my paper has achieved its purpose if it has induced a few people from other disciplines to take some interest in the results of Bayesian decision theory and in some recent developments in game theory, and in the implications both of these may have for a deeper understanding of the nature of rational behaviour.[28]

NOTES

1 The author wishes to express his thanks to the National Science Foundation for supporting this research by Grant GS-3222 to the Center for Research in Management Science, University of California, Berkeley.

2 For references, see J. C. Harsanyi, 'Rational-choice models of political behavior vs functionalist and conformist theories', *World Politics*, 21 (1969), pp. 513–38.

3 H. A. Simon, *The New Science of Management Decision* (Harper and Brothers, New York, 1960).

4 See footnote 2.

5 The concept of criterion-satisfying behavior is probably not very important in everyday life. But it is very important in ethics (see J. C. Harsanyi, 'Ethics in terms of hypothetical imperatives', *Mind*, 47 (1958), pp. 305–16.

6 Of course, in many cases, when a person has changed his goals, the most natural explanation will be that his preferences themselves have changed. In such cases, the model of rational behavior will be inapplicable, or at least will have to be supplemented by other explanatory theories, e.g. by learning theory, etc.

7 For proof, see G. Debreu, *Theory of Value* (John Wiley and Sons, New York, 1959).

8 A very simple proof of this theorum for *risk* is given in R. D. Luce and H. Raiffa, *Games and Decisions* (John Wiley and Sons, New York, 1957), pp. 23–31. But note that their Assumptions 1 and 5 could be easily stated as one axiom, whereas Assumption 6 could be omitted because it follows from the other axioms. (Of course, the use of extra axioms was intentional and made it possible for the authors to simplify their statement of the proof.) Note also that their substitutability axiom (Assumption 4) could be replaced by a form of the sure-thing principle (see below). A simple proof of the theorum for uncertainty is found in F. J. Anscombe and R. J. Aumann, 'A definition of subjective probability', *Annals of Mathematical Statistics*, 34 (1963), pp. 199–205.

9 The term 'Bayesian approach' is often restricted to the proposal of using expected-utility maximization as a definition of rational behavior in the case of uncertainty, where expected utility must be computed in terms of subjective probabilities.

10 The terms 'bet' and 'lottery' will be used interchangeably.

11 See R. Radner and J. Marschak, 'Note on some proposed decision criteria', in R. M. Thrall et al., *Decision Processes* (John Wiley and Sons, New York, 1954), pp. 61–8; J. C. Harsanyi, 'Can the maximin principle serve as a basis for morality? A critique of John Rawls's theory', *American Political Science Review*, 59 (1975), pp. 594–606.

12 J. C. Harsanyi, 'Cardinal welfare, individualistic ethics and interpersonal comparisons of utility', *Journal of Political Economy*, 63 (1955), pp. 309–21.

13 See J. C. Harsanyi, 'Cardinal utility in welfare economics and in the theory of risk-taking', *Journal of Political Economy*, 61 (1953), pp. 434–5; 'Cardinal welfare'; 'Ethics in terms of hypothetical imperatives'; 'Can the maximin principle serve as a basis for morality?'; 'Nonlinear social welfare functions', *Theory and Decision*, 7 (1975), pp. 61–80.

14 See J. C. Harsanyi, 'Games with incomplete information played by "Bayesian" players', *Management Science*, 14 (1967–68), pp. 159–82, 320–34, 486–502.

15 Cf. ibid., pp. 496–7.

16 J. F. Nash, 'Equilibrium points in *n*-person games', *Proceedings of the National Academy of Sciences*, USA, 36 (1950), pp. 48–9; 'Non-cooperative games', *Annals of Mathematics*, 54 (1951), pp. 286–95.

17 Ibid.

18 For an explanation of the name, see Luce and Raiffa, *Games and Decisions*, pp. 94–5.

19 R. Selter, Spieltheoretische Behandlung eines Oligopolmodells mit Nachfrageträgheit', *Zeitschrift fur die gesamte Staatswissenschaft*, 121 (1965), pp. 301–24, 667–89.

20 For a non-technical explanation of the terms 'normal form' and 'extensive form', see Luce and Raiffa, *Games and Decisions*.

21 From a logical point of view, strategy B_1 does satisfy the formal criteria for an equilibrium strategy because, in applying these criteria, the conditional statement defining strategy B_1 ('player 2 would make move b_1 if player 1 made move a_2') is interpreted as *material implication*. In contrast, B_1 fails to satisfy our informal criteria for a 'rational' strategy because, in applying these latter criteria, the same conditional statement is automatically interpreted as a subjunctive conditional.

22 We say that a given point of the game tree is reached by the game if it either represents the starting position in the game or is reached by a branch representing an actual move by a player or by chance. Thus, in our example, the point marked by 1 is always reached whereas the point marked by 2 is reached only if player 1 chooses to make move a_2 (rather than move a_1).

23 For a more extensive and more rigorous discussion of perfect equilibrium points and of the agent normal form see R. Setter, 'Re-examination of the perfectness concept for equilibrium points in extensive games', *International Journal of Game Theory*, 4 (1975), pp. 25–55.

24 J. von Neumann and O. Morgenstern, *Theory of Games and Economic Behavior* (Princeton University Press, Princeton, N.J., 1944).

25 Nash, 'Non-cooperative games', p. 295.

26 While Nash's proposal has many advantages, it certainly does not provide an easy routine method for solving cooperative games because, except in the very simplest cases, finding a suitable formal bargaining model for any given game – just as a modelling of any other complicated dynamic process – may be a very difficult task, requiring a good deal of insight and ingenuity, and subject to no mechanical rules.

27 J. C. Harsanyi, 'The tracing procedure: A Bayesian approach to defining a solution for n-person non-cooperative games', *International Journal of Game Theory*, 4 (1975), pp. 61–94.

28 Our theory will be described in J. C. Harsanyi and R. Selter, *A General Theory of Equilibrium Selection in Games* (MS in progress). For a preliminary outline of the theory, see J. C. Harsanyi, 'Solutions of some bargaining games under the Harsanyi–Selter solution theory', Parts I–II, *Mathematical Social Sciences*, 3 (1982), pp. 171–91, 259–79.

4

The Economic Approach to Human Behavior

GARY BECKER

Economy is the art of making the most of life.

George Bernard Shaw

In my work I use an 'economic' approach in seeking to understand human behavior in a variety of contexts and situations. Although few persons would dispute the distinctiveness of an economic approach, it is not easy to state exactly what distinguishes the economic approach from sociological, psychological, anthropological, political, or even genetical approaches. In this essay I attempt to spell out the principal attributes of the economic approach.

Let us turn for guidance first to the definitions of different fields. At least three conflicting definitions of economics are still common. Economics is said to be the study of (1) the allocation of material goods to satisfy material wants,[1] (2) the market sector,[2] and (3) the allocation of scarce means to satisfy competing ends.[3]

The definition of economics in terms of material goods is the narrowest and the least satisfactory. It does not describe adequately either the market sector or what economists 'do'. For the production of tangible goods now provides less than half of all the market employment in the United States, and the intangible outputs of the service sector are now larger in value than the outputs of the foods sector.[4] Moreover, economists are as successful in understanding the production and demand for retail trade, films, or education as they are for autos or meat. The persistence of definitions which tie economics to material goods is perhaps due to a reluctance to

This essay was first published in G. Becker, *The Economic Approach to Human Behavior* (Chicago University Press, 1976), 3–14; Copyright © Chicago University Press 1976. I am indebted to Joseph Ben-David, Milton Friedman, Victor Fuchs, Robert T. Michael, Jacob Mincer, Richard Posner, and T. W. Schultz. I am especially indebted to George J. Stigler and Robert K. Merton. None of these people should be held responsible for my arguments.

submit certain kinds of human behaviour to the 'frigid' calculus of economics.

The definition of economics in terms of scarce means and competing ends is the most general of all. It defines economics by the nature of the problem to be solved, and encompasses far more than the market sector or 'what economists do'.[5] Scarcity and choice characterize all resources allocated by the political process (including which industries to tax, how fast to increase the money supply, and whether to go to war); by the family (including decisions about a marriage mate, family size, the frequency of church attendance, and the allocation of time between sleeping and waking hours); by scientists (including decisions about allocating their thinking time, and mental energy to different research problems); and so on in endless variety. This definition of economics is so broad that it often is a source of embarrassment rather than of pride to many economists, and usually is immediately qualified to exclude most nonmarket behavior.[6]

All of these definitions of economics simply define the scope, and none tells us one iota about what the 'economic' approach is. It could stress tradition and duty, impulsive behavior, maximizing behavior, or any other behavior in analyzing the market sector or the allocation of scarce means to competing ends.

Similarly, definitions of sociology and other social sciences are of equally little help in distinguishing their approaches from others. For example, the statement that sociology 'is the study of social aggregates and groups in their institutional organization, of institutions and their organization, and of causes and consequences of changes in institutions and social organization'[7] does not distinguish the subject matter, let alone the approach, of sociology from, say, economics. Or the statement that 'comparative psychology is concerned with the behavior of different species of living organisms[8] is as general as the definitions of economics and sociology, and as uninformative.

Let us turn away from definitions, therefore, because I believe that what most distinguishes economics as a discipline from other disciplines in the social sciences is not its subject matter but its approach. Indeed, many kinds of behavior fall within the subject matter of several disciplines: for example, fertility behavior is considered part of sociology, anthropology, economics, history, and perhaps even politics. I contend that the economic approach is uniquely powerful because it can integrate a wide range of human behavior.

Everyone recognizes that the economic approach assumes maximizing behavior more explicitly and extensively than other approaches do, be it the utility or wealth function of the household, firm, union or government bureau that is maximized. Moreover, the economic approach assumes the existence of markets that with varying degrees of efficiency coordinate the actions of different participants – individuals, firms, even nations – so that their behavior becomes mutually consistent. Since economists generally have had little to contribute, especially in recent times, to the understanding of how preferences are formed, preferences are assumed not to change substantially over time, nor to be very different between wealthy and poor persons, or even between persons in different societies and cultures.

Prices and other market instruments allocate the scarce resources within a society and thereby constrain the desires of participants and coordinate their actions. In the economic approach, these market instruments perform most, if not all, of the functions assigned to 'structure' in sociological theories.[9]

The preferences that are assumed to be stable do not refer to market goods and services, like oranges, automobiles, or medical care, but to underlying objects of choice that are produced by each household using market goods and services, their own time, and other inputs. These underlying preferences are defined over fundamental aspects of life, such as health, prestige, sensual pleasure, benevolence or envy, that do not always bear a stable relation to market goods and services. The assumption of stable preferences provides a stable foundation for generating predictions about responses to various changes, and prevents the analyst from succumbing to the temptation of simply postulating the required shift in preferences to 'explain' all apparent contradictions to his predictions.

The combined assumptions of maximizing behavior, market equilibrium, and stable preferences, used relentlessly and unflinchingly, form the heart of the economic approach as I see it. They are responsible for the many theorems associated with this approach. For example, that (1) a rise in price reduces quantity demanded,[10] be it a rise in the market price of eggs reducing the demand for eggs, a rise in the 'shadow' price of children reducing the demand for children, or a rise in the office waiting time for physicians, which is one component of the full price of physician services, reducing the demand for their services; (2) a rise in price increases the quantity supplied, be it a rise in the market price of beef increasing the number of cattle raised and slaughtered, a rise in the wage rate offered to married women increasing their labor force participation, or a reduction in 'cruising' time raising the effective price received by taxicab drivers and thereby increasing the supply of taxicabs; (3) competitive markets satisfy consumer preferences more effectively than monopolistic markets, be it the market for aluminum or the market for ideas[11]; or (4) a tax on the output of a market reduces that output, be it an excise tax on gasoline that reduces the use of gasoline, punishment of criminals (which is a 'tax' on crime) that reduces the amount of crime, or a tax on wages that reduces the labor supplied to the market sector.

The economic approach is clearly not restricted to material goods and wants, nor even to the market sector. Prices, be they the money prices of the market sector or the 'shadow' imputed prices of the nonmarket sector, measure the opportunity cost of using scarce resources, and the economic approach predicts the same kind of response to shadow prices as to market prices. Consider, for example, a person whose only scarce resource is his limited amount of time. This time is used to produce various commodities that enter his preference function, the aim being to maximize utility. Even without a market sector, either directly or indirectly, each commodity has a relevant marginal 'shadow' price, namely, the time required to produce a unit change in that commodity; in equilibrium, the ratio of these prices must equal the ratio of the marginal utilities.[12] Most importantly, an increase in the relative price of any commodity – that is, an increase in the time required to produce a unit of that commodity – would tend to reduce the consumption of that commodity.

The economic approach does not assume that all participants in any market necessarily have complete information or engage in costless transactions. Incomplete information or costly transactions should not, however, be confused with irrational or volatile behavior.[13] The economic approach has developed a theory of the optimal or rational accumulation of costly information[14] that implies, for example, greater investment in information when undertaking major than minor decisions – the purchase of a house or entrance into marriage versus the purchase of a sofa or bread. The assumption that information is often seriously incomplete because it is costly to acquire is used in the economic approach to explain the same kind of behavior that is explained by irrational and volatile behavior, or traditional behavior, or 'nonrational' behavior in other discussions.

When an apparently profitable opportunity to a firm, worker, or household is not exploited, the economic approach does not take uge in assertions about irrationality, contentment with wealth ...eady acquired, or convenient *ad hoc* shifts in values (that is, preferences). Rather it postulates the existence of costs, monetary or psychic, of taking advantage of these opportunities that eliminate their profitability – costs that may not be easily 'seen' by outside observers. Of course, postulating the existence of costs closes or 'completes' the economic approach in the same, almost tautological, way that postulating the existence of (sometimes unobserved) uses of energy completes the energy system, and preserves the law of the conservation of energy. Systems of analysis in chemistry, genetics, and other fields are completed in a related manner. The critical question is whether a system is completed in a useful way; the important theorems derived from the economic approach indicate that it has been completed in a way that yields much more than a bundle of empty tautologies in good part because, as I indicated earlier, the assumption of stable preferences provides a foundation for predicting the responses to various changes.

Moreover, the economic approach does not assume that decision units are necessarily conscious of their efforts to maximize or can verbalize or otherwise describe in an informative way reasons for the systematic patterns in their behavior.[15] Thus it is consistent with the emphasis on the subconscious in modern psychology and with the distinction between manifest and latent functions in sociology.[16] In addition, the economic approach does not draw conceptual distinctions between major and minor decisions, such as those involving life and death[17] in contrast to the choice of a brand of coffee; or between decisions said to involve strong emotions and those with little emotional involvement,[18] such as in choosing a mate or the number of children in contrast to buying paint; or between decisions by persons with different incomes, education, or family backgrounds.

Indeed, I have come to the position that the economic approach is a comprehensive one that is applicable to all human behavior, be it behavior involving money prices or imputed shadow prices, repeated or infrequent decisions, large or minor decisions, emotional or mechanical ends, rich or poor persons, men or women, adults or children, brilliant or stupid persons, patients or therapists, businessmen or politicians, teachers or students. The applications of the economic approach so conceived are as extensive as the scope of economics in the definition given earlier that emphasizes scarce means and competing ends. It is an appropriate approach to go with such a broad and unqualified definition, and with the statement by Shaw that begins this essay.

For whatever its worth in evaluating this conclusion, let me indicate that I did not arrive at it quickly. In college I was attracted by the problems studied by sociologists and the analytical techniques used by economists. These interests began to merge in my doctoral study,[19] which used economic analysis to understand racial discrimination.[20] Subsequently, I applied the economic approach to fertility, education, the uses of time, crime, marriage, social interactions, and other 'sociological,' 'legal,' and 'political' problems. Only after long reflection on this work and the rapidly growing body of related work by others did I conclude that the economic approach was applicable to all human behavior.

The economic approach to human behavior is not new, even outside the market sector. Adam Smith often (but not always!) used this approach to understand political behavior. Jeremy Bentham was explicit about his belief that the pleasure-pain calculus is applicable to all human behavior: 'Nature has placed mankind under the governance of two sovereign masters, *pain and pleasure. It is for them alone to point out what we ought to do, as well as to determine what we shall do . . . . They govern us in all we do, in all we say, in all we think*'.[21] The pleasure-pain calculus is said to be applicable to *all* we do, say, and think, without restriction to monetary decisions, repetitive choices, unimportant decisions, etc. Bentham did apply his calculus to an extremely wide range of human behavior, including criminal sanctions, prison reform, legislation, usury laws and jurisprudence as well as the markets for goods and services. Although Bentham explicitly states that the pleasure-pain calculus is applicable to what we 'shall' do as well as to what we 'ought' to do, he was primarily interested in 'ought' – he was first and foremost a reformer – and did not develop a theory of actual human behavior with many testable implications. He often became bogged down in tautologies because he did not maintain the assumption of stable preferences, and because he was more concerned about making his calculus consistent with all behavior than about deriving the restrictions it imposed on behavior.

Marx and his followers have applied what is usually called an 'economic' approach to politics, marriage, and other nonmarket behavior as well as to market behavior. But to the Marxist, the economic approach means that the organization of production is decisive in determining social and political structure, and he places much emphasis upon material goods, processes, and ends, conflict between capitalists and workers, and general subjugation of one class by another. What I have called the 'economic approach' has little in common with this view. Moreover, the Marxist, like the

Benthamite, has concentrated on what ought to be, and has often emptied his approach of much predictive content in the effort to make it consistent with all events.

Needless to say, the economic approach has not provided equal insight into and understanding of all kinds of behavior: for example, the determinants of war and of many other political decisions have not yet been much illuminated by this approach (or by any other approach). I believe, however, that the limited success is mainly the result of limited effort and not lack of relevance. For, on the one hand, the economic approach has not been systematically applied to war, and its application to other kinds of political behavior is quite recent; on the other hand, much apparently equally intractable behavior – such as fertility, child-rearing, labor force participation and other decisions of families – has been greatly illuminated in recent years by the systematic application of the economic approach.

Support for the economic approach is provided by the extensive literature developed in the last twenty years that uses the economic approach to analyze an almost endlessly varied set of problems, including the evolution of language,[22] church attendance,[23] capital punishment,[24] the legal system,[25] the extinction of animals,[26] and the incidence of suicide.[27] To convey dramatically the flavor of the economic approach, I discuss briefly three of the more unusual and controversial applications.

Good health and a long life are important aims of most persons, but surely no more than a moment's reflection is necessary to convince anyone that they are not the only aims: somewhat better health or a longer life may be sacrificed because they conflict with other aims. The economic approach implies that there is an 'optial' expected length of life, where the value in utility of an addition al year is less than the utility foregone by using time and other resources to obtain that year. Therefore, a person may be a heavy smoker or so committed to work as to omit all exercise, not necessarily because he is ignorant of the consequences or 'incapable' of using the information he possesses, but because the life-span forfeited is not worth the cost to him of quitting smoking or working less intensively. These would be unwise decisions if a long life were the only aim, but as long as other aims exist, they could be informed and in this sense 'wise'.

According to the economic approach, therefore, *most* (if not all!) deaths are to some extent 'suicides' in the sense that they could have been postponed if more resources had been invested in prolonging life. This not only has implications for the analysis of what are ordinarily called suicides,[28] but also calls into question the common distinction between suicides and 'natural' deaths. Once again the economic approach and modern psychology come to similar conclusions since the latter emphasizes that a 'death wish' lies behind many 'accidental' deaths and others allegedly due to 'natural' causes.

The economic approach does not merely restate in language familiar to economists different behavior with regard to health, removing all possibility of error by a series of tautologies. The approach implies, for example, that both health and medical care would rise as a person's wage rate rose, that aging would bring declining health although expenditures on medical care would rise, and that more education would induce an increase in health even though expenditures on medical care would fall. None of these or other implications is necessarily true, but all appear to be consistent with the available evidence.[29]

According to the economic approach, a person decides to marry when the utility expected from marriage exceeds that expected from remaining single or from additional search for a more suitable mate. Similarly, a married person terminates his (or her) marriage when the utility anticipated from becoming single or marrying someone else exceeds the loss in utility from separation, including losses due to physical separation from one's children, division of joint assets, legal fees, and so forth. Since many persons are looking for mates, a *market* in marriages can be said to exist: each person tries to do the best he can, given that everyone else in the market is trying to do the best they can. A sorting of persons into different marriages is said to be an equilibrium sorting if persons not married to each other in this sorting could not marry and make each better off.

Again, the economic approach has numerous implications about behavior that could be falsified. For example, it implies that 'likes' tend to marry each other, when measured by intelligence, education, race, family background, height, and many other variables, and that 'unlikes' marry when measured by wage rates and some other variables. The implication that men with relatively high wage rates marry women with relatively low wage rates (other variables being held constant) surprises many, but appears consistent with the available data when they are adjusted for the large fraction of married women who do not work. The economic approach also implies that higher-income persons marry younger and divorce less frequently than others, implications consistent with the available evidence[30] but not with common beliefs. Still another implication is that an increase in the relative earnings of wives increases the likelihood of marital dissolution, which partly explains the greater dissolution rate among black than among white families.

According to the Heisenberg indeterminacy principle, the phenomena analyzed by physical scientists cannot be observed in a 'natural' state because their observations change these phenomena. An even stronger principle has been suggested for social scientists since they are participants as well as analysts and, therefore, are supposed to be incapable of objective observation. The economic approach makes a very different but distantly related point: namely that persons only choose to follow scholarly or other intellectual or artistic pursuits if they expect the benefits, both monetary and psychic, to exceed those available in alternative occupations. Since the criterion is the same as in the choice of more commonplace occupations, there is no obvious reason why intellectuals would be less concerned with personal rewards, more concerned with social well-being, or more intrinsically honest than others.[31]

It then follows from the economic approach that an increased demand by different interest groups or constituencies for particular intellectual arguments and conclusions would stimulate an increased supply of these arguments, by the theorem cited earlier on the effect of a rise in 'price' on quantity supplied. Similarly, a flow of foundation or government funds into particular research topics, even 'ill-advised' topics, would have no difficulty generating proposals for research on those topics. What the economic approach calls normal responses of supply to changes in demand, others may call intellectual or artistic 'prostitution' when applied to intellectual or artistic pursuits. Perhaps, but attempts to distinguish sharply the market for intellectual and artistic services from the market for 'ordinary' goods have been the source of confusion and inconsistency.[32]

I am not suggesting that the economic approach is used by all economists for all human behavior or even by most economists for most. Indeed, many economists are openly hostile to all but the traditional applications. Moreover, economists cannot resist the temptation to hide their own lack of understanding behind allegations of irrational behavior, unnecessary ignorance, folly, *ad hoc* shifts in values, and the like, which is simply acknowledging defeat in the guise of considered judgment. For example, if some Broadway theater owners charge prices that result in long delays before seats are available, the owners are alleged to be ignorant of the profit-maximizing price structure rather than the analyst ignorant of why actual prices do maximize profits. When only a portion of the variation in earnings among individuals is explained, the unexplained portion is attributed to luck or chance,[33] not to ignorance of or inability to measure additional systematic components. The coal industry is called inefficient because certain cost and output calculations point in that direction,[34] although an attractive alternative hypothesis is that the calculations are seriously in error.

War is said to be caused by madmen, and political behavior, more generally, dominated by folly and ignorance. Recall Keynes's remark about 'madmen in authority, who hear voices in the air',[35] and although Adam Smith, the principal founder of the economic approach, interpreted some laws and legislation in the same way that he interpreted market behavior, even he, without much discussion, lamely dismissed others as a result of folly and ignorance.[36]

Examples abound in the economic literature of changes in preferences conveniently introduced *ad hoc* to explain puzzling behavior. Education is said to change preferences – about different goods and services, political candidates, or family size – rather than real income or the relative cost of different choices.[37] Businessmen talk about the social responsibilities of business because their attitudes are said to be influenced by public discussions of this question rather than because such talk is necessary to maximize their profits, given the climate of public intervention. Or advertisers are alleged to take advantage of the fragility of consumer preferences, with little explanation of why, for example, advertising is heavier in some industries than others, changes in importance in a given industry over time, and occurs in quite competitive industries as well as in monopolistic ones.[38]

Naturally, what is tempting to economists nominally committed to the economic approach becomes irresistible to others without this commitment, and without a commitment to the scientific study of sociology, psychology, or anthropology. With an ingenuity worthy of admiration if put to better use, almost any conceivable behavior is alleged to be dominated by ignorance and irrationality, values and their frequent unexplained shifts, custom and tradition, the compliance somehow induced by social norms, or the ego and the id.

I do not mean to suggest that concepts like the ego and the id, or social norms, are without any scientific content. Only that they are tempting materials, as are concepts in the economic literature, for *ad hoc* and useless explanations of behavior. There is no apparent embarrassment in arguing, for example, both that the sharp rise in fertility during the late 1940s and early 1950s resulted from a renewed desire for large families, and that the prolonged decline starting just a few years later resulted from a reluctance to be tied down with many children. Or developing countries are supposed simply to copy the Americans' 'compulsiveness' about time, whereas the growing value of their own time is a more fruitful explanation of their increased effort to economize in their use of time. More generally, custom and tradition are said to be abandoned in developing countries because their young people are seduced by Western ways; it is not recognized that while custom and tradition are quite useful in a relatively stationary environment, they are often a hindrance in a dynamic world, especially for young people.[39]

Even those believing that the economic approach is applicable to all human behavior recognize that many noneconomic variables also significantly affect human behavior. Obviously, the laws of mathematics, chemistry, physics, and biology have a tremendous influence on behavior through their influence on preferences and production possibilities. That the human body ages, that the rate of population growth equals the birth rate plus the migration rate minus the death rate, that children of more intelligent parents tend to be more intelligent than children of less intelligent parents, that people need to breathe to live, that a hybrid plant has a particular yield under one set of environmental conditions and a very different yield under another set, that gold and oil are located only in certain parts of the world and cannot be made from wood, or that an assembly line operates according to certain physical laws – all these and more influence choices, the production of people and goods, and the evolution of societies.

To say this, however, is not the same as saying that, for example, the rate of population growth is itself 'noneconomic' in the sense that birth, migration, and death rates cannot be illuminated by the economic approach, or that the rate of adoption of new hybrids is 'noneconomic' because it cannot be explained by the economic approach. Indeed, useful implications about the number of children in different families have been obtained by assuming that families maximize their utility from stable preferences subject to a constraint on their resources and prices, with resources and prices partly determined by the gestation period for pregnancies, the abilities of children, and other noneconomic variables.[40] Similarly, the rate of adoption of hybrid corn in different parts of the United States has been neatly explained by assuming that farmers maximize profits: new hybrids were more profitable, and thus adopted earlier, in some parts because weather, soil, and other physical conditions were more favorable.[41]

Just as many noneconomic variables are necessary for understanding human behavior, so too are the contributions of sociologists, psychologists, sociobiologists, historians, anthropologists, political scientists, lawyers and others. Although I am arguing that the economic approach provides a useful framework for understanding all human behavior, I am not trying to downgrade the contributions of other social scientists, nor even to suggest that the economist's are more important. For example, the preferences that are given and stable in the economic approach, and that determine the predictions from this approach, are analyzed by the sociologist, psychologist, and probably most successfully by the sociobiologist.[42] How preferences have become what they are, and their perhaps slow evolution over time, are obviously relevant in predicting and understanding behavior. The value of other social sciences is not diminished even by an enthusiastic and complete acceptance of the economic approach.

At the same time, however, I do not want to soften the impact of what I am saying in the interest of increasing its acceptability in the short run. I am saying that the economic approach provides a valuable unified framework for understanding *all* human behavior, although I recognize, of course, that much behavior is not yet understood, and that noneconomic variables and the techniques and findings from other fields contribute significantly to the understanding of human behavior. That is, although a comprehensive *framework* is provided by the economic approach, many of the important concepts and techniques are provided and will continue to be provided by other disciplines.

The heart of my argument is that human behavior is not compartmentalized, sometimes based on maximizing, sometimes not, sometimes motivated by stable preferences, sometimes by volatile ones, sometimes resulting in an optimal accumulation of information, sometimes not. Rather, all human behavior can be viewed as involving participants who maximize their utility from a stable set of preferences and accumulate an optimal amount of information and other inputs in a variety of markets.

If this argument is correct, the economic approach provides a unified framework for understanding behavior that has long been sought by and eluded Bentham, Comte, Marx and others. The reader will judge for himself the power of the economic approach.

NOTES

1 '[Economics] is the social science that deals with the ways in which men and societies seek to satisfy their material needs and desires', Albert Rees, 'Economics', in *International Encyclopedia of Social Sciences*, ed. D. E. Sills (Macmillan and Free Press, New York, 1968); '[Economics is the] study of the supplying of man's physical needs and wants', article 'Economics', *The Columbia Encyclopedia*, 3rd edn, p. 624; and see also the many earlier references to Marshall, Cannan and others in L. Robbins, *The Nature and Significance of Economic Science* (Macmillan, London, 1962).

2 A. C. Pigou said '[Economic welfare is] that part of social welfare that can be brought directly or indirectly into relation with the measuring rod of money' (*The Economics of Welfare*, 4th edn (St Martin's Press, New York, 1962)).

3 'Economics is the science which studies human behavior as a relationship between ends and scarce means which have alternative uses', Robbins, *The Nature and Significance of Economic Science*; 'Economics . . . is the study of the allocation of scarce resources among unlimited and competing uses', Rees, 'Economics', and many other references.

4 V. Fuchs, *The Service Economy* (Columbia University Press for the National Bureau of Economic Research, New York, 1968).

5 This definition of economics is attributed to Jacob Viner by K. Boulding, *Economic Analysis* (Harper and Row, New York, 1966).

6 Almost immediately after giving the broad definition of economics, Rees ('Economics') gives one in terms of material needs, without explaining why he so greatly reduced the scope of economics. Even Robbins, after an excellent discussion of what an economic problem is in the first chapter of *The Nature and Significance of Economic Science*, basically restricts his analysis in later chapters to the market sector.

7 A. J. Reiso, 'Sociology', in Sills, *International Encyclopedia of Social Sciences*.

8 R. H. Waters and B. N. Brunnell, 'Comparative Psychology', in Sills, *International Encyclopedia of Social Sciences*.

9 An excellent statement of structural analysis can be found in R. K. Merton, *Social Theory and Social Structure* (Free Press, New York, 1968).

10 That maximizing behavior is not necessary to reach this conclusion is shown in chapter 8 of G. Becker, *The Economic Approach to Human Behavior* (Chicago University Press, Chicago, 1976).

11 A. Director, 'The parity of the economic market place', *Journal of Law and Economics* (1964) October; R. H. Coase, 'The market for goods and the market for ideas', *American Economic Review*, 64 (1974) May.

12 He maximizes $U = U(Z_1 \ldots Z_m)$ subject to $Z_1 = f_i(t_i)$, and $\sum t_i = t$,

where Z_i is the ith commodity, f_i the production function for Z_i, and t_i is the time input into Z_i. The well-known first-order equilibrium conditions for the allocation of his scarce resource, time, are:

$$\frac{\partial U}{\partial Z_t} = \lambda\frac{\partial t_t}{\partial Z_t} = \frac{\lambda}{\partial Z_t/\partial t_t} = \frac{\lambda}{MP_{t_i}}$$

where λ is his marginal utility of time.

13 J. Schumpeter (*Capitalism, Socialism and Democracy* (reprinted Harper, New York, 1950) chapter 21, 'Human Nature in Politics') appears to confuse them, although with considerable modification.

14 The pioneering paper is G. Stigler, 'The economics of information', *Journal of Political Economy*, 69 (1961) June.

15 This point is stressed in Milton Friedman's seminal article, 'The methodology of positive economics' in *Essays in Positive Economics* (Chicago University Press, Chicago, 1953).

16 Merton, *Social Theory*.

17 The length of life itself is a decision variable in the important study by M. Grossman, *The Demand for Health: A Theoretical and Empirical Investigation* (Columbia University Press for the National Bureau of Economic Research, New York, 1972).

18 Jeremy Bentham said 'As to the proposition that passion does not calculate, this, like most of these very general and oracular propositions is not true . . . I would not say that even a madman does not calculate. Passion calculates, more or less, in every man.' He does add, however, that 'of all passions, the most given to calculation . . . [is] the motive of pecuniary interest.' *An Introduction to the Principles of Morals and Legislation* (Harper, New York, 1963).

19 Actually, a little earlier in an essay that applied economic analysis to political behavior.

20 G. C. Becker, *The Economics of Discrimination*, 2nd edn (University of Chicago Press, Chicago, 1971).

21 Bentham, *An Introduction to the Principles of Morals and Legislation*.

22 J. Marschak, 'Economics of Language', *Behavioral Science*, 10 (1965), April.

23 C. Azzi and R. Ehrenberg, 'Household allocation of time and church attendance', *Journal of Political Economy*, 83 (1975), February.

24 I. Ehrlich, 'Capital punishment: A case of life or death', *American Economic Review* (1975), June.

25 R. Posner, *Economic Analysis of Law* (Little, Brown, Boston, 1973); G. S. Becker and W. M. Lands (eds), *Essays in the Economics of Crime and Punishment* (Columbia University Press for the National Bureau of Economic Research, New York, 1974).

26 V. Smith, 'The primitive hunter culture, Pleistocene extinction, and the rise of agriculture', *Journal of Political Economy*, 83 (1975), August.

27 D. Hammermesh and N. M. Soss, 'An economic theory of suicide', *Journal of Political Economy*, 82 (1974), January/February.

28 Some of these implications are developed in Hammermesh and Soss, ibid.

29 These implications are derived and the evidence is examined in M. Grossman, 'The economics of joint production in the household' (Report 7145, Center for Mathematical Studies in Business and Economics, University of Chicago, 1971).

30 See M. C. Keeley, 'A model of marital formation: the determinants of the optimal age of first marriage and differences in age of marriage', PhD dissertation, University of Chicago, 1974.

31 This example is taken from G. J. Stigler, 'Do economists matter?', *Southern Economic Journal*, 42 (1976). See also the discussion of the reward system in science and of related issues in R. K. Merton, *The Sociology of Science* (University of Chicago Press, Chicago, 1973), esp. part 4.

32 See Director, 'The parity of the economic market place'; Coase, 'The market for goods'.

33 An extreme example is C. Jencks, *Inequality* (Basic Books, New York, 1972). Jencks even grossly understates the portion that can be explained because he neglects the important work by Mincer and others (see, especially, J. Mincer, *Schooling, Experience, and Earnings* (Columbia University Press for the National Bureau of Economic Research, New York, 1974)).

34 See J. M. Henderson, *The Efficiency of the Coal Industry: An Application of Linear Programming* (Harvard University Press, Cambridge, Mass., 1958).

35 J. M. Keynes, *The General Theory of Employment, Interest, and Money* (Harcourt Brace and World, New York, 1962), p. 383.

36 See G. J. Stigler, 'Smith's travels on the ship of state', *History of Political Economy* (1971), Fall. Smith does not indicate why ignorance is dominant in the passage of certain laws and not others.

37 For an interpretation of the effects of education on consumption entirely in terms of income and price effects, see R. T. Michael, *The Effect of Education on Efficiency in Consumption* (National Bureau of Economic Research, New York, 1972).

38 For an analysis of advertising that is consistent with stable preferences, and implies that advertising might even be more important in competitive than monopolistic industries, see G. J. Stigler and G. S. Becker, 'De gustibus non est disputandum', *American Economic Review*, 67 (1977), December. For a good discussion of advertising that also does not rely on shifts in preferences, see P. J. Nelson, 'The economic consequence of advertising', *Journal of Business*, 48 (1975), April.

39 See Stigler and Becker, 'De gustibus non est disputandum'.

40 See also T. W. Schultz (ed.), *Economics of the Family* (University of Chicago Press, Chicago, 1975).

41 Z. Grilichers, 'Hybrid corn: an exploration in the economics of "technical change" ', *Econometrica*, 25 (1957), October.

42 See E. O. Wilson, *Sociobiology* (Harvard University Press, Cambridge, Mass., 1975).

5

The Framing of Decisions and the Psychology of Choice

AMOS TVERSKY AND DANIEL KAHNEMAN

Explanations and predictions of people's choices, in everyday life as well as in the social sciences, are often founded on the assumption of human rationality. The definition of rationality has been much debated, but there is general agreement that rational choices should satisfy some elementary requirements of consistency and coherence. In this article we describe decision problems in which people systematically violate the requirements of consistency and coherence, and we trace these violations to the psychological principles that govern the perception of decision problems and the evaluation of options.

A decision problem is defined by the acts or options among which one must choose, the possible outcomes or consequences of these acts, and the contingencies or conditional probabilities that relate outcomes to acts. We use the term 'decision frame' to refer to the decision-maker's conception of the acts, outcomes, and contingencies associated with a particular choice. The frame that a decision-maker adopts is controlled partly by the formulation of the problem and partly by the norms, habits, and personal characteristics of the decision-maker.

It is often possible to frame a given decision problem in more than one way. Alternative frames for a decision problem may be compared to alternative perspectives on a visual scene. Veridical perception requires that the perceived relative heights of two neighboring mountains, say, should not reverse with changes of vantage point. Similarly, rational choice requires that the preference between options should not reverse with changes of frame. Because of imperfections of human perception and decision, however, changes of perspective often reverse the relative apparent size of objects and the relative desirability of options.

We have obtained systematic reversals of preference by variations in the framing of acts, contingencies, or outcomes. These

This essay was first published in *Science* 211 (1981), pp. 453–8, copyright 1981 by the American Association for the Advancement of Science.

effects have been observed in a variety of problems and in the choices of different groups of respondents. Here we present selected illustrations of preference reversals, with data obtained from students at Stanford University and at the University of British Columbia who answered brief questionnaires in a classroom setting. The total number of respondents for each problem is denoted by N, and the percentage who chose each option is indicated in brackets.

The effect of variations in framing is illustrated in problems 1 and 2.

Problem 1 [$N = 152$]: Imagine that the US is preparing for the outbreak of an unusual Asian disease, which is expected to kill 600 people. Two alternative programs to combat the disease have been proposed. Assume that the exact scientific estimates of the consequences of the programs are as follows:

If Program A is adopted, 200 people will be saved. [72 per cent]

If Program B is adopted, there is 1/3 probability that 600 people will be saved, and 2/3 probability that no people will be saved. [28 per cent]

Which of the two programs would you favor?

The majority choice in this problem is risk averse: the prospect of certainly saving 200 lives is more attractive than a risky prospect of equal expected value, that is, a one-in-three chance of saving 600 lives.

A second group of respondents was given the cover story of problem 1 with a different formulation of the alternative programs, as follows:

Problem 2 [$N = 155$]:

If Program C is adopted 400 people will die. [22 per cent]

If Program D is adopted there is 1/3 probability that nobody will die, and 2/3 probability that 600 people will die. [78 per cent]

Which of the two programs would you favor?

The majority choice in problem 2 is risk taking: the certain death of 400 people is less acceptable than the two-in-three chance that 600 will die. The preferences in problems 1 and 2 illustrate a common pattern: choices involving gains are often risk averse and choices involving losses are often risk taking. However, it is easy to see that the two problems are effectively identical. The only difference between them is that the outcomes are described in problem 1 by the number of lives saved and in problem 2 by the number of lives lost. The change is accompanied by a pronounced shift from risk aversion to risk taking. We have observed this reversal in several groups of respondents, including university faculty and physicians. Inconsistent responses to problems 1 and 2 arise from the conjunction of a framing effect with contradictory attitudes toward risks involving gains and losses. We turn now to an analysis of these attitudes.

THE EVALUATION OF PROSPECTS

The major theory of decision-making under risk is the expected utility model. This model is based on a set of axioms, for example, transitivity of preferences, which provide criteria for the rationality of choices. The choices of an individual who conforms to the axioms can be described in terms of the utilities of various outcomes for that individual. The utility of a risky prospect is equal to the expected utility of its outcomes, obtained by weighting the utility of each possible outcome by its probability. When faced with a choice, a rational decision-maker will prefer the prospect that offers the highest expected utility.[1,2]

As will be illustrated below, people exhibit patterns of preference which appear incompatible with expected utility theory. We have presented elsewhere[3] a descriptive model, called prospect theory, which modifies expected utility theory so as to accommodate these observations. We distinguish two phases in the choice process: an initial phase in which acts, outcomes, and contingencies are framed, and a subsequent phase of evaluation.[4] For simplicity, we restrict the formal treatment of the theory to choices involving stated numerical probabilities and quantitative outcomes, such as money, time, or number of lives.

Consider a prospect that yields outcome x with probability p, outcome y with probability q, and the status quo with probability $1 - p - q$. According to prospect theory, there are values $v(.)$ associated with outcomes, and decision weights $\pi(.)$ associated with probabilities, such that the overall value of the prospect equals $\pi(p) v(x) + \pi(q) v(y)$. A slightly different equation should be applied if all outcomes of a prospect are on the same side of the zero point.[5]

In prospect theory, outcomes are expressed as positive or negative deviations (gains or losses) from a neutral reference outcome, which is assigned a value of zero. Although subjective values differ among individuals and attributes, we propose that the value function is commonly S-shaped, concave above the reference point and convex below it, as illustrated in figure 5.1. For example, the difference in subjective value between gains of $10 and $20 is greater than the subjective difference between gains of $110 and $120. The same relation between value differences holds for the corresponding losses. Another property of the value function is that the response to losses is more extreme than the response to gains. The displeasure associated with losing a sum of money is generally greater than the pleasure associated with winning the same amount, as is reflected in people's reluctance to accept fair bets on a toss of a coin. Several studies of decision[3,6] and judgment[7] have confirmed these properties of the value function.[8]

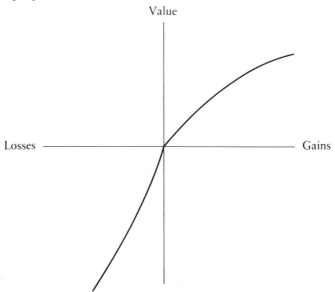

Figure 5.1.   A hypothetical value function

The second major departure of prospect theory from the expected utility model involves the treatment of probabilities. In expected utility theory the utility of an uncertain outcome is weighted by its probability; in prospect theory the value of an uncertain outcome is multiplied by a decision weight $\pi(p)$, which is a monotonic function of p but is not a probability. The weighting function π has the following properties. First, impossible events are discarded, that is, $\pi(0) = 0$, and the scale is normalized so that $\pi(1) = 1$, but the function is not well behaved near the endpoints. Second, for low probabilities $\pi(p) > p$, but $\pi(p) + \pi(1 - p) \leq 1$. Thus low probabilities are overweighted, moderate and high probabilities are underweighted, and the latter effect is more pronounced than the former. Third, $\pi(pq)/\pi(p) < \pi(pqr)/\pi(pr)$ for all $0 < p, q, r \leq 1$. That is, for any fixed probability ratio q, the ratio of decision weights is closer to unity when the probabilities are low than when they are high, for example, $\pi(.1)/\pi(.2) > \pi(.4)/\pi(.8)$. A hypothetical weighting function which satisfies these properties is shown in figure 5.2. The major qualitative properties of decision weights can be extended to cases in which the probabilities of outcomes are subjectively assessed rather than explicitly given. In these situations, however, decision weights may also be affected by other characteristics of an event, such as ambiguity or vagueness.[9]

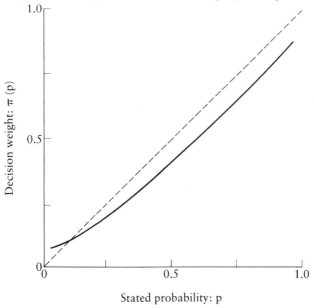

Figure 5.2. A hypothetical weighting function

Prospect theory, and the scales illustrated in figures 5.1 and 5.2, should be viewed as an approximate, incomplete, and simplified description of the evaluation of risky prospects. Although the properties of v and π summarize a common pattern of choice, they are not universal: the preferences of some individuals are not well

128   *Amos Tversky and Daniel Kahneman*

described by an S-shaped value function and a consistent set of decision weights. The simultaneous measurement of values and decision weights involves serious experimental and statistical difficulties.[10]

If π and v were linear throughout, the preference order between options would be independent of the framing of acts, outcomes, or contingencies. Because of the characteristic nonlinearities of π and v, however, different frames can lead to different choices. The following three sections describe reversals of preference caused by variations in the framing of acts, contingencies, and outcomes.

THE FRAMING OF ACTS

Problem 3 [$N = 150$]: Imagine that you face the following pair of concurrent decisions. First examine both decisions, then indicate the options you prefer.

Decision (i). Choose between:

    A. a sure gain of $240 [84 per cent]
    B. 25% chance to gain $1000 and
        75% chance to gain nothing [16 per cent]

Decision (ii). Choose between:

    C. a sure loss of $750 [13 per cent]
    D. 75% chance to lose $1000, and
        25% chance to lose nothing [87 per cent]

The majority choice in decision (i) is risk averse: a riskless prospect is preferred to a risky prospect of equal or greater expected value. In contrast, the majority choice in decision (ii) is risk taking: a risky prospect is preferred to a riskless prospect of equal expected value. This pattern of risk aversion in choices involving gains and risk seeking in choices involving losses is attributable to the properties of v and π. Because the value function is S-shaped, the value associated with a gain of $240 is greater than 25 per cent of the value associated with a gain of $1000, and the (negative) value associated with a loss of $750 is smaller than 75 per cent of the value associated with a loss of $1000. Thus the shape of the value function contributes to risk aversion in decision (i) and to risk seeking in decision (ii). Moreover, the underweighting of moderate and high probabilities contributes to the relative attractiveness of the sure gain in (i) and to the relative aversiveness of the sure loss in (ii). The same analysis applies to problems 1 and 2.

Because (i) and (ii) were presented together, the respondents had in effect to choose one prospect from the set: A and C, B and C, A and D, B and D. The most common pattern (A and D) was chosen by 73 per cent of respondents, while the least popular pattern (B and C) was chosen by only 3 per cent of respondents. However, the combination of B and C is definitely superior to the combination A and D, as is readily seen in problem 4.

Problem 4 [N = 86]: Choose between:

A & D. 25% chance to win $240, and
        75% chance to lose $760. [0 per cent]

B & C. 25% chance to win $250, and
        75% chance to lose $750. [100 per cent]

When the prospects were combined and the dominance of the second option became obvious, all respondents chose the superior option. The popularity of the inferior option in problem 3 implies that this problem was framed as a pair of separate choices. The respondents apparently failed to entertain the possibility that the conjunction of two seemingly reasonable choices could lead to an untenable result.

The violations of dominance observed in problem 3 do not disappear in the presence of monetary incentives. A different group of respondents who answered a modified version of problem 3, with real payoffs, produced a similar pattern of choices.[11] Other authors have also reported that violations of the rules of rational choice, originally observed in hypothetical questions, were not eliminated by payoffs.[12]

We suspect that many concurrent decisions in the real world are framed independently, and that the preference order would often be reversed if the decisions were combined. The respondents in problem 3 failed to combine options, although the integration was relatively simple and was encouraged by instructions.[13] The complexity of practical problems of concurrent decisions, such as portfolio selection, would prevent people from integrating options without computational aids, even if they were inclined to do so.

THE FRAMING OF CONTINGENCIES

The following triple of problems illustrates the framing of contingencies. Each problem was presented to a different group of respondents. Each group was told that one participant in ten, preselected at random, would actually be playing for money. Chance events were realized, in the respondents' presence, by drawing a single ball from a bag containing a known proportion of balls of the winning color, and the winners were paid immediately.

Problem 5 [N = 77]: Which of the following options do you prefer?

A. a sure win of $30 [78 per cent]
B. 80% chance to win $45 [22 per cent]

Problem 6 [N = 85]: Consider the following two-stage game. In the first stage, there is a 75% chance to end the game without winning anything, and a 25% chance to move into the second stage. If you reach the second stage you have a choice between:

C. a sure win of $30 [74 per cent]
D. 80% chance to win $45 [26 per cent]

Your choice must be made before the game starts, i.e., before the outcome of the first stage is known. Please indicate the option you prefer.

Problem 7 [N = 81]: Which of the following options do you prefer?

E. 25% chance to win $30 [42 per cent]
F. 20% chance to win $45 [58 per cent]

Let us examine the structure of these problems. First, note that problems 6 and 7 are identical in terms of probabilities and outcomes, because prospect C offers a .25 chance to win $30 and prospect D offers a probability of .25 × .80 = .20 to win $45. Consistency therefore requires that the same choice be made in problems 6 and 7. Second, note that problem 6 differs from problem 5 only by the introduction of a preliminary stage. If the second stage of the game is reached, then problem 6 reduces to problem 5; if the game ends at the first stage, the decision does not affect the outcome. Hence there seems to be no reason to make a different choice in problems 5 and 6. By this logical analysis, problem 6 is equivalent to problem 7 on the one hand and problem 5 on the other. The participants, however, responded similarly to problems 5 and 6 but differently to problem 7. This pattern of responses exhibits two phenomena of choice: the certainty effect and the pseudocertainty effect.

The contrast between problems 5 and 7 illustrates a phenomenon discovered by Allais,[14] which we have labeled the certainty effect: a reduction of the probability of an outcome by a constant factor has more impact when the outcome was initially certain than when it was merely probable. Prospect theory attributes this effect to the properties of π. It is easy to verify, by applying the equation of prospect theory to problems 5 and 7, that people for whom the value ratio $v(30)/v(45)$ lies between the weight ratios $\pi(.20)/\pi(.25)$ and $\pi(.80)/\pi(1.0)$ will prefer A to B and F to E, contrary to expected utility theory. Prospect theory does not predict a reversal of preference for every individual in problems 5 and 7. It only requires that an individual who has no preference between A and B prefer F to E. For group data, the theory predicts the observed directional shift of preference between the two problems.

The first stage of problem 6 yields the same outcome (no gain) for both acts. Consequently, we propose, people evaluate the options conditionally, as if the second stage had been reached. In this framing, of course, problem 6 reduces to problem 5. More generally, we suggest that a decision problem is evaluated conditionally when (1) there is a state in which all acts yield the same outcome, such as failing to reach the second stage of the game in problem 6, and (2) the stated probabilities of other outcomes are conditional on the nonoccurrence of this state.

The striking discrepancy between the responses to problems 6 and 7, which are identical in outcomes and probabilities, could be described as a pseudocertainty effect. The prospect yielding $30 is relatively more attractive in problem 6 than in problem 7, as if it had the advantage of certainty. The sense of certainty associated with option C is illusory, however, since the gain is in fact contingent on reaching the second stage of the game.[15]

We have observed the certainty effect in several sets of problems, with outcomes ranging from vacation trips to the loss of human lives. In the negative domain, certainty exaggerates the aversiveness of losses that are certain relative to losses that are merely probable. In a question dealing with the response to an epidemic, for example, most respondents found 'a sure loss of 75 lives' more aversive than '80% chance to lose 100 lives' but preferred '10% chance to lose 75 lives' over '8% chance to lose 100 lives', contrary to expected utility theory.

We also obtained the pseudocertainty effect in several studies where the description of the decision problems favored conditional evaluation. Pseudocertainty can be induced either by a sequential formulation, as in problem 6, or by the introduction of causal contingencies. In another version of the epidemic problem, for instance, respondents were told that risk to life existed only in the event (probability .10) that the disease was carried by a particular virus. Two alternative programs were said to yield 'a sure loss of 75 lives' or '80% chance to lose 100 lives' if the critical virus was involved, and no loss of life in the event (probability .90) that the disease was carried by another virus. In effect, the respondents were asked to choose between 10 per cent chance of losing 75 lives and 8 per cent chance of losing 100 lives, but their preferences were the same as when the choice was between a sure loss of 75 lives and 80 per cent chance of losing 100 lives. A conditional framing was evidently adopted in which the contingency of the noncritical virus was eliminated, giving rise to a pseudocertainty effect. The certainty effect reveals attitudes toward risk that are inconsistent with the axioms of rational choice, whereas the pseudocertainty effect violates the more fundamental requirement that preferences should be independent of problem description.

Many significant decisions concern actions that reduce or eliminate the probability of a hazard, at some cost. The shape of π in the range of low probabilities suggests that a protective action which reduces the probability of a harm from 1 per cent to zero, say, will be valued more highly than an action that reduces the probability of the same harm from 2 per cent to 1 per cent. Indeed, probabilistic insurance, which reduces the probability of loss by half, is judged to be worth less than half the price of regular insurance that eliminates the risk altogether.[3]

It is often possible to frame protective action in either conditional or unconditional form. For example, an insurance policy that covers fire but not flood could be evaluated either as full protection against the specific risk of fire or as a reduction in the overall probability of property loss. The preceding analysis suggests that insurance should appear more attractive when it is presented as the elimination of risk than when it is described as a reduction of risk. P. Slovic, B. Fischhoff, and S. Lichtenstein, in an unpublished study, found that a hypothetical vaccine which reduces the probability of contracting a disease from .20 to .10 is less attractive if it is described as effective in half the cases than if it is presented as fully effective against one of two (exclusive and equiprobable) virus strains that produce identical symptoms. In accord with the present analysis of pseudocertainty, the respondents valued full protection against an identified virus more than probabilistic protection against the disease.

The preceding discussion highlights the sharp contrast between lay responses to the reduction and the elimination of risk. Because no form of protective action can cover all risks to human welfare, all insurance is essentially probabilistic: it reduces but does not eliminate risk. The probabilistic nature of insurance is commonly masked by formulations that emphasize the completeness of protection against identified harms, but the sense of security that such formulations provide is an illusion of conditional framing. It appears that insurance is bought as protection against worry, not only against risk, and that worry can be manipulated by the labeling of outcomes and by the framing of contingencies. It is not easy to determine whether people value the elimination of risk too much or the reduction of risk too little. The contrasting attitudes to the two forms of protective action, however, are difficult to justify on normative grounds.[16]

THE FRAMING OF OUTCOMES

Outcomes are commonly perceived as positive or negative in relation to a reference outcome that is judged neutral. Variations of the reference point can therefore determine whether a given outcome is evaluated as a gain or as a loss. Because the value function is generally concave for gains, convex for losses, and steeper for losses than for gains, shifts of reference can change the value difference between outcomes and thereby reverse the preference order between options.[6] Problems 1 and 2 illustrated a preference reversal induced by a shift of reference that transformed gains into losses.

For another example, consider a person who has spent an afternoon at the race track, has already lost $140, and is considering a $10 bet on a 15:1 long shot in the last race. This decision can be framed in two ways, which correspond to two natural reference points. If the status quo is the reference point, the outcomes of the bet are framed as a gain of $140 and a loss of $10. On the other hand, it may be more natural to view the present state as a loss of $140, for the betting day, and accordingly frame the last bet as a chance to return to the reference point or to increase the loss to $150. Prospect theory implies that the latter frame will produce more risk seeking than the former. Hence, people who do not adjust their reference point as they lose are expected to take bets that they would normally find unacceptable. This analysis is supported by the observation that bets on long shots are most popular on the last race of the day.[17]

Because the value function is steeper for losses than for gains, a difference between options will loom larger when it is framed as a disadvantage of one option rather than as an advantage of the other option. An interesting example of such an effect in a riskless context has been noted by Thaler.[18] In a debate on a proposal to pass to the consumer some of the costs associated with the processing of credit-card purchases, representatives of the credit-card industry requested that the price difference be labeled a cash discount rather than a credit-card surcharge. The two labels induce different reference points by implicitly designating as normal reference the higher or the lower of the two prices. Because losses loom larger than gains, consumers are less willing to accept a surcharge than to forego a discount. A similar effect has been observed in experimental studies of insurance: the proportion of respondents who preferred a sure loss to a larger probable loss was significantly greater when the former was called an insurance premium.[19,20]

These observations highlight the lability of reference outcomes, as well as their role in decision-making. In the examples discussed so far, the neutral reference point was identified by the labeling of outcomes. A diversity of factors determine the reference outcome in everyday life. The reference outcome is usually a state to which one has adapted; it is sometimes set by social norms and expectations; it sometimes corresponds to a level of aspiration, which may or may not be realistic.

We have dealt so far with elementary outcomes, such as gains or losses in a single attribute. In many situations, however, an action gives rise to a compound outcome, which joins a series of changes in a single attribute, such as a sequence of monetary gains and losses, or a set of concurrent changes in several attributes. To describe the framing and evaluation of compound outcomes, we use the notion of a psychological account, defined as an outcome frame which specifices (1) the set of elementary outcomes that are evaluated jointly and the manner in which they are combined and (2) a reference outcome that is considered neutral or normal. In the account that is set up for the purchase of a car, for example, the cost of the purchase is not treated as a loss nor is the car viewed as a gift. Rather, the transaction as a whole is evaluated as positive, negative, or neutral, depending on such factors as the performance of the car and the price of similar cars in the market. A closely related treatment has been offered by Thaler.[18]

We propose that people generally evaluate acts in terms of a minimal account, which includes only the direct consequences of the act. The minimal account associated with the decision to accept a gamble, for example, includes the money won or lost in that gamble and excludes other assets or the outcome of previous gambles. People commonly adopt minimal accounts because this mode of framing (1) simplifies evaluation and reduces cognitive strain, (2) reflects the intuition that consequences should be causally linked to acts, and (3) matches the properties of hedonic experience, which is more sensitive to desirable and undesirable changes than to steady states.

There are situations, however, in which the outcomes of an act affect the balance in an account that was previously set up by a related act. In these cases, the decision at hand may be evaluated in terms of a more inclusive account, as in the case of the bettor who views the last race in the context of earlier losses. More generally, a sunk-cost effect arises when a decision is referred to an existing account in which the current balance is negative. Because of the nonlinearities of the evaluation process, the minimal account and a more inclusive one often lead to different choices.

Problems 8 and 9 illustrate another class of situations in which an existing account affects a decision:

Problem 8 [N = 183]: Imagine that you have decided to see a play where admission is $10 per ticket. As you enter the theater you discover that you have lost a $10 bill.
Would you still pay $10 for a ticket for the play?
Yes [88 per cent]   No [12 per cent]

Problem 9 [N = 200]: Imagine that you have decided to see a play and paid the admission price of $10 per ticket. As you enter the theater you discover that you have lost the ticket. The seat was not marked and the ticket cannot be recovered.
Would you pay $10 for another ticket?
Yes [46 per cent]   No [54 per cent]

The marked difference between the responses to problems 8 and 9 is an effect of psychological accounting. We propose that the purchase of a new ticket in problem 9 is entered in the account that was set up by the purchase of the original ticket. In terms of this account, the expense required to see the show is $20, a cost which many of our respondents apparently found excessive. In problem 8, on the other hand, the loss of $10 is not linked specifically to the ticket purchase and its effect on the decision is accordingly slight.

The following problem, based on examples by Savage[2] and Thaler,[18] further illustrates the effect of embedding an option in different accounts. Two versions of this problem were presented to different groups of subjects. One group (N = 93) was given the values that appear in parentheses, and the other group (N = 88) the values shown in square brackets.

Problem 10: Imagine that you are about to purchase a jacket for ($125) [$15], and a calculator for ($15) [$125]. The calculator salesman informs you that the calculator you wish to buy is on sale for ($10) [$120] at the other branch of the store, located 20 minutes drive away. Would you make the trip to the other store?

The response to the two versions of problem 10 were markedly different: 68 per cent of the respondents were willing to make an extra trip to save $5 on a $15 calculator; only 29 per cent were willing to exert the same effort when the price of the calculator was $125. Evidently the respondents do not frame problem 10 in the minimal account, which involves only a benefit of $5 and a cost of some inconvenience. Instead, they evaluate the potential saving in a more inclusive account, which includes the purchase of the calculator but not of the jacket. By the curvature of v, a discount of $5 has a greater impact when the price of the calculator is low than when it is high.

A closely related observation has been reported by Pratt, Wise, and Zeckhauser,[21] who found that the variability of the prices at which a given product is sold by different stores is roughly proportional to the mean price of that product. The same pattern was observed for both frequently and infrequently purchased items. Overall, a ratio of 2:1 in the mean price of two products is associated with a ratio of 1.86:1 in the standard deviation of the respective quoted prices. If the effort that consumers exert to save each dollar on a purchase, for instance by a phone call, were independent of price, the dispersion of quoted prices should be about the same for all products. In contrast, the data of Pratt et al.[21] are consistent with the hypothesis that consumers hardly exert more effort to save $15 on a $150 purchase than to save $5 on a $50 purchase.[18] Many readers will recognize the temporary devaluation of money which facilitates extra spending and reduces the significance of small discounts in the context of a large expenditure, such as buying a house or a car. This paradoxical variation in the value of money is incompatible with the standard analysis of consumer behavior.

DISCUSSION

In this article we have presented a series of demonstrations in which seemingly inconsequential changes in the formulation of choice problems caused significant shifts of preference. The inconsistencies were traced to the interaction of two sets of factors: variations in the framing of acts, contingencies, and outcomes, and the characteristic nonlinearities of values and decision weights. The demonstrated effects are large and systematic, although by no means universal. They occur when the outcomes concern the loss of human lives as well as in choices about money; they are not restricted to hypothetical questions and are not eliminated by monetary incentives.

Earlier we compared the dependence of preferences on frames to the dependence of perceptual appearance on perspective. If while traveling in a mountain range you notice that the apparent relative heights of mountain peaks vary with your vantage point, you will conclude that some impressions of relative height must be erroneous, even when you have no access to the correct answer. Similarly, one may discover that the relative attractiveness of options varies when the same decision problem is framed in different ways. Such a discovery will normally lead the decision-maker to reconsider the original preferences, even when there is no simple way to resolve the inconsistency. The susceptibility to perspective effects is of special concern in the domain of decision-making because of the absence of objective standards such as the true height of mountains.

The metaphor of changing perspective can be applied to other phenomena of choice, in addition to the framing effects with which we have been concerned here.[19] The problem of self-control is naturally construed in these terms. The story of Ulysses' request to be bound to the mast of the ship in anticipation of the irresistible temptation of the Sirens' call is often used as a paradigm case.[22] In this example of precommitment, an action taken in the present renders inoperative an anticipated future preference. An unusual feature of the problem of intertemporal conflict is that the agent who views a problem from a particular temporal perspective is also aware of the conflicting views that future perspectives will offer. In most other situations, decision-makers are not normally aware of the potential effects of different decision frames on their preferences.

The perspective metaphor highlights the following aspects of the psychology of choice. Individuals who face a decision problem and have a definite preference (1) might have a different preference in a different framing of the same problem, (2) are normally unaware of alternative frames and of their potential effects on the relative attractiveness of options, (3) would wish their preferences to be independent of frame, but (4) are often uncertain how to resolve detected inconsistencies.[23] In some cases (such as problems 3 and 4 and perhaps problems 8 and 9) the advantage of one frame becomes evident once the competing frames are compared, but in other cases (problems 1 and 2 and problems 6 and 7) it is not obvious which preferences should be abandoned.

These observations do not imply that preference reversals, or other errors of choice or judgment,[24] are necessarily irrational. Like other intellectual limitations, discussed by Simon[25] under the heading of 'bounded rationality', the practice of acting on the most readily available frame can sometimes be justified by reference to the mental effort required to explore alternative frames and avoid potential inconsistencies. However, we propose that the details of the phenomena described in this article are better explained by prospect theory and by an analysis of framing than by *ad hoc* appeals to the notion of cost of thinking.

The present work has been concerned primarily with the descriptive question of how decisions are made, but the psychology of choice is also relevant to the normative question of how decisions ought to be made. In order to avoid the difficult problem of justifying values, the modern theory of rational choice has adopted the coherence of specific preferences as the sole criterion of rationality. This approach enjoins the decision-maker to resolve inconsistencies but offers no guidance on how to do so. It implicitly assumes that the decision-maker who carefully answers the question 'What do I really want?' will eventually achieve coherent preferences. However, the susceptibility of preferences to variations of framing raises doubt about the feasibility and adequacy of the coherence criterion.

Consistency is only one aspect of the lay notion of rational behavior. As noted by March,[26] the common conception of rationality also requires that preferences or utilities for particular outcomes should be predictive of the experiences of satisfaction or displeasure associated with their occurrence. Thus, a man could be judged irrational either because his preferences are contradictory or because his desires and aversions do not reflect his pleasures and pains. The predictive criterion of rationality can be applied to resolve inconsistent preferences and to improve the quality of decisions. A predictive orientation encourages the decision-maker to focus on future experience and to ask 'What will I feel then?' rather than 'What do I want now?' The former question, when answered with care, can be the more useful guide in difficult decisions. In particular, predictive considerations may be applied to select the decision frame that best represents the hedonic experience of outcomes.

Further complexities arise in the normative analysis because the framing of an action sometimes affects the actual experience of its outcomes. For example, framing outcomes in terms of overall wealth or welfare rather than in terms of specific gains and losses may attenuate one's emotional response to an occasional loss. Similarly, the experience of a change for the worse may vary if the change is framed as an uncompensated loss or as a cost incurred to achieve some benefit. The framing of acts and outcomes can also reflect the acceptance or rejection of responsibility for particular consequences, and the deliberate manipulation of framing is commonly used as an instrument of self-control.[22] When framing influences the experience of consequences, the adoption of a decision frame is an ethically significant act.

NOTES

1 J. Von Neumann and O. Morgenstern, *Theory of Games and Economic Behavior* (Princeton University Press, Princeton, N.J., 1947); H. Raiffa, *Decision Analysis: Lectures on Choices Under Uncertainty* (Addison-Wesley, Reading, Mass., 1968); P. Fishburn, *Utility Theory for Decision Making* (Wiley, New York, 1970).
2 L. J. Savage, *The Foundations of Statistics* (Wiley, New York, 1954).
3 D. Kahneman and A. Tversky, *Econometrica* 47 (1979), p. 263.
4 The framing phase includes various editing operations that are applied to simplify prospects, for example by combining events or outcomes or by discarding negligible components. See Kahneman and Tversky, 1979.
5 If $p + q = 1$ and either $x > y > 0$ or $x < y < 0$, the equation in the text is replaced by $v(y) + \pi(p) [v(x) - v(y)]$, so that decision weights are not applied to sure outcomes.
6 P. Fishburn and G. Kochenberger, *Decision Sci.*, 10 (1979), p. 503; D. J. Laughhunn, J. W. Payne, R. Crum, *Manage Sci.*, 26 (1980), pp. 1039–60; J. W. Payne, D. J. Laughhunn, R. Crum, *Manage Sci.*, 27 (1981), pp. 953–8; S. A. Eraker and H. C. Sox, *Med. Decision Making*, 1 (1981), pp. 29–39. In the last study several hundred clinic patients made hypothetical choices between drug therapies for severe headaches, hypertension, and chest pain. Most patients were risk averse when the outcomes were described as postitive (for example,

reduced pain or increased life expectancy) and risk taking when the outcomes were described as negative (increased pain or reduced life expectancy). No significant differences were found between patients who actually suffered from the ailments described and patients who did not.

7 E. Galanter and P. Pliner, in *Sensation and Measurement*, H. R. Moskowitz et al. eds (Reidel, Dordrecht, 1974), pp. 65–76.

8 The extension of the proposed value function to multiattribute options, with or without risk, deserves careful analysis. In particular, indifference curves between dimensions of loss may be concave upward, even when the value functions for the separate losses are both convex, because of marked subadditivity between dimensions.

9 D. Ellsberg, *Q. J. Econ.* 75 (1961), p. 643; W. Fellner, *Probability and Profit – A Study of Economic Behavior Along Bayesian Lines* (Irwin, Homewood, Ill., 1965).

10 The scaling of v and π by pair comparisons requires a large number of observations. The procedure of pricing gambles is more convenient for scaling purposes, but it is subject to a severe anchoring bias: the ordering of gambles by their cash equivalents diverges systematically from the preference order observed in direct comparisons (S. Lichtenstein and P. Slovic, *J. Exp. Psychol.* 89 (1971), p. 46).

11 A new group of respondents ($N = 126$) was presented with a modified version of problem 3, in which the outcomes were reduced by a factor of 50. The participants were informed that the gambles would actually be played by tossing a pair of fair coins, that one participant in ten woud be selected at random to play the gambles of his or her choice. To ensure a positive return for the entire set, a third decision, yielding only positive outcomes, was added. These payoff conditions did not alter the pattern of preferences observed in the hypothetical problem: 67 per cent of respondents chose prospect A and 86 per cent chose prospect D. The dominated combination of A and D was chosen by 60 per cent of respondents, and only 6 per cent favored the dominant combination of B and C.

12 S. Lichtenstein and P. Slovic, *J. Exp. Psychol.* 101 (1973), p. 16; D. M. Grether and C. R. Plott, *Am. Econ. Rev.* 69 (1979), p. 623; I. Lieblich and A. Lieblich, *Percept. Mot. Skills* 29 (1969), p. 467; D. M. Grether, *Social Science Working Paper No. 245* (California Institute of Technology, Pasadena, 1979).

13 Other demonstrations of a reluctance to integrate concurrent options have been reported: P. Slovic and S. Lichtenstein, *J. Exp. Psychol.* 78 (1968), p. 646; J. W. Payne and M. L. Braunstein, ibid. 87 (1971), p. 13.

14 M. Allais, *Econometrica* 21 (1953), p. 503; K. McCrimmon and S. Larsson, in *Expected Utility Hypotheses and the Allais Paradox*, M. Allais and O. Hagan, eds (Reidel, Dordrecht, 1979).

15 Another group of respondents ($N = 205$) was presented with all three problems, in different orders, without monetary payoffs. The joint

frequency distribution of choices in problems 5, 6, and 7 was as follows: ACE, 22; ACF, 65; ADE, 4; ADF, 20; BCE, 7; BCF, 18; BDE, 17; BDF, 52. These data confirm in a within-subject design the analysis of conditional evaluation proposed in the text. More than 75 per cent of respondents made compatible choices (AC or BD) in problems 5 and 6, and less than half made compatible choices in problems 6 and 7 (CE or DF) or 5 and 7 (AE or BF). The elimination of payoffs in these questions reduced risk aversion but did not substantially alter the effects of certainty and pseudocertainty.

16 For further discussion of rationality in protective action see H. Kunreuther, *Disaster Insurance Protection: Public Policy Lessons* (Wiley, New York, 1978).

17 W. H. McGlothlin, *Am. J. Psychol.* 69 (1956), p. 604.

18 R. Thaler, *J. Econ. Behav. Organ.* 1 (1980), p. 39.

19 B. Fischhoff, P. Slovic, S. Lichtenstein, in *Cognitive Processes in Choice and Decision Behavior*, T. Wallsten, ed. (Erlbaum, Hillsdale, N.J., 1980).

20 J. C. Hershey and P. J. H. Schoemaker, *J. Risk Insur.*, 47 (1980), pp. 111–32.

21 J. Pratt, A. Wise, R. Zeckhauser, *Q. J. Econ.* 93 (1979), p. 189.

22 R. H. Strotz, *Rev. Econ. Stud.* 23 (1955), p. 165; G. Ainslie, *Psychol. Bull.* 82 (1975), p. 463; J. Elster, *Ulysses and the Sirens: Studies in Rationality and Irrationality* (Cambridge University Press, London, 1979; R. Thaler and H. M. Shifrin, *J. Polit. Econ.*, 89 (1981), pp. 392–406.

23 P. Slovic and A. Tversky, *Behav. Sci.* 19 (1974), p. 368.

24 A. Tversky and D. Kahneman, *Science* 185 (1974), p. 1124; P. Slovic, B. Fischhoff, S. Lichtenstein, *Annu. Rev. Psychol.* 28 (1977), p. 1; R. Nisbett and L. Ross, *Human Inference: Strategies and Shortcomings of Social Judgment* (Prentice-Hall, Englewood Cliffs, N.J., 1980); H. Einhorn and R. Hogarth, *Annu. Rev. Psychol.* 32 (1981), p. 53.

25 H. A. Simon, *Q. J. Econ.* 69 (1955), p. 99; *Psychol. Rev.* 63 (1956), p. 129.

26 J. March, *Bell J. Econ.* 9 (1978), p. 587.

27 This work was supported by the Office of Naval Research under contract N00014-79-C-0077 to Stanford University.

6

Bounded Rationality, Ambiguity, and the Engineering of Choice

JAMES G. MARCH

Rational choice involves two guesses, a guess about uncertain future consequences and a guess about uncertain future preferences. Partly as a result of behavioral studies of choice over a twenty-year period, modifications in the way the theory deals with the first guess have become organized into conceptions of bounded rationality. Recently, behavioral studies of choice have examined the second guess, the way preferences are processed in choice behavior. These studies suggest possible modifications in standard assumptions about tastes and their role in choice. This chapter examines some of those modifications, some possible approaches to working on them, and some complications.

I THE ENGINEERING OF CHOICE AND ORDINARY CHOICE BEHAVIOR

Recently I gave a lecture on elementary decision theory, an introduction to rational theories of choice. After the lecture, a student asked whether it was conceivable that the practical procedures for decision-making implicit in theories of choice might make actual human decisions worse rather than better. What is the empirical evidence, he asked, that human choice is improved by knowledge of decision theory or by application of the various engineering forms of rational choice? I answered, I think correctly, that the case for the usefulness of decision engineering rested primarily not on the kind of direct empirical confirmation that he sought, but on two other things: on a set of theorems proving the superiority of particular procedures in particular situations if the situations are correctly specified and the procedures correctly applied, and on the willingness of clients to purchase the services of experts with skills in decision sciences.

The answer may not have been reasonable, but the question clearly was. It articulated a classical challenge to the practice of

This essay was first published in the *Bell Journal of Economics*, 9 (1978), 587–608.

rational choice, the possibility that processes of rationality might combine with properties of human beings to produce decisions that are less sensible than the unsystematized actions of an intelligent person, or at least that the way in which we might use rational procedures intelligently is not self-evident. Camus[1] argued, in effect, that man was not smart enough to be rational, a point made in a different way at about the same time by Herbert A. Simon.[2] Twenty years later, tales of horror have become contemporary clichés of studies of rational analysis in organizations.[3]

I do not share the view of some of my colleagues that microeconomics, decision science, management science, operations analysis and the other forms of rational decision engineering are mostly manufacturers of massive mischief when they are put into practice. It seems to me likely that these modern technologies of reason have, on balance, done more good than harm, and that students of organizations, politics, and history have been overly gleeful in their compilation of disasters. But I think there is good sense in asking how the practical implementation of theories of choice combines with the ways people behave when they make decisions, and whether our ideas about the engineering of choice might be improved by greater attention to our descriptions of choice behavior.

At first blush, pure models of rational choice seem obviously appropriate as guides to intelligent action, but more problematic for predicting behavior. In practice, the converse seems closer to the truth for much of economics. So long as we use individual choice models to predict the behavior of relatively large numbers of individuals or organizations, some potential problems are avoided by the familiar advantages of aggregation. Even a small signal stands out in a noisy message. On the other hand, if we choose to predict small numbers of individuals or organizations or give advice to a single individual or organization, the saving graces of aggregation are mostly lost. The engineering of choice depends on a relatively close articulation between choice as it is comprehended in the assumptions of the model and choice as it is made comprehensible to individual actors.

This relation is reflected in the historical development of the field. According to conventional dogma, there are two kinds of theories of human behavior: descriptive (or behavioral) theories that purport to describe actual behavior of individuals or social institutions, and prescriptive (or normative) theories that purport to prescribe optimal behavior. In many ways, the distinction leads to an intelligent and fruitful division of labor in social science, reflecting differences in techniques, objectives and professional cultures. For a variety of historical and intellectual reasons, however, such a division has not characterized the development of the theory of choice. Whether one considers ideas about choice in economics, psychology, political science, sociology or philosophy, behavioral and normative theories have developed as a dialectic rather than as separate domains. Most modern behavioral theories of choice take as their starting point some simple ideas about rational human behavior. As a result, new developments in normative theories of choice have quickly affected behavioral theories. Contemplate, for example, the impact of game theory, statistical decision theory, and information theory on behavioral theories of human problem-solving, political decision-making, bargaining and organizational behavior.[4] It is equally obvious that prescriptive theories of choice have been affected by efforts to understand actual choice behavior. Engineers of artificial intelligence have modified their perceptions of efficient problem solving procedures by studying the actual behavior of human problem solvers.[5] Engineers of organizational decision-making have modified their models of rationality on the basis of studies of actual organizational behavior.[6]

Modern students of human choice frequently assume, at least implicitly, that actual human choice behavior in some way or other is likely to make sense. It can be understood as being the behavior of an intelligent being or a group of intelligent beings. Much theoretical work searches for the intelligence in apparently anomalous human behavior. This process of discovering sense in human behavior is conservative with respect to the concept of rational man and to behavioral change. It preserves the axiom of rationality; and it preserves the idea that human behavior is intelligent, even when it is not obviously so. But it is not conservative with respect to prescriptive models of choice. For if there is sense in the choice behavior of individuals acting contrary to standard engineering procedures for rationality, then it seems reasonable to suspect that there may be something inadequate about our normative theory of choice or the procedures by which it is implemented.

Rational choice involves two kinds of guesses: guesses about future consequences of current actions and guesses about future preferences for those consequences.[7] We try to imagine what will happen in the future as a result of our actions and we try to imagine how we shall evaluate what will happen. Neither guess is necessarily easy. Anticipating future consequences of present decisions is often subject to substantial error. Anticipating future preferences is often confusing. Theories of rational choice are primarily theories of these two guesses and how we deal with their complications. Theories of choice under uncertainty emphasize the complications of guessing future consequences. Theories of choice under conflict or ambiguity emphasize the complications of guessing future preferences.

Students of decision-making under uncertainty have identified a number of ways in which a classical model of how alternatives are assessed in terms of their consequences is neither descriptive of behavior nor a good guide in choice situations. As a result of these efforts, some of our ideas about how the first guess is made and how it ought to be made have changed. Since the early writings of Herbert A. Simon,[8] for example, bounded rationality has come to be recognized widely, though not universally, both as an accurate portrayal of much choice behavior and as a normatively sensible adjustment to the costs and character of information gathering and processing by human beings.[9]

The second guess has been less considered. For the most part, theories of choice have assumed that future preferences are exogenous, stable, and known with adequate precision to make decisions unambiguous. The assumptions are obviously subject to question. In the case of collective decision-making, there is the problem of conflicting objectives representing the values of different participants.[10] In addition, individual preferences often appear to be fuzzy and inconsistent, and preferences appear to change over time, at least in part as a consequence of actions taken. Recently, some students of choice have been examining the ways individuals and organizations confront the second guess under conditions of ambiguity (i.e., where goals are vague, problematic, inconsistent, or unstable).[11] Those efforts are fragmentary, but they suggest that ignoring the ambiguities involved in guessing future preferences leads both to misinterpreting choice behavior and to mis-stating the normative problem facing a decision-maker. The doubts are not novel; John Stuart Mill[12] expressed many of them in his essay on Bentham. They are not devastating; the theory of choice is probably robust enough to cope with them. They are not esoteric; Hegel is relevant, but may not be absolutely essential.

II BOUNDED RATIONALITY

There is a history. A little over twenty years ago, Simon published two papers that became a basis for two decades of development in the theory of choice.[13] The first of these examined the informational and computational limits on rationality by human beings. The paper suggested a focus on stepfunction utility functions and a process of information gathering that began with a desired outcome and worked back to a set of antecedent actions sufficient to produce it. The second paper explored the consequences of simple payoff functions and search rules in an uncertain environment. The two papers argued explicitly that descriptions of decision-making in terms of such ideas conformed more to actual human behavior than did descriptions built upon classical rationality, that available evidence designed to test such models against classical ones tended to support the alternative ideas.

Because subsequent developments were extensive, it is well to recall that the original argument was a narrow one. It started from the proposition that all intendedly rational behavior is behavior within constraints. Simon added the idea that the list of technical constraints on choice should include some properties of human beings as processors of information and as problem solvers. The limitations were limitations of computational capability, the organization and utilization of memory, and the like. He suggested that human beings develop decision procedures that are sensible, given the constraints, even though they might not be sensible if the constraints were removed. As a short-hand label for such procedures, he coined the term 'satisficing'.

Developments in the field over the past twenty years have expanded and distorted Simon's original formulation. But they have retained some considerable flavor of his original tone. He emphasized the theoretical difficulty posed by self-evident empirical truths. He obscured a distinction one might make between individual and organizational decision-making, proposing for the most part the same general ideas for both. He obscured a possible distinction between behavioral and normative theories of choice, preferring to view differences between perfect rationality and bounded rationality as explicable consequences of constraints. Few of the individual scholars who followed had precisely the same interests or commitments as Simon, but the field has generally maintained the same tone. Theoretical puzzlement with respect to the simplicity of decision behavior has been extended to puzzlement with respect to decision inconsistencies and instabilities, and the extent to which individuals and organizations do things without apparent reason.[14] Recent books on decision-making move freely from studies of organizations to studies of individuals.[15] And recent books on normative decision-making accept many standard forms of organizational behavior as sensible.[16]

Twenty years later, it is clear that we do not have a single, widely-accepted, precise behavioral theory of choice. But I think it can be argued that the empirical and theoretical efforts of the past twenty years have brought us closer to understanding decision processes. The understanding is organized in a set of conceptual vignettes rather than a single, coherent structure; and the connections among the vignettes are tenuous. In effect, the effort has identified major aspects of some key processes that appear to be reflected in decision-making; but the ecology of those processes is not well captured by any current theory. For much of this development, Simon bears substantial intellectual responsibility.

Simon's contributions have been honored by subsumption, extension, elaboration, and transformation. Some writers have felt it important to show that aspiration level goals and goal-directed search can be viewed as special cases of other ideas, most commonly classical notions about rational behavior.[17] Others have taken ideas about individual human behavior and extended them to organizations (both business firms and public bureaucracies) and to other institutions, for example, universities.[18] Simon's original precise commentary on specific difficulties in rational models has been expanded to a more general consideration of problems in the assumptions of rationality, particularly the problems of subjective understanding, perception, and conflict of interest.[19] The original articles suggested small modifications in a theory of economic behavior, the substitution of bounded rationality for omniscient rationality. But the ideas ultimately have led to an examination of the extent to which theories of choice might subordinate the idea of rationality altogether to less intentional conceptions of the causal determinants of action.[20]

III   ALTERNATIVE RATIONALITIES

The search for intelligence in decision-making is an effort to rationalize apparent anomalies in behavior. In a general way, that effort imputes either calculated or systemic rationality to observed choice behavior. Action is presumed to follow either from explicit calculation of its consequences in terms of objectives, or from rules of behavior that have evolved through processes that are sensible but which obscure from present knowledge full information on the rational justification for any specific rule.

Most efforts to rationalize observed behavior have attempted to place that behavior within a framework of calculated rationality.

The usual argument is that a naïve rational model is inadequate either because it focuses on the wrong unit of analysis, or because it uses an inaccurate characterization of the preferences involved. As a result, we have developed ideas of limited rationality, contextual rationality, game rationality, and process rationality.

Ideas of *limited rationality* emphasize the extent to which individuals and groups simplify a decision problem because of the difficulties of anticipating or considering all alternatives and all information.[21] They introduce, as reasonable responses, such things as step-function tastes, simple search rules, working backward, organizational slack, incrementalism and muddling through, uncertainty avoidance, and the host of elaborations of such ideas that are familiar to students of organizational choice and human problem solving.

Ideas of *contextual rationality* emphasize the extent to which choice behavior is embedded in a complex of other claims on the attention of actors and other structures of social and cognitive relations.[22] They focus on the way in which choice behavior in a particular situation is affected by the opportunity costs of attending to that situation and by the apparent tendency for people, problems, solutions, and choices to be joined by the relatively arbitrary accidents of their simultaneity rather than by their *prima facie* relevance to each other.

Ideas of *game rationality* emphasize the extent to which organizations and other social institutions consist of individuals who act in relation to each other intelligently to pursue individual objectives by means of individual calculations of self-interest.[23] The decision outcomes of the collectivity in some sense amalgamate those calculations, but they do so without imputing a super-goal to the collectivity or invoking collective rationality. These theories find reason in the process of coalition formation, sequential attention to goals, information bias and interpersonal gaming, and the development of mutual incentives.

Ideas of *process rationality* emphasize the extent to which decisions find their sense in attributes of the decision process, rather than in attributes of decision outcomes.[24] They explore those significant human pleasures (and pains) found in the ways we act while making decisions, and in the symbolic content of the idea and procedures of choice. Explicit outcomes are viewed as secondary and decision-making becomes sensible through the intelligence of the way it is orchestrated.

All of these kinds of ideas are theories of intelligent individuals making calculations of the consequences of actions for objectives, and acting sensibly to achieve those objectives. Action is presumed to be consequential, to be connected consciously and meaningfully to knowledge about personal goals and future outcomes, to be controlled by personal intention.

Although models of calculated rationality continue to be a dominant style, students of choice have also shown considerable interest in a quite different kind of intelligence, systemic rather than calculated. Suppose we imagine that knowledge, in the form of precepts of behavior, evolves over time within a system and accumulates across time, people, and organizations without complete current consciousness of its history. Then sensible action is taken by actors without comprehension of its full justification. This characterizes models of adaptive rationality, selected rationality, and posterior rationality.

Ideas of *adaptive rationality* emphasize experiential learning by individuals or collectivities.[25] Most adaptive models have the property that if the world and preferences are stable and the experience prolonged enough, behavior will approach the behavior that would be chosen rationally on the basis of perfect knowledge. Moreover, the postulated learning functions normally have properties that permit sensible adaptation to drifts in environmental or taste attributes. By storing information on past experiences in some simple behavioral predilections, adaptive rationality permits the efficient management of considerable experiential information; but it is in a form that is not explicitly retrievable – particularly across individuals or long periods of time. As a result, it is a form of intelligence that tends to separate current reasons from current actions.

Ideas of *selected rationality* emphasize the process of selection among individuals or organizations through survival or growth.[26] Rules of behavior achieve intelligence not by virtue of conscious calculation of their rationality by current role players but by virtue of the survival and growth of social institutions in which such rules are followed and such roles are performed. Selection theories focus on the extent to which choice is dominated by standard operating procedures and the social regulation of social roles.

Ideas of *posterior rationality* emphasize the discovery of intentions as an interpretation of action rather than as a prior position.[27] Actions are seen as being exogenous and as producing experiences that are organized into an evaluation after the fact. The valuation is in terms of preferences generated by the action and its consequences, and choices are justified by virtue of their posterior consistency with goals that have themselves been developed through a critical interpretation of the choice. Posterior rationality models maintain the idea that action should be consistent with preferences, but they conceive action as being antecedent to goals.

These explorations into elements of systemic rationality have, of course, a strong base in economics and behavioral science,[28] but they pose special problems for decision engineering. On the one hand, systemic rationality is not intentional. That is, behavior is not understood as following from a calculation of consequences in terms of prior objectives. If such a calculation is asserted, it is assumed to be an interpretation of the behavior but not a good predictor of it. On the other hand, these models claim, often explicitly, that there is intelligence in the suspension of calculation. Alternatively, they suggest that whatever sense there is in calculated rationality is attested not by its formal properties but by its survival as a social rule of behavior, or as an experientially verified personal propensity.

In a general way, these explications of ordinary behavior as forms of rationality have considerably clarified and extended our understanding of choice. It is now routine to explore aspects of limited, contextual, game, process, adaptive, selected, and posterior rationality in the behavioral theory of choice. We use such ideas to discover and celebrate the intelligence of human behavior. At the same time, however, this discovery of intelligence in the ordinary behavior of individuals and social institutions is an implicit pressure for reconstruction of normative theories of choice, for much of the argument is not only that observed behavior is understandable as a human phenomenon, but that it is, in some important sense, intelligent. If behavior that apparently deviates from standard procedures of calculated rationality can be shown to be intelligent, then it can plausibly be argued that models of calculated rationality are deficient not only as descriptors of human behavior but also as guides to intelligent choice.

IV   THE TREATMENT OF TASTES

Engineers of intelligent choice sensibly resist the imputation of intelligence to all human behavior. Traditionally, deviations of choice behavior from the style anticipated in classical models were treated normatively as errors, or correctable faults, as indeed many of them doubtless were. The objective was to transform subjective rationality into objective rationality by removing the needless informational, procedural, and judgmental constraints that limited the effectiveness of persons proceeding intelligently from false or incomplete informational premises.[29] One of Simon's contributions to the theory of choice was his challenge of the self-evident proposition that choice behavior necessarily would be improved if it were made more like the normative model of rational choice. By asserting that certain limits on rationality stemmed from properties of the human organism, he emphasized the possibility that actual human choice behavior was more intelligent than it appeared.

Normative theories of choice have responded to the idea. Substantial parts of the economics of information and the economics of attention (or time) are tributes to the proposition that information gathering, information processing, and decision-making impose demands on the scarce resources of a finite capacity human organism.[30] Aspiration levels, signals, incrementalism, and satisficing rules for decision-making have been described as sensible under fairly general circumstances.[31]

These developments in the theory of rational choice acknowledge important aspects of the behavioral critique of classical procedures for guessing the future consequences of present action. Normative response to behavioral discussions of the second guess, the estimation of future preferences, has been similarly conservative but perceptible. That standard theories of choice and the engineering procedures associated with them have a conception of preferences that differs from observations of preferences has long been noted.[32] As in the case of the informational constraints on rational choice, the first reaction within decision engineering was to treat deviations from well-defined, consistent preference functions as correctable faults. If individuals had deficient (i.e., inconsistent, incomplete) preference functions, they were to be induced to generate proper ones, perhaps through revealed preference techniques and education. If groups or organizations exhibited conflict, they were to be induced to resolve that conflict through prior discussion, prior side payments (e.g., an employment contract), or prior bargaining. If individuals or organizations exhibited instability in preferences over time, they were to be induced to minimize that instability by recognizing a more general specification of the preferences so that apparent changes became explicable as reflecting a single, unchanging function under changing conditions or changing resources.

Since the specific values involved in decision-making are irrelevant to formal models of choice, both process rationality and contextual rationality are, from such a perspective, versions of simple calculated rationality. The criterion function is changed, but the theory treats the criterion function as any arbitrary set of well-ordered preferences. So long as the preferences associated with the process of choice or the preferences involved in the broader context are well defined and well behaved, there is no deep theoretical difficulty. But, in practice, such elements of human preference functions have not filtered significantly into the engineering of choice.

The record with respect to problems of goal conflict, multiple, lexicographic goals, and loosely coupled systems is similar. Students of bureaucracies have argued that a normative theory of choice within a modern bureaucratic structure must recognize explicitly the continuing conflict in preferences among various actors.[33] Within such systems 'decisions' are probably better seen as strategic first-move interventions in a dynamic internal system than as choices in a classical sense. Decisions are not expected to be implemented, and actions that would be optimal if implemented are suboptimal as first moves. This links theories of choice to game-theoretic conceptions of politics, bargaining, and strategic actions in a productive way. Although in this way ideas about strategic choice in collectivities involving conflict of interest are well established in part of the choice literature,[34] they have had little impact on such obvious applied domains as bureaucratic decision-making or the design of organizational control systems. The engineering of choice has been more explicitly concerned with multiple criteria decision procedures for dealing with multiple, lexicographic, or political goals.[35] In some cases these efforts have considerably changed the spirit of decision analysis, moving it toward a role of exploring the implications of constraints and away from a conception of solution.

Behavioral inquiry into preferences has, however, gone beyond the problems of interpersonal conflict of interest in recent years and into the complications of ambiguity. The problems of ambiguity are partly problems of disagreement about goals among individuals, but they are more conspicuously problems of the relevance, priority, clarity, coherence, and stability of goals in both individual and organizational choice. Several recent treatments of organizational choice behavior record some major ways in which explicit goals seem neither particularly powerful predictors of outcomes nor particularly well represented as either stable, consistent preference orders or well-defined political constraints.[36]

It is possible, of course, that such portrayals of behavior are perverse. They may be perverse because they systematically misrepresent the actual behavior of human beings or they may be perverse because the human beings they describe are, in so far as the description applies, stupid. But it is also possible that the description is accurate and the behavior is intelligent, that the ambiguous way human beings sometimes deal with tastes is, in fact, sensible. If such a thing can be imagined, then its corollary may also be imaginable: perhaps we treat tastes inadequately in our engineering of choice. When we start to discover intelligence in decision-making where goals are unstable, ill-defined, or apparently irrelevant, we are led to asking some different kinds of questions about our normative conceptions of choice and walk close not only to some issues in economics but also to some classical and modern questions in literature and ethics, particularly the role of clear prior purpose in the ordering of human affairs.

Consider the following properties of tastes as they appear in standard prescriptive theories of choice:

Tastes are *absolute*. Normative theories of choice assume a formal posture of moral relativism. The theories insist on morality of action in terms of tastes; but they recognize neither discriminations among alternative tastes, nor the possibility that a person reasonably might view his own preferences and actions based on them as morally distressing.

Tastes are *relevant*. Normative theories of choice require that action be taken in terms of tastes, that decisions be consistent with preferences in the light of information about the probable consequences of alternatives for valued outcomes. Action is willful.

Tastes are *stable*. With few exceptions, normative theories of choice require that tastes be stable. Current action is taken in terms of current tastes. The implicit assumption is that tastes will be unchanged when the outcomes of current actions are realized.

Tastes are *consistent*. Normative theories of choice allow mutually inconsistent tastes only in so far as they can be made irrelevant by the absence of scarcity or reconcilable by the specification of trade-offs.

Tastes are *precise*. Normative theories of choice eliminate ambiguity about the extent to which a particular outcome will satisfy tastes, at least in so far as possible resolutions of that ambiguity might affect the choice.

Tastes are *exogenous*. Normative theories of choice presume that tastes, by whatever process they may be created, are not themselves affected by the choices they control.

Each of these features of tastes seems inconsistent with observations of choice behavior among individuals and social institutions. Not always, but often enough to be troublesome. Individuals commonly find it possible to express both a taste for something and a recognition that the taste is something that is repugnant to moral standards they accept. Choices are often made without respect to tastes. Human decision-makers routinely ignore their own, fully conscious, preferences in making decisions. They follow rules, traditions, hunches, and the advice or actions of others. Tastes change over time in such a way that predicting future tastes is often difficult. Tastes are inconsistent. Individuals and organizations are aware of the extent to which some of their preferences conflict with other of their preferences; yet they do nothing to resolve those inconsistencies. Many preferences are stated in forms that lack precision. It is difficult to make them reliably operational in evaluating possible outcomes. While tastes are used to choose among actions, it is often also true that actions and experience with their consequences affect tastes. Tastes are determined partly endogenously.

Such differences between tastes as they are portrayed by our models and tastes as they appear in our experience produce ordinary behavioral phenomena that are not always well accommodated within the structure of our prescriptions.

We manage our preferences. We select actions now partly in terms of expectations about the effect of those actions upon future preferences. We do things now to modify our future tastes. Thus, we know that if we engage in some particularly tasty, but immoral, activity, we are likely to come to like it more. We know that if we develop competence in a particular skill, we shall often come to favor it. So we choose to pursue the competence, or not, engage in an activity, or not, depending on whether we wish to increase or decrease our taste for the competence or activity.

We construct our preferences. We choose preferences and actions jointly, in part, to discover – or construct – new preferences that are currently unknown. We deliberately specify our objectives in vague terms to develop an understanding of what we might like to become. We elaborate our tastes as interpretations of our behavior.

We treat our preferences strategically. We specify goals that are different from the outcomes we wish to achieve. We adopt preferences and rules of actions that if followed literally would lead us to outcomes we do not wish, because we believe that the final outcome will only partly reflect our initial intentions. In effect, we consider the choice of preferences as part of an infinite game with ourselves in which we attempt to deal with our propensities for acting badly by anticipating them and outsmarting ourselves. We use deadlines and make commitments.

We confound our preferences. Our deepest preferences tend often to be paired. We find the same outcome both attractive and repulsive, not in the sense that the two sentiments cancel each other and we remain indifferent, but precisely that we simultaneously want and do not want an outcome, experience it as both pleasure and pain, love and hate it.[37]

We avoid our preferences. Our actions and our preferences are only partly linked. We are prepared to say that we want something, yet should not want it, or wish we did not want it. We are prepared to act in ways that are inconsistent with our preferences, and to maintain that inconsistency in the face of having it demonstrated. We do not believe that what we do must necessarily result from a desire to achieve preferred outcomes.

We expect change in our preferences. As we contemplate making choices that have consequences in the future, we know that our attitudes about possible outcomes will change in ways that are substantial but not entirely predictable. The subjective probability distribution over possible future preferences (like the subjective probability distribution over possible future consequences) increases its variance as the horizon is stretched. As a result, we have a tendency to want to take actions now that maintain future options for acting when future preferences are clearer.

We suppress our preferences. Consequential argument, the explicit linking of actions to desires, is a form of argument in which some people are better than others. Individuals who are less competent at consequential rationalization try to avoid it with others who are more competent, particularly others who may have a stake in persuading them to act in a particular way. We resist an explicit formulation of consistent desires to avoid manipulation of our choices by persons cleverer than we at that special form of argument called consistent rationality.

It is possible, on considering this set of contrasts between decision-making as we think it ought to occur and decision-making as we think it does occur to trivialize the issue into a 'definitional problem'. By suitably manipulating the concept of tastes, one can save classical theories of choice as 'explanations' of behavior in a formal sense, but probably only at the cost of stretching a good idea into a doubtful ideology.[38] More importantly from the present point of view, such a redefinition pays the cost of destroying the practical relevance of normative prescriptions for choice. For prescriptions are useful only if we see a difference between observed procedures and desirable procedures.

Alternatively, one can record all of the deviations from normative specifications as stupidity, errors that should be corrected; and undertake to transform the style of existing humans into the styles anticipated by the theory. This has, for the most part, been the strategy of operations and management analysis for the past twenty years; and it has had its successes. But it has also had failures.

It is clear that the human behavior I have described may, in any individual case, be a symptom of ignorance, obtuseness, or deviousness. But the fact that such patterns of behavior are fairly common among individuals and institutions suggests that they might be sensible under some general kinds of conditions – that goal ambiguity, like limited rationality, is not necessarily a fault in human choice to be corrected but often a form of intelligence to be refined by the technology of choice rather than ignored by it.

Uncertainty about future consequences and human limitations in dealing with them are relatively easily seen as intrinsic in the decision situation and the nature of the human organism. It is much harder to see in what way ambiguous preferences are a necessary property of human behavior. It seems meaningful in ordinary terms to assert that human decision-makers are driven to techniques of limited rationality by the exigencies of the situation in which they find themselves. But what drives them to ambiguous and changing goals? Part of the answer is directly analogous to the formulations of limited rationality. Limitations of memory organization and retrieval and of information capacity affect information processing about preferences just as they affect information processing about consequences.[39] Human beings have unstable, inconsistent, incompletely evoked, and imprecise goals at least in part because human abilities limit preference orderliness. If it were possible to be different at reasonable cost, we probably would want to be.

But viewing ambiguity as a necessary cost imposed by the information processing attributes of individuals fails to capture the extent to which similar styles in preferences would be sensible, even if the human organism were a more powerful computational system. We probably need to ask the more general question: Why might a person or institution intelligently choose to have ambiguous tastes? The answer, I believe, lies in several things, some related to ideas of bounded rationality, others more familiar to human understanding as it is portrayed in literature and philosophy than to our theories of choice.

First, human beings recognize in their behavior that there are limits to personal and institutional integration in tastes. They know that no matter how much they may be pressured both by their own prejudices for integration and by the demands of others, they will be left with contradictory and intermittent desires partially ordered but imperfectly reconciled. As a result, they engage in activities designed to manage preferences or game preferences. These activities make little sense from the point of view of a conception of human choice that assumes people know what they want and will want, or a conception that assumes wants are morally equivalent. But ordinary human actors sense that they might come to want something that they should not, or that they might make unwise or inappropriate choices under the influence of fleeting, but powerful, desires if they do not act now either to control the development of tastes or to buffer action from tastes.[40]

Second, human beings recognize implicitly the limitations of acting rationally on current guesses. By insisting that action, to be justified, must follow preferences and be consistent both with those preferences and with estimates of future states, we considerably exaggerate the relative power of a choice based consistently upon two guesses compared to a choice that is itself a guess. Human beings are both proponents for preferences and observers of the process by which their preferences are developed and acted upon. As observers of the process by which their beliefs have been formed and consulted, they recognize the good sense in perceptual and moral modesty.[41]

Third, human beings recognize the extent to which tastes are constructed, or developed, through a more or less constant confrontation between preferences and actions that are inconsistent with them, and among conflicting preferences. As a result, they appear to be comfortable with an extraordinary array of unreconciled sources of legitimate wants. They maintain a lack of coherence both within and among personal desires, social demands, and moral codes. Though they seek some consistency, they appear to see inconsistency as a normal, and necessary, aspect of the development and clarification of tastes.[42]

Fourth, human beings are conscious of the importance of preferences as beliefs independent of their immediate action consequences. They appear to find it possible to say, in effect, that they believe something is more important to good action than they are able (or willing) to make it in a specific case. They act as though some aspects of their beliefs are important to life without necessarily being consistent with actions, and important to the long-run quality of choice behavior without controlling it completely in the short run. They accept a degree of personal and social wisdom in ordinary hypocrisy.[43]

Fifth, human beings know that some people are better at rational argument than others, and that those skills are not particularly well correlated with either morality or sympathy. As a result, they recognize the political nature of argumentation more clearly, and more personally, than the theory of choice does. They are unwilling to gamble that God made clever people uniquely virtuous. They protect themselves from cleverness by obscuring the nature of their preferences; they exploit cleverness by asking others to construct reasons for actions they wish to take.[44]

V　TASTES AND THE ENGINEERING OF CHOICE

These characteristics of preference processing by individual human beings and social institutions seem to me to make sense under rather general circumstances. As a result, it seems likely to me that our engineering of choice behavior does not make so much sense as we sometimes attribute to it. The view of human tastes and their proper role in action that we exhibit in our normative theory of choice is at least as limiting to the engineering applicability of that theory as the perfect knowledge assumptions were to the original formulations.

Since it has taken us over twenty years to introduce modest elements of bounded rationality and conflict of interest into prescriptions about decision-making, there is no particular reason to be sanguine about the speed with which our engineerings of choice will accept and refine the intelligence of ambiguity. But there is hope. The reconstruction involved is not extraordinary, and in some respects has already begun. For the doubts I have expressed about engineering models of choice to be translated into significant changes, they will have to be formulated a bit more precisely in terms that are comprehensible within such theories, even though they may not be consistent with the present form of the theories or the questions the theories currently address. I cannot accomplish such a task in any kind of complete way, but I think it is possible to identify a few conceptual problems that might plausibly be addressed by choice theorists and a few optimization problems that might plausibly be addressed by choice engineers.

The conceptual problems involve discovering interesting ways to reformulate some assumptions about tastes, particularly about the stability of tastes, their exogenous character, their priority, and their internal consistency.

Consider the problem of *intertemporal comparison* of preferences.[45] Suppose we assume that the preferences that will be held at every relevant future point in time are known. Suppose further that those preferences change over time but are, at any given time, consistent. If action is to be taken now in terms of its consequences over a period of time during which preferences change, we are faced with having to make intertemporal comparisons. As long as the changes are exogenous, we can avoid the problem if we choose to do so. If we can imagine an individual making a complete and transitive ordering over possible outcomes over time, then intertemporal comparisons are implicit in the preference orderings and cause no particular difficulty beyond the heroic character of the assumption about human capabilities. If, on the other hand, we think of the individual as having a distinct, complete, and consistent preference relation defined over the outcomes realized in a particular time period, and we imagine that those preferences change over time, then the problem of intertemporal comparisons is more difficult. The problem is technically indistinguishable from the problem of interpersonal comparison of utilities. When we compare the changing preferences of a single person over time to make tradeoffs across time, we are in the identical position to when we attempt to make comparisons across different individuals at a point in time. The fact that the problems are identical has the advantage of immediately bringing to bear on the problems of intertemporal comparisons the apparatus developed to deal with interpersonal comparisons.[46] It has the disadvantage that that apparatus allows a much weaker conception of solution than is possible within a single, unchanging set of preferences. We are left with the weak theorems of social welfare economics, but perhaps with a clearer recognition that there is no easy and useful way to escape the problem of incomparable preference functions by limiting our attention to a single individual, as long as tastes change over time and we think of tastes as being defined at a point in time.

Consider the problem of *endogenous change* in preferences.[47] Suppose we know that future tastes will change in a predictable way as a consequence of actions taken now and the consequences of those actions realized over time. Then we are in the position of choosing now the preferences we shall have later. If there is risk involved, we are choosing now a probability distribution over future preferences. If we can imagine some 'super goal', the problem becomes tractable. We evaluate alternative preferences in terms of their costs and benefits for the 'super goal'. Such a strategy preserves the main spirit of normal choice theory but allows only a modest extension into endogenous change. This is the essential strategy adopted in some of the engineering examples below. In such cases desirable preferences cannot always be deduced from the 'super goal', but alternative preferences can be evaluated. In somewhat the same spirit, we can imagine adaptive preferences as a possible decision procedure and examine whether rules for a sequence of adaptations in tastes can be specified that lead to choice outcomes better in some easily recognized sense than those obtained through explicit calculated rationality at the start of the process. One possible place is the search for cooperative solutions in games in which calculated rationality is likely to lead to outcomes desired by no one.[48] Also in the same general spirit, we might accept the strict morality position and attempt to select a strategy for choice that will minimize change in values. Or we might try to select a strategy that maximizes value change. All of these are possible explorations, but they are not fully attentive to the normative management of adaptation in tastes. The problem exceeds our present concepts: how do we act sensibly now to manage the development of preferences in the future when we do not have now a criterion for evaluating future tastes that will not itself be affected by our actions? There may be some kind of fixed-point theorem answer to such a problem, but I suspect that a real conceptual confrontation with endogenous preferences will involve some reintroduction of moral philosophy into our understanding of choice.[49]

Consider the problem of *posterior preferences*.[50] The theory of choice is built on the idea of prior intentions. Suppose we relax the requirement of priority, allow preferences to rationalize action after the fact in our theories as well as our behavior. How do we act in such a way that we conclude, after the fact, that the action was intelligent, and also are led to an elaboration of our preferences that we find fruitful? Such a formulation seems closer to a correct representation of choice problems in politics, for example, than is conventional social welfare theory. We find meaning and merit in our actions after they are taken and the consequences are observed and interpreted. Deliberate efforts to manage posterior constructions of preferences are familiar to us. They include many elements of child rearing, psychotherapy, consciousness raising, and product advertising. The terms are somewhat different. We talk of development of character in child rearing, of insight in psychotherapy, of recognition of objective reality in political, ethnic or sexual consciousness raising, and of elaboration of personal needs in advertising. But the technologies are more similar than their ideologies. These techniques for the construction (or excavation) of tastes include both encouraging a reinterpretation of experience and attempting to induce current behavior that will facilitate posterior elaboration of a new understanding of personal preferences. I have tried elsewhere to indicate some of the possibilities this suggests for intelligent foolishness and the role of ambiguity in sensible action.[51] The problem is in many ways indistinguishable from the problem of poetry and the criticism of poetry (or art and art criticism). The poet attempts to write a poem that has meanings intrinsic in the poem but not necessarily explicit at the moment of composition.[52] In this sense, at least, decisions, like poems, are open; and good decisions are those that enrich our preferences and their meanings. But to talk in such a manner is to talk the language of criticism and aesthetics, and it will probably be necessary for choice theory to engage that literature in some way.[53]

Finally, consider the problem of *inconsistency* in preferences.[54] From the point of view of ordinary human ideas about choice, as well as many philosophical and behavioral conceptions of choice, the most surprising thing about formal theories of choice is the tendency to treat such terms as values, goals, preferences, tastes, wants and the like as either equivalent or as reducible to a single objective function with properties of completeness and consistency. Suppose that instead of making such an assumption, we viewed the decision-maker as confronted simultaneously with several orderings of outcomes. We could give them names, calling one a moral code, another a social role, another a personal taste, or whatever. From the present point of view what would be critical would be that the several orderings were independent and irreducible. That is, they could not be deduced from each other, and they could not be combined into a single order. Then instead of taking the conventional step of imputing a preference order across these incomparables by some kind of revealed preference procedure, we treat them as truly incomparable and examine solutions to internal inconsistency that are more in the spirit of our efforts to provide intelligent guidance to collectivities in which we accept the incomparability of preferences across individuals. Then we could give better advice to individuals who want to treat their own preferences strategically, and perhaps move to a clearer recognition of the role of contradiction and paradox in human choice.[55] The strategic problems are amenable to relatively straightforward modifications of our views of choice under conflict of interest; the other problems probably require a deeper understanding of contradiction as it appears in philosophy and literature.[56]

Formulating the conceptual problems in these ways is deliberately conservative *vis-à-vis* the theory of choice. It assumes that thinking about human behavior in terms of choice on the basis of some conception of intention is useful, and that the tradition of struggle between normative theories of choice and behavioral theories of choice is a fruitful one. There are alternative paradigms for understanding human behavior that are in many situations likely to be more illuminating. But it is probably unwise to think that every paper should suggest a dramatic paradigm shift, particularly when the alternative is seen only dimly.

Such strictures become even more important when we turn to the engineering of choice. Choice theorists have often discussed complications in the usual abstract representation of tastes. But those concerns have had little impact on ideas about the engineering of choice, perhaps because they pose the problems at a level of philosophic complexity that is remote from decision engineering. Thus, although I think the challenges that ambiguity makes to our models of choice are rather fundamental, my engineering instincts are to sacrifice purity to secure tractability. I suspect we should ask the engineers of choice not initially to reconstruct a philosophy of tastes but to reexamine, within a familiar framework, some presumptions of our craft, and to try to make the use of ambiguity somewhat less of a mystery, somewhat more of a technology. Consider, for example, the following elementary problems in engineering.

The optimal ambition problem. The level of personal ambition is not a decision variable in most theories of choice; but as a result of the work by Simon and others on satisficing, there has been interest in optimal levels of aspiration. These efforts consider an aspiration level as a trigger that either begins or ends the search for new alternatives. The optimization problem is one of balancing the expected costs of additional search with the expected improvements to be realized from the effort.[57]

But there is another, rather different, way of looking at the optimum ambition problem. Individuals and organizations form aspirations, goals, targets, or ambitions for achievement. These ambitions are usually assumed to be connected to outcomes in at least two ways: they affect search (either directly or through some variable like motivation) and thereby performance; they affect (jointly with performance) satisfaction.[58] Suppose we wish to maximize some function of satisfaction over time by selecting among alternative ambitions over time, alternative initial ambitions, or alternatives defined by some other decision variable that affects ambition. Examples of the latter might be division of income between consumption and savings, tax policies, or choice among alternative payment schemes. In effect, we wish to select a preference function for achievement that will, after the various behavioral consequences of that selection are accounted for, make us feel that we have selected the best ambition. It is a problem much more familiar to the real world of personal and institutional choice than it is to the normative theory of choice, but it is something about which some things could be said.

The optimal clarity problem. Conventional notions about intelligent choice often begin with the presumption that good decisions require clear goals, and that improving the clarity of goals unambiguously improves the quality of decision-making. In fact, greater precision in the statement of objectives and the measurement of performance with respect to them is often a mixed blessing. There are arguments for moderating an unrestrained enthusiasm for precise performance measures: where contradiction and confusion are essential elements of the values, precision misrepresents them. The more precise the measure of performance, the greater the motivation to find ways of scoring well on the measurement index without regard to the underlying goals. And precision in objectives does not allow creative interpretation of what the goal might mean.[59] Thus, the introduction of precision into the evaluation of performance involves a tradeoff between the gains in outcomes attributable to closer articulation between action and performance on an index of performance and the losses in outcomes attributable to misrepresentation of goals, reduced motivation to development of goals, and concentration of effort on irrelevant ways of beating the index. Whether one is considering developing a performance evaluation scheme for managers, a testing procedure for students, or an understanding of personal preferences, there is a problem of determining the optimum clarity in goals.

The optimal sin problem. Standard notions of intelligent choice are theories of strict morality. That is, they presume that a person should do what he believes right and believe that what he does is right. Values and actions are to be consistent. Contrast that perspective with a view, somewhat more consistent with our behavior (as well as some theology), that there is such a thing as sin, that individuals and institutions sometimes do things even while recognizing that what they do is not what they wish they did, and that saints are a luxury to be encouraged only in small numbers. Or contrast a theory of strict morality with a view drawn from Nietzsche[60] or Freud[61] (see also Jones[62]) of the complicated contradiction between conscience and self-interest. Although the issues involved are too subtle for brief treatment, a reasonably strong case can be made against strict morality and in favor of at least some sin, and therefore hypocrisy. One of the most effective ways of maintaining morality is through the remorse exhibited and felt at immoral action. Even if we are confident that our moral codes are correct, we may want to recognize human complexities. There will be occasions on which humans will be tempted by desires that they recognize as evil. If we insist that they maintain consistency between ethics and actions, the ethics will often be more likely to change than the actions. Hypocrisy is a long-run investment in morality made at some cost (the chance that, in fact, action might otherwise adjust to morals). To encourage people always to take responsibility for their actions is to encourage them to deny that bad things are bad – to make evil acceptable. At the same time, sin is an experiment with an alternative morality. By recognizing sin, we make it easier for persons to experiment with the possibility of having different tastes. Moral systems need those experiments, and regularly grant licenses to experiment to drunks, lovers, students, or sinners. These gains from sin are purchased by its costs. Thus, the optimization problem.

The optimal rationality problem. Calculated rationality is a technique for making decisions. In standard versions of theories of choice it is the only legitimate form of intelligence. But it is obvious that it is, in fact, only one of several alternative forms of intelligence, each with claims to legitimacy. Learned behavior, with its claim to summarize an irretrievable but relevant personal history, or conventional behavior and rules, with their claims to capture the intelligence of survival over long histories of experience more relevant than that susceptible to immediate calculation, are clear alternative contenders. There are others: revelation or intuition, by which we substitute one guess for two; or imitation, or expertise, by which we substitute the guess of someone else for our own. Among all of these, only calculated rationality really uses conscious preferences of a current actor as a major consideration in making decisions. It is easy to show that there exist situations in which any one of these alternative techniques will make better decisions than the independent calculation of rational behavior by ordinary individuals or institutions. The superiority of learned or conventional behavior depends, in general, on the amount of experience it summarizes and the similarity between the world in which the experience was accumulated and the current world. The superiority of imitation depends, in general, on the relative competence of actor and expert and the extent to which intelligent action is reproducible but not comprehendible. At the same time, each form of intelligence exposes an actor to the risks of corruption. Imitation risks a false confidence in the neutrality of the process of diffusion; calculated rationality risks a false confidence in the neutrality of rational argument; and so on. It is not hard to guess that the relative sizes of these risks vary from individual to individual, or institution to institution. What is harder to specify in any very precise way is the extent and occasions on which a sensible person would rely on calculated rationality rather than the alternatives.

VI A ROMANTIC VISION

Prescriptive theories of choice are dedicated to perfecting the intelligence of human action by imagining that action stems from reason and by improving the technology of decision. Descriptive theories of choice are dedicated to perfecting the understanding of human action by imagining that action makes sense. Not all behavior makes sense; some of it is unreasonable. Not all decision technology is intelligent; some of it is foolish. Over the past twenty years, the contradiction between the search for sense in behavior and the search for improvement in behavior has focused on our interpretation of the way information about future consequences is gathered and processed. The effort built considerably on the idea of bounded rationality and a conception of human decision-making as limited by the cognitive capabilities of human beings. Over the next twenty years, I suspect the contradiction will be increasingly concerned with an interpretation of how beliefs about future preferences are generated and utilized. The earlier confrontation led theories of choice to a slightly clearer understanding of information processing and to some modest links with the technologies of computing, inference and subjective probability. So perhaps the newer confrontation will lead theories of choice to a slightly clearer understanding of the complexities of preference processing and to some modest links with the technologies of ethics, criticism, and aesthetics. The history of theories of choice and their engineering applications suggests that we might appropriately be pessimistic about immediate, major progress. The intelligent engineering of tastes involves questions that encourage despair over their difficulty.[63] But though hope for minor progress is a romantic vision, it may not be entirely inappropriate for a theory built on a romantic view of human destiny.

NOTES

1 A. Camus, *L'Homme Révolté* (Gallimard, Paris, 1951). Published in English as *The Rebel*.
2 H. A. Simon, *Models of Man* (Wiley, New York, 1957).
3 A. Wildavsky, *A Revolt Against the Masses and Other Essays on Politics and Public Policy* (Basic Books, New York, 1971); A. Wildavsky and H. Pressman, *Implementation* (University of California

Press, Berkeley, 1973); D. P. A. Warwick, *A Theory of Public Bureaucracy: Politics, Personality, and Organization in the State Department* (Harvard University Press, Cambridge, Mass., 1975).

4 A. Rapoport, *Fights, Games, and Debates* (University of Michigan Press, Ann Arbor, 1960); V. H. Vroom, *Work and Motivation* (Wiley, New York, 1964); R. Binkley, R. Bronaugh and A. Marras (eds), *Agent, Action, and Reason* (University of Toronto Press, Toronto, (1971); A. Tversky and D. Kahneman, 'Judgment under uncertainty: heuristics and biases', *Science*, 185 (1974), pp. 1124–31; D. R. Mayhew, *Congress: The Electoral Connection* (Yale University Press, New Haven, Conn., 1974).

5 H. A. Simon, *The Science of the Artificial* (MIT Press, Cambridge, Mass., 1969); A. Newell and H. A. Simon, *Human Problem Solving* (Prentice-Hall, Englewood Cliffs, N.J., 1972).

6 A. Charnes and W. W. Cooper, 'Deterministic equivalents for optimizing and satisficing under chance constraints', *Operations Research*, 11 (1963), pp. 18–39; P. G. W. Keen, 'The evolving concept of optimality', *TIMS Studies in the Management Sciences*, 6 (1977), pp. 31–57.

7 L. J. Savage, *Foundations of Statistics* (Wiley, New York, 1954); J. Thompson, *Organizations in Action* (McGraw-Hill, New York, 1967).

8 Simon, *Models of Man.*

9 R. Radner, 'A behavioral model of cost reduction', *The Bell Journal of Economics*, 6 (1975), Spring, pp. 196–215; Idem, 'Satisficing', *Journal of Mathematical Economics*, 2 (1975), pp. 253–62; Idem and M. Rothschild, 'On the allocation of effort', *Journal of Economic Theory*, 10 (1975), pp. 358–76; T. Connolly, 'Information processing and decision making in organisations', in B. M. Staw and G. R. Salancik (eds), *New Directions in Organizational Behavior* (St Clair, Chicago, 1977).

10 J. G. March, 'The business firm as a political coalition', *Journal of Politics*, 24 (1962), pp. 662–78; M. Olson, *The Logic of Collective Action* (Schocken, New York, 1965); M. Taylor, 'The theory of collective choice', in F. I. Greenstein and N. W. Polsby (eds), *Handbook of Political Science*, vol. 3 (Addison-Wesley, Reading, Mass., 1975); J. Pfeffer, 'Power and resource allocation in organisations', in Staw and Salancik, *New Directions in Organizational Behavior.*

11 M. D. Cohen and J. G. March, *Leadership and Ambiguity: The American College President* (McGraw-Hill, New York, 1974); K. W. Weick, 'Educational organizations as loosely coupled systems', *Administrative Science Quarterly*, 21 (1976), pp. 1–18; J. G. March and J. P. Olsen (eds), *Ambiguity and Choice in Organizations* (Universitetsforlaget, Bergen, 1976); M. Crozier and E. Friedberg, *L'Acteur et le Système* (Seuil, Paris, 1977).

12 J. S. Mill, *Bentham* (1838). Reprinted in *Mill on Bentham and Coleridge* (Chatto and Windus, London, 1950).

13 H. A. Simon, 'A behavioral model of rational choice', *Quarterly Journal of Economics*, 69 (1955), pp. 99–118; Idem, 'Rational choice and

the structure of the environment', *Psychological Review*, 63 (1956), pp. 129–38.

14 March and Olsen, *Ambiguity and Choice*.

15 I. L. Janis and L. Mann, *Decision Making* (Free Press, New York, 1977).

16 Keen, 'The evolving concept of optimality'.

17 W. Riker and P. Ordeshook, *An Introduction to Positive Political Theory* (Prentice-Hall, Englewood Cliffs, N.J., 1973).

18 J. L. Bower, 'Descriptive decision theory from the "administrative" viewpoint', in R. A. Bauer and K. J. Gergen (eds), *The Study of Policy Formation* (Free Press, New York, 1968); G. T. Allison, *Essence of Decision: Explaining the Cuban Missile Crisis* (Little, Brown, Boston); J. D. Steinbruner, *The Cybernetic Theory of Decision* (Princeton University Press, Princeton, 1974); O. E. Williamson, *Markets and Hierarchies* (Free Press, New York, 1975).

19 R. M. Cyert and J. G. March, *A Behavioral Theory of the Firm* (Prentice-Hall, Englewood Cliffs, N.J., 1963); A. M. Porat and J. A. Haas, 'Information effects on decision making', *Behavioral Science*, 14 (1969), pp. 98–104; E. E. Carter, 'The behavioral theory of the firm and top-level corporate decisions', *Administrative Science Quarterly*, 16 (1971), pp. 413–29; R. N. Taylor, 'Psychological determinants of bounded rationality: Implications for decision-making strategies', *Decision Sciences*, 6 (1975), pp. 409–29; P. Slovic, B. Fischhoff and S. Lichtenstein, 'Behavioral decision theory', *Annual Review of Psychology*, 28 (1977), pp. 1–39.

20 March and Olsen, *Ambiguity and Choice*.

21 J. G. March and H. A. Simon, *Organizations* (Wiley, New York, 1958); C. E. Lindblom, 'The science of muddling through', *Public Administration Review*, 19 (1959), pp. 79–88; Idem, *The Intelligence of Democracy* (Macmillan, New York, 1965); Radner, 'A behavioral model of cost reduction'; Idem, 'Satisficing'.

22 N. E. Long, 'The local community as an ecology of games', *American Journal of Sociology*, 44 (1958), pp. 251–61; T. Schelling, 'On the ecology of micro-motives', *Public Interest*, 25 (1971), pp. 59–98; M. D. Cohen, J. G. March and J. P. Olsen, 'A garbage can model of organizational choice', *Administrative Science Quarterly*, 17 (1972), pp. 1–25; S. S. Weiner, 'Participation, deadlines, and choice', in March and Olsen, *Ambiguity and Choice*; L. S. Sproull, S. S. Weiner and D. B. Wolf, *Organizing an Anarchy* (University of Chicago Press, Chicago, 1978).

23 R. Farquharson, *Theory of Voting* (Yale University Press, New Haven, 1969; J. C. Harsanyi and R. Selten, 'A generalized Nash solution for two-person bargaining games with incomplete information', *Management Science*, 18 (1972), pp. 80–106; S. J. Brams, *Game Theory and Politics* (Free Press, New York, 1975).

24 M. Edelman, *The Symbolic Uses of Politics* (University of Illinois Press, Champaign, Ill., 1964); Cohen and March, *Leadership and Ambiguity*;

K. Kreiner, 'Ideology and management in a garbage can situation', in March and Olsen, *Ambiguity and Choice*; S. Christensen, 'Decision making and socialization', ibid.

25 Cyert and March, *A Behavioral Theory of the Firm*; R. H. Day and T. Groves (eds), *Adaptive Economic Models* (Academic Press, New York, 1975).

26 S. G. Winter, 'Economic "natural selection" and the theory of the firm', *Yale Economic Essays*, 4 (1964), pp. 225–72; idem, 'Satisficing, selection, and the innovating remnant', *Quarterly Journal of Economics*, 85 (1971), pp. 237–61; idem, 'Optimization and evolution in the theory of the firm', in Day and Groves, *Adaptive Economic Models*; R. R. Nelson and S. G. Winter, 'Towards an evolutionary theory of economic capabilities', *The American Economic Review*, 63 (1973), pp. 440–9.

27 A. O. Hirschman, *Development Projects Observed* (The Brookings Institution, Washington, D.C., 1967); K. E. Weick, *The Social Psychology of Organizing* (Addison-Wesley, Reading, Mass., 1969); J. G. March, 'Model bias in social action', *Review of Educational Research*, 42 (1973), pp. 413–29.

28 E. O. Wilson, *Sociobiology* (Harvard University Press, Cambridge, Mass., 1975); G. S. Becker, 'Altruism, egoism, and genetic fitness: economics and sociobiology', *Journal of Economic Literature*, 14 (1976), pp. 817–26.

29 R. L. Ackoff and M. W. Sasieni, *Fundamentals of Operations Research* (Wiley, New York, 1968).

30 G. J. Stigler, 'The economics of information', *Journal of Political Economy*, 69 (1961), pp. 213–25; G. S. Becker, 'A theory of the allocation of time', *Economic Journal*, 75 (1965), pp. 493–517; C. B. McGuire and R. Radner (eds), *Decision and Organization* (North-Holland, Amsterdam, 1972); J. Marschak and R. Radner, *Economic Theory of Teams* (Yale University Press, New Haven, 1972); M. Rothschild and J. Stiglitz, 'Equilibrium in competitive insurance markets: an essay on the economics of imperfect information', *Quarterly Journal of Economics*, 90 (1976), pp. 629–49.

31 A. O. Hirschman and C. E. Lindblom, 'Economic development, research and development, policy making: some converging views', *Behavioral Science*, 7 (1962), pp. 211–22; A. M. Spence, *Market Signalling* (Harvard University Press, Cambridge, Mass., 1974); Radner, 'A behavioral model of cost reduction'; idem, 'Satisficing'; Radner and Rothschild, 'On the allocation of effort'.

32 E. Johnson, *Studies in Multiobjective Decision Models* (Lund, Studentlitteratur, 1968).

33 G. Tullock, *The Politics of Bureaucracy* (Public Affairs, Washington, D.C., 1965); A. Downs, *Inside Bureaucracy* (Little, Brown, Boston, 1967); G. T. Allison and M. H. Halperin, 'Bureaucratic politics: paradigm and some policy implications', in R. Tanter and R. H. Ullman (eds), *Theory and Policy in International Relations* (Princeton University Press, Princeton, N.J., 1972); M. H. Halperin, *Bureaucratic*

Politics and Foreign Policy (The Brookings Institution, Washington, D.C., 1974).

34 J. Elster, *Logic and Society* (Wiley, London, 1977).

35 S. M. Lee, *Goal Programming for Decision Analysis* (Auerbach, Philadelphia, 1972); P. K. Pattanaik, 'Group choice with lexicographic individual orderings', *Behavioral Science*, 18 (1973), pp. 118–23.

36 Cohen and March, *Leadership and Ambiguity*; Weick, 'Educational organisations'; March and Olsen, *Ambiguity and Choice*; Sproull, Weiner and Wolf, *Organizing an Anarchy*.

37 G. V. Catullus, Carmina, 85 (Rome, 58 BC).

38 G. J. Stigler and G. S. Becker, 'De gustibus non est disputandum', *The American Economic Review*, 67 (1977), March, pp. 76–90.

39 March and Simon, *Organizations*; Cyert and March, *Behavioral Theory of the Firm*; H. A. Simon, 'The structure of ill-structured problems', *Artificial Intelligence*, 4 (1973), pp. 181–201; J. G. March and P. J. Romelaer, 'Position and presence in the drift of decisions', in March and Olsen, *Ambiguity and Choice*.

40 J. Elster, 'Ulysses and the sirens: a theory of imperfect rationality', *Social Science Information*, 16 (1977), pp. 469–526.

41 B. A. O. Williams, *Problems of the Self* (Cambridge University Press, Cambridge, 1973); J. Elster, 'Some unresolved problems in the theory of rational behaviour', in *Ulysses and the Sirens* (Cambridge University Press, Cambridge, 1979).

42 March, 'Model bias in social action'.

43 N. Chomsky, *Language and Mind* (Harcourt, Brace and World, New York, 1968); March, 'Model bias in social action'; L. R. Pondy and M. L. Olson, 'Organization and performance', unpublished manuscript.

44 W. Shakespeare, *Hamlet, Prince of Denmark* (Stratford-upon-Avon, 1623).

45 R. H. Strotz, 'Myopia and inconsistency in dynamic utility maximization', *Review of Economic Studies*, 23 (1956); T. C. Koopmans, 'On flexibility of future preferences', in M. W. Shelley and G. L. Bryan (eds), *Human Judgments and Optimality*, (Wiley, New York, 1964); M. J. Bailey and M. Olson, 'Pure time preference, revealed marginal utility, and Friedman-Savage gambles', unpublished manuscript, 1977; H. M. Shefrin and R. Thaler, 'An economic theory of self-control', unpublished manuscript, 1977.

46 D. C. Mueller, 'Public choice: a survey', *Journal of Economic Literature*, 14 (1976), pp. 395–433.

47 C. C. von Weiszäcker, 'Notes on endogenous change of taste', *Journal of Economic Theory*, 3 (1971), pp. 345–72; M. Olson, 'Exchange, integration, and grants', in M. Pfaff (ed.), *Essays in Honor of Kenneth Boulding* (North-Holland, Amsterdam, 1976).

48 R. M. Cyert and M. H. de Groot, 'An analysis of co-operation and learning in a duopoly context', *The American Economic Review*, 63 (1973), March, pp. 1–25; idem, 'Adaptive Utility' in Day and Groves, *Adaptive Economic Models*.

49 M. Friedman, *To Deny our Nothingness: Contemporary Images of Man* (Delacorte, New York, 1967); Williams, *Problems of the Self*; L. W. Beck, *The Actor and the Spectator* (Yale University Press, New Haven, Conn., 1975).

50 A. Schutz, *The Phenomenology of the Social World* (Northwestern, Evanston, Ill., 1967); Hirschman, *Development Projects Observed*; Weick, *The Social Psychology of Organizing*; J. Elster, 'A note on hysteresis in the social sciences', *Synthese*, 33 (1976), pp. 371–91.

51 March, 'Model bias in social action'; idem, 'Administrative Leadership in Education', unpublished manuscript, 1977.

52 J. Ciardi, *How Does a Poem Mean?* (Houghton Mifflin, Cambridge, Mass., 1960).

53 T. S. Eliot, *The Use of Poetry and the Use of Criticism* (Harvard University Press, Cambridge, Mass., 1933); S. Cavell, *Must We Mean What We Say?* (Scribner, New York, 1969); L. Steinberg, *Other Criteria: Confrontations with Twentieth Century Art* (Oxford University Press, New York, 1972); H. Rosenberg, *Art on the Edge: Creators and Situations* (Macmillan, New York, 1975).

54 Elster, 'Some unresolved problems'.

55 L. Farber, *Lying, Despair, Jealousy, Envy, Sex, Suicide, Drugs, and the Good Life* (Basic Books, New York, 1976); Elster, 'Some unresolved problems'.

56 Elster, 'Some unresolved problems'.

57 March and Simon, *Organizations*.

58 Ibid.

59 J. G. March, 'American public school administration: a short analysis', *School Review*, 86 (1978), pp. 217–50.

60 F. Nietzsche, *The Genealogy of Morals* (Boni and Liveright, New York, 1918).

61 S. Freud, *The Ego and the Id* (Hogarth, London, 1927).

62 E. Jones, 'The origin and structure of the Superego', *International Journal of Psychoanalysis*, 7 (1926), pp. 303–11.

63 Savage, *Foundations of Statistics*.

7

The Logic of Relative Frustration

RAYMOND BOUDON

This text, theoretical in nature, is intended as a contribution to a particular debate. This debate is concerned with the paradox in there being a relation between both inequality and satisfaction *and* material plenty and satisfaction. In fact classical sociology is full of paradoxical statements of this sort. For Tocqueville greater equality tends to produce envious comparisons: as they become more equal individuals find their inequality harder and harder to bear. C. Wright Mills has also taken up this theme. For Durkheim individual happiness does not increase in direct ratio to the quantity of available goods. The relation between happiness and goods has the form of a reversed U-shaped curve: on this side of and beyond a particular optimum satisfaction decreases. Again, for Tocqueville, dissatisfaction and frustration may grow when each person's opportunities begin to open out and improve. In *Marienthal*, Lazarsfeld observes the converse of Tocqueville's theorem: when an individual's future is blocked, recriminations against the social system may well be weak. Stouffer's works show that individuals may well grow more discontented with the social system to which they belong as it offers them what are, on average, better opportunities for success and promotion.

In short Tocqueville, Durkheim, Lazarsfeld, Stouffer and also Merton, Runciman and Hyman, authors who surely differ massively in their various methodological, theoretical and political orientations, agree to acknowledge the complex and (since there is no need to reject the word when it is given an exact meaning) *dialectical* character of the relation between material plenty and equality on the one hand, and between material plenty and individual satisfaction on the other.

By contrast there are many more recent authors who interpret

This essay is reprinted from R. Boudon, *The Unintended Consequences of Social Action* © Presses Universitaires de France 1981 by permission of St. Martin's Press Inc. and MacMillan, London and Basingstoke.

this relation in a manner that would seem to have no other virtue apart from its simplicity: some clearly think that an intolerable and potentially explosive situation is created as soon as the poorest five per cent have a salary that is less than half the national average. There are others who think that a reduction in inequalities is invariably, regardless of the context, positive.

The following text reaffirms its links with the sociological tradition. It argues that the paradoxical relationships that the classical works of sociology point to can be deduced from simple models inspired by game theory. The basic virtue of these models lies in their ability to show that (among other things) there is no simple way in which one can associate a particular degree of collective happiness, frustration or satisfaction with the various possible distributions of goods.

The simple models presented here bring out complex effects of composition (which may account for the paradoxical appeal of the propositions referred to above).

> Now let us consider the effect of this public prosperity on the private happiness of citizens. First of all, if these riches are distributed equally, it is certain that they will not long remain in this state of equality, or that, if they did, they would be as if non-existent for those who possessed them. For, in everything beyond immediate necessity the advantages of fortune only make themselves felt in terms of differences.
>
> Jean-Jacques Rousseau, *Political Fragments*

The notions of relative deprivation and of reference group together make up a conceptual whole whose success is doubtless attributable to the way in which it allows one to account – with the help of commonsense propositions – for paradoxical observations. As Runciman notes, the two notions derive from a familiar truism, namely 'that people's attitudes, aspirations and grievances largely depend on the frame of reference within which they are conceived.'[1] Observation in fact shows that in most cases it is impossible to understand why an individual A will feel envious of B but not of C if one does not know 'the frame of reference' of A. How is one to explain why it is that A envies his right-hand neighbour's Peugeot if one does not know that A can hope to raise himself up to his right-hand neighbour's level but not to that of his left-hand neighbour? Suppose we use the excellent definition of relative deprivation proposed by Runciman: 'A strict definition is difficult. But we can roughly say that A is relatively deprived when (1) he does not have x, (2) he sees some other person or persons, which may include himself at some previous or anticipated time, as having *x* (whether or not this will in fact be the case), (3) he wants *x* and (4) he sees it as feasible that he should have *x*. Possession of *x* may of course mean avoidance of or exemption from *y*.'

The difficulty with this definition, as Runciman acknowledges, is the notion of *feasibility*: people only desire what they can plausibly hope to obtain. But what rules determine the things that one can or cannot obtain? Does *A*'s envy of *B* decrease in ratio to the feasibility of *A* obtaining the object *x* that *B* possesses? Suppose I take this argument a little further. By defining the notion of relative deprivation in terms of the concept of *feasibility* is one not setting up a kind of vicious circle? I understand that the Jaguar owner does not belong to *A*'s reference group, a group that includes the Peugeot 504's owner. I also understand that *A* envies the second but not the first. But the first proposition sheds no light on the second: the notion of reference group is simply a rephrasing of the proposition that has it that *A* feels envious of the Peugeot 504 owner but not of the Jaguar owner.

I do not propose to analyse here the important literature to which the two notions of reference group and relative deprivation have given rise. I think however that it is fair to say that the following two propositions contain the most comprehensive summary of this literature:

1. The two notions make it possible to account for certain fundamental social phenomena. Take, for instance, Tocqueville's famous law. This law holds that the improvement of the condition of all may well increase rather than diminish the general sense of discontent. When prosperity increases, Tocqueville writes, 'people seem, however, more uneasy and anxious in their minds; public discontent is aggravated; hate against all the old institutions increases [. . .] What is more, the parts of France which must be the principal focus for this revolution are the very ones in which progress is most apparent [. . .] it could fairly be said that the French have found their position increasingly unbearable as it became better.'[2]

One can clearly also postulate a link between the notions of reference group and relative deprivation and the law of Durkheim's that has it that the satisfaction that the individual experiences depends less on the plentiful supply of goods that are at the collectivity's disposal and more on the tendency the collectivity has to instil desires in the individual that are limited to what he can hope to obtain: 'Under this pressure, each, in his own sphere, becomes vaguely aware of the furthest point to which his ambitions may reach, and aspires to nothing beyond it if, at least, he is respectful of rules and has a docile attitude to collective authority, i.e., if he has a healthy moral constitution, he feels that it is not right to demand more. A goal and a limit are thus marked out for the passions. But this determination doubtless has nothing rigid or absolute about it. The economic ideal assigned to each category of citizens is itself understood to have certain limits, within which desires may freely move. But it is not without these limits. *It is this relative limitation, and the moderation that it entails, which makes men happy with their lot, while at the same time stimulating them, within reason, to improve it* (my italics, R.B.); and it is this average contentment that gives rise to that feeling of calm and active joy, that pleasure in being and living which, for societies as for individuals, is what characterises health.'³

Lastly I will call to mind the famous conclusion of *The American Soldier*, the book that marks the beginning of the literature on relative deprivation and on reference groups. Military policemen, who belong to a group in which promotion is rare, declare themselves satisfied with the system of promotion that governs their lives. Pilots, on the other hand, though belonging to a group in which promotion is frequent, declare themselves to be unsatisfied with the system of promotion.⁴ Everything happens as if an objectively greater upwards mobility brought with it weaker overall satisfaction.

2. There is no doubt that the apparently paradoxical phenomena covered by Tocqueville's, Durkheim's or Stouffer's laws are fundamental ones. But that would clearly be the second conclusion that one would draw from an analysis of the literature, i.e. however useful the concepts of reference group and relative deprivation are, they only enable one to grasp very imperfectly the logic underlying these laws.

In the notes that follow I hope to show that the sociological notions of collective relative deprivation and reference group may be more clearly defined if one has recourse to simple models derived from game theory. These simple models suggest that the appearance of relative deprivation phenomena is, in some situations anyway, the 'natural' product of structures of interaction (of competition) within which individuals are located. In other words it would seem that some structures of competition incite a more or less significant proportion of individuals to participate in 'rivalries' from which some amongst them must necessarily emerge as losers. This proportion, and consequently, the general rate of deprivation, varies with the properties of these structures. I will devote the rest of this article to a presentation of these elementary structures of competition and to an analysis of certain of their logical properties. As the reader will observe, even extremely simple structures of competition give rise to relatively complex analyses. It is incidentally worth noting that the *counter-intuitive* character of the properties of these structures of competition may well explain their capacity to fascinate: the consequences that they entail correspond to data that are often observed but only with some difficulty explained.

On a theoretical plane the simple models developed below make it possible to specify the purchase that Tocqueville's, Durkheim's and Stouffer's 'laws' enjoy, to demonstrate that it is not a question of universally valid laws, as Durkheim thought, but of propositions which may be conditionally true. In other words it is not true that in general an increase in the opportunities or goods offered to individuals will in every case bring about the higher degree of dissatisfaction observed by Tocqueville. On the other hand it is true that the phenomenon can, in certain cases, occur. By 'certain cases' I mean as a function of modifications in the structures of competition that the increase in opportunities or goods offered to individuals by the 'social structure' has provoked.

We therefore arrive at a completely different interpretation of his law than Durkheim himself does. In *Suicide*, and perhaps even more clearly in *The Division of Labour*, Durkheim has recourse to propositions that are well established in the psycho-physiology of the period in order to explain that dissatisfaction may grow with the increasing number of goods on offer: 'Indeed, it is a truth generally recognised today that pleasure accompanies neither the very intense states of conscience nor those that are too weak. There is a pain when the functional activity is insufficient, but excessive activity produces the same effects [. . .] This proposition is, besides, a corollary of Weber's and Fechner's law. It is not without reason that human experience sees the condition of happiness in the *golden mean*.'[5]

The reader will see below that this interpretation rests on hypotheses that are both needlessly ponderous and probably false.

As Runciman suggests, in the text quoted above, there is relative deprivation when there exists a good x that A possesses and that B does not have. The notion of relative deprivation does, in other words, imply the notion of competition for a good.

Imagine a simple competition model in which there is a group comprising N individuals. 'Society' proposes the following option to each of the N individuals: (1) They can either reap a profit B ($>C$) for a stake C, with a probability that diminishes as the number of competitors rises; (2) or they can choose not to participate in the competition. This very general structure characterises a whole number of situations in which there is competition: should I 'invest' in order to try and be promoted to the rank of office head, given that the majority of my colleagues are doubtless driven by the same objective? I would like to make it clear that throughout the first part of this article I shall assume individuals are equal and regard each other as such. This hypothesis will be abandoned in the last part of the article.

It is worth introducing a methodological proviso at this point: I am aware that in many situations of competition individuals are not equal and do not consider themselves as such. It is clear enough that, through sociology, a statistical correlation between social origins and a whole range of other characteristics could be elicited. One is nevertheless entitled, from the methodological point of view, to neglect this fact during the first stages of the analysis. This strategy has the added advantage of highlighting in all its purity the *perverse* character of the effects of composition that structures of competition generate. In the last part of the analysis I will openly abandon the egalitarian hypothesis in order to postulate the existence of groups that tend to be endowed with different levels of resources. These groups can be called classes. One will not of course obtain identical perverse effects when one advances an essentially unrealistic hypothesis – that all are equal – as when one admits that classes do exist, but in either case one will still observe them. They tend, *ceteris paribus*, to be more marked when the egalitarian hypothesis is posited.

Quite apart from its methodological interest, recourse to the fiction of equality allows one to obtain a sociologically significant result, namely, that equality of opportunity does not necessarily lead to deprivation being minimalised. We thus come back to another of Tocqueville's classic themes, and one that C. Wright Mills later revives: that equal conditions tend to stir up rather than to curb envy. I will come back to these points later.

In order to fix these ideas in the reader's mind and in order to make the logic of interaction shown by the preceding model more concrete I propose to give its parameters an arithmetical value. Let N therefore equal 20: the set of individuals to whom the option is available comprises twenty individuals. Let us also imagine that stake and profit are quantifiable, which is clearly not always the case in social life, and that C, the stake, equals £1, while B, the profit, equals £5. Finally we will only allow $n = 5$ winners. Thus if fifteen out of twenty persons decide to put down a stake, only five of these fifteen will draw a profit of £5. The other ten will lose their stake. We will presume that the distribution between winners and losers is random and occurs through drawing of lots (it would naturally be possible to construct more complex examples but there is some interest in beginning with the analysis of the simplest cases.) What will happen? How many of the twenty potential players will in fact decide to re-enter the game? How many losers or frustrated people will the game create? In this example the answers to these questions are not difficult to provide. If we take just one of the twenty players and presume that he is perfectly well informed about the situation, he will make the following calculations:

1 If I suppose that I, Jones, am the only person playing, I know that in staking £1 I am absolutely certain to get back £5. I will therefore make a bet.

2 This also applies if one, two, three or four colleagues play. In each case I am assured of a net profit of £4 (£5 profit less my stake of £1) since there are five winners.

3 If five of my colleagues play, there are six of us competing for the five winners' places. I have therefore five out of six chances of winning £4 (£5 profit less a stake of £1) and one chance of losing my stake, i.e., of obtaining a negative profit, or as one would be more likely to put it, a loss of £1. My 'expectations' of a profit therefore stand, in statistical terms, at $(5/6)(4) + (1/6)(-1) = 3.2$. I clearly run the risk of losing my stake but I have a good chance of winning £4. It is likely that I will decide to make a bet.

4 If six of my colleagues play, my expectation of a profit will then be: $(5/7)(4) + (2/7)(-1) = 2.6$. I therefore make a bet.

5 If 7, 8, 9, 10 . . . 16, 17, 18 of my colleagues play, my expectations of a profit will diminish accordingly but will still be positive: the value of my possible profit, multiplied by the probability of obtaining it, exceeds the value of the possible loss incurred, multiplied by the possibility of suffering it. I have five out of nineteen chances of winning £4 and fourteen out of nineteen of losing £1. My expectation of profit is therefore $(5/19)(4) + (14/19)(-1) = 0.3$. Supposing I consider it quite reasonable to make a bet when my expectation of profit is positive: I will then bet on the assumption that the number of other gamblers is equal to eighteen. If everyone bets, my expectation of making a profit is still positive: $(5/20)(4) + (15/20)(-1) = 0.25$. I will therefore make a bet.[6]

We are therefore dealing with a structure of competition in which each person, regardless of the behaviour of others, reckons that it is in his interests to bet. As a result there will naturally be fifteen losers. The example simulates a situation of competition in which each of the group's members feels justified in entering the lists. Nothing forces potential players to rejoin the game, except the encouragement given by the fact that expectations of profit are positive irrespective of the number of players. The players therefore invest in the game not because of any constraint but because a good understanding of their individual interests inspires them to do so. Now the combined effect of these interests is to turn three-quarters of the group's members into losers. The structure generates a collective deprivation that can be measured in terms of the number of losers: in the above game, fifteen out of twenty individuals appear to be so deprived. Their contribution was the same as that of the five winners. It was no more unreasonable for them to bet than it was for those who came out of the game without losses. These individuals cannot help adopting the five winners as a reference group and therefore feeling *relatively deprived* in relation to them. In this case the structure helps to generate a level of dissatisfaction typical of the upper level. It perhaps helps to throw some light on Stouffer's observations: when promotions are relatively numerous it is in everyone's interest to bet on promotion. But all those not promoted (the majority in this case) are then deprived. Ease of promotion generates a considerable degree of overall frustration.

The previous game brings to mind the case of the aviators who figure in Stouffer's famous analysis. The game's structure offers individuals objective opportunities for profit – or, in another language, for promotion or increased mobility – that are by no means negligible. But it therefore encourages an excessive number of players and consequently a considerable collective deprivation.

Before proceeding any further I will introduce a new methodological proviso. In the previous model I used a fairly unpopular version of *homo sociologicus*. Sociologists tend to recoil from the idea of assimilating *homo sociologicus* to a calculating individual intent on pursuing his own interests. In fact the model does not at all imply such a narrow representation of the determinants of his behaviour. Although it would make my mode of exposition and argument far more ponderous, I could eliminate the apparently shocking nature of the hypotheses used. I could for instance suppose that individuals were moved not only by the idea of profit but by other motives (pleasure at playing, for example), or that some work out the lottery's value, in a more or less confused way, before deciding, whilst others decide to take part in the game because they believe their luck is in, or decide to abstain because they are plagued by ill-fortune. (I will leave to one side the question raised by the unrealistic hypothesis of *equality* between individuals, which, once again, will be taken up again below.) I could put forward hypotheses as to the frequency with which individuals decide as a function of their own interests. It is not hard to see that, under a wide range of conditions (i.e., if one supposes that social agents do *on average* tend to follow their own interests rather than setting them to one side), my previous conclusions hold good, in the sense that a perverse effect will invariably appear. The brutal simplification implicit in positing a rational *homo sociologicus* does have the considerable methodological advantage of making the exposition and demonstration less ponderous. It would be purely and simply a misunderstanding to interpret this hypothesis as an ontological statement. It is also incidentally worth noting that if one postulates a minority of individuals who fail to recognise their own best interests and make their decision on the basis of irrational sentiments (ill luck, chance etc.), the collective level of deprivation will, paradoxically, be attenuated.

Suppose we now simulate the second case presented in Stouffer's classic analysis, that of the military police. Here promotion is, objectively speaking, rare. This feature can be represented by supposing that the number n of winners no longer equals 5, as before, but equals 2, for example.[7] Thus, the proportion of winners to group members is no more than two out of twenty. For the rest, I will keep the parameters of the previous example and consider military policeman Jones's line of reasoning:

1 If I, Jones, make a bet, and if at the most one of my colleagues also bets, I have a guaranteed win of £4.
2 If two colleagues bet, I have two in three chances of winning £4 and one chance in three of losing £1. My hope of winning is then: $(2/3)(4) + (1/3)(-1) = 2.3$.
3 If 3, 4, 5, 6, 7, 8, 9 colleagues bet, my chances of winning are progressively reduced and in the final case, become nil. In fact $(2/10)(4) + (8/10)(-1) = 0$.
4 If more than nine colleagues bet, my expectations of winning are negative and the 'hoped for' loss will rise in ratio to the number of people who bet. Then, for fifteen people betting altogether, Jones's expectation of winning is $(2/15)(4) + (13/15)(-1) = 0.33$. When there are twenty people altogether who bet, Jones's chance of winning amounts to: $(2/20)(4) + (18/20)(-1) = 0.50$.

What will Jones do? Imagine that he has no information about the possible behaviour of the others and that the same goes for them: each must then decide whether to participate or not in the game, given a totally solipsistic context.[8] In this case Jones and each of his colleagues reckons that, if there turned out to be 11, 12, 13 . . . 20 people betting in all, this would result in an unfavourable situation in which expectations of profit would be negative (expectations of loss). Beyond solipsism a sort of solidarity must then be introduced: with no one having control over the behaviour of others, each will do everything in his power to ensure that the total number of people betting does not exceed ten.

It is worth giving this point some thought, for, in spite of the fact that the model's hypotheses tend to simplify things, the structure of interdependence that it generates is of extreme complexity. Let me repeat the proposition that I have just formulated: 'Each will do everything in his power to ensure that the total number of people betting does not exceed ten.' In reality, although it is in everyone's interest to obtain this result, no one can assume responsibility for it, since it clearly depends on the collaboration of all. But a collaboration of this sort was ruled out by definition. Suppose we imagine that the lottery simulates a choice that the educational system offers a public of potential students: those who play clearly cannot, in such circumstances, confer amongst themselves. What should one do in such a contradictory situation? If Ego assumes that each will take his chance, it is in his interests to abstain. But everyone might reason like this. In reality Ego stands to gain most if, in the hope that the others will do likewise, he allows himself one chance in two of participating in the game.[9] If everybody acts thus, the number of participants will be of the order of a dozen. Interestingly enough the structure of interdependence commits the players to a form of tacit cooperation that I defined above in terms of the notion of quasi-solidarity. It is worth making at this point a methodological observation of the sort I had made above, although in a different context: the model attributes to policeman Jones the capacity to make subtle calculations. But it is important to recognise that the relevance of the hypothesis is purely *methodological*. In other words it is a caricature of the more realistic proposition that, in a situation in which upwards mobility is rare, the potential players will hesitate more before investing their energies in the search for a difficult promotion. In hesitating thus they will, without wishing to and perhaps without knowing it, be manifesting a behaviour of *quasi-solidarity*.

Let us now return to the model and suppose that each will allow his own bet to be decided by the toss of a coin. Let us suppose that Jones and the others employ this strategy. Each will then hope to gain: $(1/2)(0) + (1/2)[(2/10)(4) + (8/10)(-1)] = 0$.

This clearly is not a brilliant result but it is preferable to the one that Jones could hope to obtain by deciding, for instance, to allow himself more than a 1/2 chance of participating in the game. The term in brackets does in this case become negative, since the coefficient of 4 would then be lower than 2/10 and that of (-10) higher than 8/10. Jones therefore imposes on himself, and consequently on the others, a negative expectation of profit.

One can in short admit that, in a situation of this sort, the behaviour of a rational player can broadly be described by supposing that he will allow a toss of the coin to decide his participation in the game. There will then be ten people betting (if we admit, for the sake of simplicity, that the twenty tosses of the coin will give heads ten times and tails ten times).[10] Once again a result like this is only a semblance of what one actually observes. But at the same time, it is not entirely unrealistic. One often enough finds that an individual who wants to obtain a good but perceives, more or less clearly, that the number of individuals who desire it make his chances of obtaining it purely 'random' uses a dice throw to decide whether or not to participate in the game.

Once this process of *self-selection* has occurred, we find that the situation for ten people betting is analogous to the first situation examined; out of the ten, eight will emerge losers and two as winners, since it was stated that only two individuals could win the £5 prize.

The game that corresponds to the second example – the one simulating the result given in *The American Solidier* for the military police – can in short be summed up as follows:

1 Ten potential players do not take part in the competition game. They win nothing, but lose nothing. Their nonparticipation in the game is the result of a considered and reasonable procedure. I have shown how this abstention can be interpreted as a result of the *quasi-solidarity* imposed by the structure of competition.
2 Two players bet and win.
3 Three players bet and lose.

What sort of consequences does this result lead to, with respect to frustration? The two winning players do of course have no reason to feel frustrated. As for the eight players who have made bets and lost, they will probably be tempted to compare their fate to that of the two winners, i.e., to consider them as their reference group: their *contribution* is equal to that of the winners, their *reward* less. This difference in treatment received will tend to be perceived as illegitimate, and frustration is in this case the most likely response to the situation. The case of the ten players who have abstained and have therefore won nothing has to be considered separately. The situation is different from that of the two other groups of players, for the zero value of their reward is the proper remuneration for the zero value of their contribution. From another angle their abstention has been described as the product of deliberation. But abstention only appeared to them to be a reasonable strategy because of the existence of the structure of interdependence. They can therefore consider themselves to be frustrated. Nevertheless frustration is very probably more likely here than when the players have lost their stake out of a feeling of resignation. I will define their reaction in terms of the notion of *resigned* frustration. One can conclude from this that the collective frustration engendered by the lottery is lower in this case than in the preceding model. More precisely, the number of individuals who are likely to feel frustrated and cheated at the outcome of the game, and who will therefore contest its legitimacy, will doubtless be lower in this case than in the preceding example. This can therefore be summarised by saying that a frustration leading to *quarrels* will be least frequent in the latter case. It is worth noting, incidentally, that the model, in spite of the simplicity of the original psychological hypotheses, generates complex distinctions regarding the situations in which individuals find themselves at the start of the game, and therefore regarding the sentiments which ought to correspond to these situations. We have in short to deal with a situation that is objectively less favourable than the first one was for the potential players. In the first situation the number of potential winners was five, whereas in the second it is two. But, on the other hand, the first situation incites each player to participate in the game, while in the second it would be quite reasonable for each player to decide whether to participate in the game by tossing a coin. The first situation thus generates fifteen cases of frustration *leading to quarrels* in a group comprising twenty persons, while the second only produces eight cases of this type. In this latter case we therefore have a situation comparable to that of the military police analysed by Stouffer: there is less chance of promotion there than in the air force, but the general level of frustration produced by the system of promotion is much weaker. To be more exact frustration *leading to quarrels* is less likely to appear.

To conclude I will recall an important methodological observation: in the two cases analysed above, I presumed that individuals would evaluate in the same way a fixed profit and a lottery linked to expectations that are, mathematically, of equivalent value. In actual fact it tends to be the case that individuals only treat a lottery and a fixed profit identically when the expectations of profit linked to the lottery are higher than those in the case of the fixed profit.[11] In applying this principle to the results of the two examples above, I would conclude that my analysis gives a maximum estimate of the rates of frustration for both. But, whatever hypothesis one retains as to the value of the difference between the fixed profit and the expectation of profit, it is important to realise that the rate of frustration leading to quarrels is higher in the first case, although individuals' objective opportunities are greater.

It is of some interest to formalise the above argument. I will posit a group of N persons, who are then offered a possible win of B_1 for a stake $C_1(B_1 > C_1)$ or B_2 for a stake $C_2(B_2 > C_2)$, with $B_1 > B_2$, $C_1 > C_2$. If $B_2 = C_2 = 0$, one again finds the two situations cited in the previous section (either one tries to obtain B_1 with a stake C_1 or one does not participate in the game). Let n_1 and n_2 be the numbers of winners of lots B_1 and B_2 respectively (supposing $n_1 + n_2 = N$). It is worth noting, incidentally, that the fact of introducing positive values for B_2 and C_2 is of more interest at the level of sociological interpretation than at the formal level. In fact, in the case of B_2 and C_2 not being nil, the game amounts to proposing to the players an additional stake $C_1 - C_2$, with the clear option of abstaining, i.e., in this case obtaining nil (additional) profit as against nil (additional) stake.

When $x_1(> n_1)$ players stake C_1, the expectation of profit $E_1(x_1)$ of a player also betting C_1 is:

$$E_1(x_1) = (B_1 - C_1)\frac{n_1}{x_1} + (B_2 - C_1)\frac{x_1 - n_1}{x_1}$$

$$= (B_1 - B_2)\frac{n_1}{x_1} + B_2 - C_1 \qquad [1]$$

The expectation of profit $E_2(x_1)$ of a player betting C_2 when $x_1(> n_1)$ players stake C_1, is, however:

$$E_2(x_1) = B_2 - C_2 \qquad [2]$$

Thus when $x_1 (> n_1)$ players take C_1, a player is advised to stake C_1 rather than C_2 if:

$$E_1(x_1) > E_2(x_2)$$

or

$$(B_1 - B_2)\frac{n_1}{x_1} + B_2 - C_1 > B_2 - C_2 \qquad [3]$$

More simply, it is advisable to stake C_1 if:

$$(B_1 - B_2)\frac{n_1}{x_1} \geq C_1 - C_2$$

or

$$\frac{B_1 - B_2}{C_1 - C_2} \geq \frac{x_1}{n_1} \qquad [4]$$

I will now apply this relation to the two examples given in the previous section. In the first example, $B_2 = C_2 = 0$. Potential players are in effect offered the possibility either of trying to win $B_1 = 5$ by betting $C_1 = 1$, or of not playing. Resolution [4] here becomes:

$$B_1/C_1 > x_1/n_1 \qquad [5]$$

In other words so long as the relation B_1/C_1 – which amounts to $5/1 = 5$ in the example given – is higher than x_1/n_1, it is reasonable for a player to stake C_1. Since x_1 cannot be higher than the total number of members of the group ($N = 20$ in the first example), and given that n_1 equals 5, x_1/n_1 cannot be higher than $20/5 = 4$. The example is therefore structured in such a way that inequality [5] is always satisfied for all possible values of x_1. It is therefore reasonable for each player to stake C_1.[12]

In the second example x_1/n_1 is higher than B_1/C_1, once x_1 is higher than 10, since $n_1 = 2$. The reader will recall that a player's expectation of profit does in fact become negative if the number of people betting exceeds ten.

This simple formalisation makes it easier for us to analyse the consequences of the system $\{B_1 - B_2; C_1 - C_2; n_1; N\}$. Suppose, for instance, we study the variations in the level of overall frustration, as defined by the proportion of individuals who find themselves in the tiresome position of acquiring at the high price C_1 the lot of least value, B_2.[13] If lot B_1 is considerably more attractive than lot B_2, or, to be more exact, if the difference between them is much greater than the difference in cost, to the effect that $(B_1 - B_2)/(C_1 - C_2) > N/n_1$, all potential players will stake C_1 and the rate of frustration will amount to $(N - n_1)/N$. If, on the other hand, $(B_1$

$- B_2)/(C_1 - C_2)$ amounts to $k/n_1 < N/n_1$, the number of individuals staking C_1 will be k and the rate of frustration will amount to $(k - n_1)/N$.

In order to study the relation between the structure of competition and the phenomenon of frustration, I have drawn up two tables. Table 7.1 gives the percentage $100x_1/N$ of players considered as a function of the relation between the additional advantage $B_1 - B_2$ and the cost of the additional stake $C_1 - C_2$ on the one hand, and the percentage of winners $100n_1/N$ on the other. Table 7.2 gives the proportion of frustrated members considered in relation to the different values holding between the stake $(B_1 - B_2)/(C_1 - C_2)$ and the percentage $100n_1/N$ of winners. The table brings out the complex manner in which the overall rate of frustration depends, on the one hand, on the individual being given back $(B_1 - B_2)/(C_1 - C_2)$ an increase in his investment, and on the frequency of high-level lots on the other. When $100n_1/N = 100$, the number of lots of high value is the same as that of the members of the group. Each person invests C_1 and receives a lot B_2. In this case none of the group's members is frustrated (last column in the table). When $(B_1 - B_2)/(C_1 - C_2) = 1$ (first line of the table) the number of investors will be exactly n_1: the first line of the table corresponds to a situation in which the number of individuals choosing the investment C_1 corresponds to the number of lots of value B_1. None of the group's members is frustrated, since the group is here divided

Table 7.1   *Percentage of players as a function of the relation between the stake and the percentage of winners*

Expected gain $= \dfrac{B_1 - B_2}{C_1 - C_2}$	Percentage of winners: $100\dfrac{n_1}{N}$										
	0	10	20	30	40	50	60	70	80	90	100
1	0	10	20	30	40	50	60	70	80	90	100
2	0	20	40	60	80	100	100	100	100	100	100
3	0	30	60	90	100	100	100	100	100	100	100
4	0	40	80	100	100	100	100	100	100	100	100
5	0	50	100	100	100	100	100	100	100	100	100
6	0	60	100	100	100	100	100	100	100	100	100
7	0	70	100	100	100	100	100	100	100	100	100
8	0	80	100	100	100	100	100	100	100	100	100
9	0	90	100	100	100	100	100	100	100	100	100
10	0	100	100	100	100	100	100	100	100	100	100

into two categories: those who make a high investment C_1 and receive B_1 in return, and those who make a low investment C_2 and receive B_2 in return. One ends up here with a stratified system without relative frustration.

In every other case a proportion of the group's members appears to be frustrated. Thus when the rise in profit is twice as rapid as the rise in cost (second line of the table) and the number of lots of value B_1 amounts to 30 per cent of the number of players N (fourth column of the table), for those making a bet to avoid an expectation of negative profit the percentage of betters $100x_1/N$ must be lower than $100(n_1/N)(B_1 - B_2)/(C_1 - C_2)$, that is, in this case, 100.0, 30.2 = 60. Each individual will thus stake C_1, with a probability 6/10, from which it follows that six out of ten individuals will stake (on average) C_1. As there are only three lots of value B_1 for ten individuals, three individuals out of ten will end up being frustrated.

The rest of table 7.2 may be reconstituted by applying [4] in an analogous way.

Table 7.2   Percentage of frustrated people as a function of the relation between the stake and the percentage of winners

Expected gain $= \dfrac{B_1 - B_2}{C_1 - C_2}$	\multicolumn{11}{c}{Percentage of winners: $100\,\dfrac{n_1}{N}$}
	0	10	20	30	40	50	60	70	80	90	100
1	0	0	0	0	0	0	0	0	0	0	0
2	0	10	20	30	40	50	40	30	20	10	0
3	0	20	40	60	60	50	40	30	20	10	0
4	0	30	60	70	60	50	40	30	20	10	0
5	0	40	80	70	60	50	40	30	20	10	0
6	0	50	80	70	60	50	40	30	20	10	0
7	0	60	80	70	60	50	40	30	20	10	0
8	0	70	80	70	60	50	40	30	20	10	0
9	0	80	80	70	60	50	40	30	20	10	0
10	0	90	80	70	60	50	40	30	20	10	0

What general propositions can we deduce from these tables?

1 If we follow the lines in table 7.2 down the page we find situations in which the profits distributed to the group's members attain a greater and greater overall importance. The

rate of frustration grows along with the hopes raised by investment, i.e., with the formal equivalent of those Durkheimian
considerations as to the link between individual happiness and
the limitation of desires: when n_1/N, for instance, amounts to
20 per cent, it is preferable, where the general rate of frustration is concerned, that the profits obtained by an additional
investment should be weak rather than strong.

2 The highest levels of frustration occur in cases in which high-
value lots are distributed among small minorities.

3 Moderate lots $(B_1 - B_2)/(C_1 - C_2)$ have the advantage of
generating a moderate level of frustration, except when they
are generously distributed.

4 Equivalent levels of frustration are obtained by distributing
important lots parsimoniously or less important lots generously. Note, for instance, that when $100n_1/N = 30$ and $(B_1
- B_2)/(C_1 - C_2) = 3$, the overall rate of frustration is 60,
and that the same rate is attained when the return on the
additional investment amounts to 7 but the lots are parsimoniously distributed $(100n_1/N = 10)$.

5 Generally speaking the curves corresponding to identical
degrees of frustration have a complex trajectory. Comparison
of tables 7.1 and 7.2 does nevertheless bring out the general
shape of the phenomenon: in that part of the table representing the situation in which everyone bets $(x_1 = 10)$ we find a
linear progression of the overall rate of frustration, which is
inversely related to the rate of winners. This 'plateau' is eroded
at the point at which constraint is no longer operative (the
'slope's line of change' is the mode of distribution of each line
in the table), and this *curve of maximum discontent* expresses
a balance: expected gain = k/probability of winning.

The two preceding sections provide us with a general model
through which we can formally define the different classes of
situations of competition and study the proportion of individuals
who, in each case, decide to enter the lists at such and such a level.
Analysis confirms the basic intuition; namely that, in the vast
majority of cases, the structures of competition determine the
appearance of frustrated players, whose number, b, varies according to the characteristics of the structure. The preceding model is
therefore a sort of theoretical machine that allows one to simulate,
by simplifying them, the more complex structures of competition
that one encounters in social life. The model's interest also lies in

the fact that it provides a simple explanation for certain phenomena sometimes considered paradoxical in classical sociology. Thus by scanning, for example, lines 2, 3 or 4 of table 7.2 from left to right, one obtains a simple simulation of Stouffer's famous example: given the same relation of additional investment, overall frustration grows as the number of winners increases (up to a certain point, at any rate). It is therefore not at all surprising that satisfaction, with regard to promotion, is greater in a system in which it is in fact rare: in this case it is irrational to invest and consequently absurd to complain if one does not get any dividends. On the other hand in situations of competition in which it is rational to invest (frequent promotion, significant chances of mobility), the fact that for some dividends are nil is necessarily felt not merely to be frustrating but to be illegitimate: this resembles Homans' notion regarding the balance between contribution and reward.[14] But it so happens that situations of competition that culminate, at the individual level, in a balance between contribution and reward, are special ones (margins of table 7.2). In the majority of cases structures of competition determine whether participation in the competition is excessive or insufficient. These excesses are, moreover, a means normally used to select individuals with regard to the collective interest, it being left up to the collectivity to create the legitimacy of the selection thus effected.

It would now be of interest to ask what happens when individuals are no longer presumed equal or perceive themselves to be equal, as was the case in previous sections of this chapter, but have, for instance, different resources. To simplify, let us imagine that the competitive games in sections 1 and 2 are presented to two categories of potential players, whom I will call the rich and the poor. I am, in other words, using the very simplest hypothesis that one could advance with respect to the structure of a system of stratification: there exist two social classes. And, in order to avoid vicarious connotations, I use banal terms. One can then imagine that the difference in resources finds expression in the poor being more hesitant in taking risks. Thus it is not enough for them to know that applying a particular strategy gives a negative or positive expectation of profit. They also take into account the structure of the lottery that is offered to them. Thus one can imagine that the value of a lottery giving them an expectation of profit G is equal to G for rich and, for the poor, lower than G, in that the risk of losing is all the greater. Whatever definition one finally adopts here, there will still be less probability of the poor person making a high bet than of the rich person doing so.

Consider, for instance, the structure

$$n_1/N = 1/6, (B_1 - B_2)/(C_1 - C_2) = 4, N = 20$$

and imagine that there are six rich people and fourteen poor people. Suppose the rich person reckons one strategy as being at least of equal value to another if the expectation of profit associated with it is at least equal, and that a poor person adds to this condition a maximin-type condition: that the probability of losing should not be higher than r. To make this more concrete, imagine $r = 40$ per cent. That means that the poor person prefers the certainty of a nil profit to a lottery in which he would have fifty chances out of a hundred of winning £2 and fifty chances out of a hundred of losing £1. Even though the expectation of profit associated with the second strategy is positive, the poor person is presumed to prefer the first. Suppose we analyse this structure.

The strategy of 'investing' (betting C_1) gives, through [4], a positive expectation of profit if a maximum of 2/3 potential players take part in the game (bet C_1). The rich will therefore (if they are ignorant of the behaviour of the poor) bet C_1 with a probability of 2/3. Consider now the case of the poor. Given that $n_1 = 3$, the probability that a player will lose his bet exceeds $2/5 = 40$ per cent, once the number of people betting is higher than five. The result of these hypotheses is that the poor will bet C_1 with a probability of $5/20 = 1/4$.[15] Thus between three and four poor persons, on the one hand, and four rich persons, on the other hand, will bet C_1. Stratification therefore has the effect: (1) of attenuating the general rate of frustration; (2) of determining effects of self-reproduction of classes: the rich are the beneficiaries of the relatively more intense withdrawal of the poor.

One could introduce any number of further complications into the models outlined above. There is probably no point in doing more here than suggest those that are possible at the present stage in the argument.

1 Let us simply recall the family of variants that have just been outlined. It rests on the hypothesis of a preliminary *stratification* between potential players, this stratification having the effect of differentiating the players' attitudes with regard to risk.

2 One could also complicate things by making B_1 a function of n_1; by introducing, for example, the hypothesis that B_1 decreases with n_1. This sort of hypothesis is clearly useful for simulating those processes of competition for the acquisition

of goods whose value, as is the case with prestige, sinks perceptibly with the rise of the number of people to whom they are distributed. This observation suggests that the logic of relative frustration may be thought to change with the nature of the goods considered (prestige, money . . .).

3 In order to refresh the reader's memory, I will simply mention variants of a more mechanical nature, such as the one that consists of offering players the choice of three options: C_1, the necessary but not the sufficient condition for obtaining B_1; C_2, the necessary but not the sufficient condition for obtaining B_2; C_3, the necessary but not the sufficient condition for obtaining B_3 (with $B_1 > B_2 > B_3$, $C_1 > C_2 > C_3$).

4 Instead of supposing that a stake, C_1, is the necessary (but not sufficient) condition for the acquisition of a lot of value B_1, one may suppose that the stake C_1 allows access to a lottery characterised by a particular distribution of lots, the stake C_2 allowing access to another sort of lottery.

5 It is worth noting, incidentally, that the model also provides the logical skeleton for a research project in experimental social psychology that would very probably lead to some very instructive results and would perhaps put one in a better position to understand phenomena like envy.

What I have tried to suggest is that simple competition models can readily provide an account of effects which have for a long time perplexed sociologists. They clearly show that the level of overall frustration does not necessarily decrease along with the diffusion of hopes of profit: an increase in opportunities for promotion for all may in fact lead to a still more rapid increase in the obstacles to promotion. The model's advantage lies in its clearly showing the sort of conditions under which this occurs, and its results make it possible to formulate more exactly the intuitive propositions advanced, in various forms, by Tocqueville, Durkheim and by those authors who used the notions of reference group and of relative deprivation, i.e., Hyman, Merton and Stouffer.

The model confirms Tocqueville's analysis of the effects of the differences between individuals being attenuated. Everything else being equal, when differences in individual resources are attenuated, one observes an increase in the number of cases of frustration of the sort that leads to quarrels. In other words the attenuation of distances between social 'strata' must, *ceteris paribus*, increase the level of frustration leading to quarrels. One should however insist on the limiting clause of *ceteris paribus*: if distances between individuals decrease, if, in other words, equality of opportunity increases, the general level of frustration tends – as an effect of this change – to grow; but this effect can be reinforced or, on the other hand, limited, as table 7.2 shows, when opportunities open to individuals grow as much as when they lessen. Consider, for example, line 8 of this table. There one sees that, when the number of winners goes from 10 per cent to 20 per cent, the rate of frustration shifts from 70 per cent to 80 per cent; but when the number of winners goes from 20 per cent to 30 per cent the rate of frustration falls from 80 per cent to 70 per cent. If one combines this result with the effect of a diminution or of an increase in the inequality of opportunities, it is clear that all possible configurations can in theory be observed. In other words an increase in the number of winners or, to shift from the language of games to that of sociology, an increase in social mobility may coincide with either an increase or a diminution in the overall frustration. It may also coincide with a constant level of overall frustration, in the hypothetical case of an increase in mobility and a simultaneous diminution in the inequality of opportunity having effects that would compensate for each other at the level of collective frustration.

One of the model's essential virtues therefore lies in the fact that it allows one to clarify the logical status of those results in classical sociology that I have cited throughout this article. It does, for instance, show that the proposition of Tocqueville's that has it that the attenuation in differences between individuals must increase frustration and envious comparison is, *ceteris paribus*, true. On the other hand the proposition linking increase in mobility to the level of frustration is only valid if one presents it as a possibility: it is *possible* (but not necessary) that the increase in mobility should provoke an increase in the overall level of frustration. The model thus has a double advantage. Firstly it completely eliminates the mystery contained in Tocqueville's paradox: it is sufficient to posit individuals preoccupied with the pursuit of their interests and to confront them with a lottery having a determined structure, in order to simulate Tocqueville's proposition. But from another angle the model shows that one can observe an inverse correlation between mobility and general level of frustration. That does not mean that one is faced with an independence between the two phenomena. They are, on the contrary, closely dependent on each other, but the direction of this dependence depends on the properties of the structure of interdependence linking the individuals.

The model does of course show, in the same way, that Durkheim's 'law' *may* in certain cases give the impression of being valid but in other cases may not be so. Applied to Stouffer's example, the analysis likewise shows that one could in other circumstances expect to find an inversion in the links observed. I mean that, as the model shows, one *may* encounter situations in which weaker promotion opportunities are associated with *greater* dissatisfaction, just as one *may* encounter the situation described in *The American Soldier*, in which a *lesser* dissatisfaction is associated with weaker promotion opportunities. This does not mean, let me stress once more, that opportunities for mobility and satisfaction are phenomena without any relation one to another, but that the structures of interdependence are different in the two cases.

These remarks have a corollary whose importance I would emphasise. It is in vain to wonder if, *in general*, an increase in mobility or in the accessibility of these *goods*, whatever the nature of these goods, or in the equality of opportunity, produces an increase in individual satisfaction. The question is not liable to a general answer. Not because individual satisfaction is a random phenomenon, and one that is independent of the individual's social position and of the opportunities that the collectivity offers him, but because the direction of the dependence in question rests on structures of interdependence.

The above notes are clearly just a sketch. But they do indicate a possible direction for research that could turn out to be important. They show that it is possible to construct a theory allowing one, for instance, to link the rate of overall satisfaction with the characteristics of situations of competition. They also show that it is possible, on the basis of the model that was fleetingly invoked in the final section, to analyse the problem of the reproduction of inequalities and handicaps by means of a 'light' model, i.e., one that does not imply the unwieldy and banal hypothesis which crops up so often in the work of certain sociologists, which has it that the persistence of inequalities is the effect of a dominant group oppressing a dominated one. Generally speaking it may be that the neo-individualist perspective[16] adopted here allows one to reiterate certain questions bearing on the study of social stratification. The models outlined above do clearly define the reference groups imposed on actors because of the conditions of interaction. They lead to definitions of the different types of frustration and envy and include, in filigree, a theory of *envy* in which this sentiment would not be the consequence of every single occurrence of inequality, as many sociologists implicitly admit, but a response to particular situations generated by definite structures of interdependence.

One could further complicate the preceding models by questioning the legitimacy of the structures of competition thus introduced:

thus, if it is a question of choosing future doctors, a structure characterised by $(B_1 - B_2)/(C_1 - C_2) = 1$ is perhaps satisfying to the extent that it minimises the overall frustration. On the other hand it is definitely not the sort that will lead to the best and most motivated candidates being selected.

From another angle consideration of the theory – defended by authors like Jencks and Easterlin – that has it that industrial societies automatically generate phenomena of generalised envy and frustration suggests that, in terms of the perspective in use here, it is perhaps unnecessarily pessimistic.[17] As the present article indicates, it is not self-evident that every difference between two individuals generates envy and frustration. One must at least distinguish between that situation in which two individuals receive different rewards, each having made a similar contribution, and that situation in which each has made a different one. It is not certain that industrial societies, by improving the situation of all while at the same time maintaining and sometimes even aggravating relative differences, do for that reason generate frustration. Nor is it certain that, as Jencks would claim, overall frustration is narrowly tied to the distribution of goods being dispersed.

Finally the model developed above makes it reasonable to suggest that the real relation between the objective opportunities that society offers individuals and the level of collective satisfaction may be a negative one, as Durkheim and Tocqueville propose. The profound intuition of these two authors is quite opposed to the simplicity of the theory presented by Easton: 'We can expect that direct satisfaction of demand will at least generate specific support; and the longer such satisfactions are felt, the more likely it is that a higher level of political good will develop.'[18] In fact the preceding models show that one can only guarantee that a system will bring about a weak or a non-existent level of frustration if one advances the absurd hypothesis that it could eliminate every institution of competition. For the rest one must be prepared for the eventuality that, having succeeded in *increasing* and *levelling out* the opportunities of all, it will nevertheless see its audience decrease, because this improvement in the lot of all will have increased the general level of frustration, leading to quarrels.

NOTES

1 W. G. Runciman, *Relative Deprivation and Social Justice* (University of California Press, Berkeley, 1966).
2 A. de Tocqueville, *L'Ancien Régime*, trans. M. W. Patterson (Basil Blackwell, Oxford, 1933), pp. 185–6. See also James C. Davis,

'Toward a theory of revolution', *American Sociological Review*, 1962, pp. 5–19.

3 E. Durkheim, *Suicide*, trans. John A. Spaulding and George Simpson, Edited with an introduction by George Simpson (Routledge and Kegan Paul, London, 1970), p. 287.

4 Samuel A. Stouffer, *The American Soldier*, vol. 1 (Wiley, New York, 1965); R. K. Merton and A. S. Rossi, 'Contributions to the theory of reference group behaviour', in R. K. Merton (ed.), *Social Theory and Social Structure* (The Free Press, Glencoe, Ill., 1957). Along with Durkheim, de Tocqueville and Stouffer, one could cite the Danish sociologist, Kaare Svalastoga, who, in *Prestige, Class and Society* (Gyldendal, Copenhagen, 1959), defends the notion of a curvilinear relation between social mobility and individual satisfaction.

5 E. Durkheim, *The Division of Labour in Society*, trans. George Simpson (Collier-Macmillan, London, 1964), p. 235.

6 The hypothesis implicitly adopted here, according to which an expectation of a gain of a given value is seen as equivalent to an assured gain of the same value, is clearly a simplification, which is meant to place my argument in terms of the simplest examples. In fact, it is generally admitted (cf. Arrow, *Essays in the Theory of Risk-Bearing* (North-Holland, Amsterdam, 1971), that a lottery where there is an expectation of gain X offers the individual an assured gain to the value of X − h (where h is positive). It is obvious that, by supposing individuals to be indifferent to the risk involved (h = o), one maximises the rate of frustration.

7 One thus supposes that the objective opportunities offered to individuals are weaker than in the previous case. Another way of simulating the deterioration in objective opportunities would consist in reducing the amount of gains offered by the society or by the organiser of the game.

8 There is a considerable difference between the two structures corresponding to my first two examples. In the first case, each player has a dominant strategy, and therefore has no need for any information about the behaviour of the other. In the second case, on the contrary, Ego's interest in each of his strategies depends on the number of others adopting the same strategy as he does. If the group in question was a face to face one, the emergence of a structure of this sort would give rise to *negotiations* between the actors. In the case I am considering here, although, in order to simplify the analysis, I took it that N = 20, I presume that individuals cannot negotiate with each other. This is a characteristic situation, for instance, in educational behaviour or in behaviour affecting mobility.

9 One could well contest the 'solution' of the game in this example. The maximin strategy could be defended. The 'solution' employed here relies on the following observation: if each player employs the strategy that consists in giving himself x chances out of N of participating in the game, in the case where a number of players greater than x entails a negative expectation for each, this combination of strategies results in

an *equilibrium*. In fact, a player who would unilaterally abandon this strategy, in order to give himself a greater chance than x/N of participating in the game, would be punishing himself. What would happen if $x = 10$? Suppose that all the players decide to allow themselves $x/N = 1/2$ chances of participating in the game. Each person's expectation is then $1/2[(2/10)4 + (8/10)(-1)] = 0$. In choosing unilaterally to participate in the game when he is certain, the player lowers his own expectations, since the sum between brackets becomes negative. On the other hand, if all the players allow themselves a probability p lower than $x/10$ of participating in the game, it is in the interests of each to choose a value higher than p. The solution here is naturally far more difficult to determine than in the previous example. But the important thing to note is that the difference in structure, with respect to the preceding example, must entail a corresponding fall in participation. If, like Rapoport, one admits that, when no dominant strategy exists for anyone, and multiple Pareto equilibria exist, 'rationality' consist necessarily in minimising risks, participation is zero. The 'solution' envisaged here corresponds to a less marked fall in participation.

10 I have applied this type of formalisation to problems in the politics of education, thus giving rise to an interesting reaction on the part of Jon Elster, in 'Boudon, education and game theory', *Social Sciences Information*, 15 (1976), 4–5, pp. 733–40. Jon Elster asks if one may realistically apply game theory to situations of competition in which hundreds of thousands of students in a country like France are, *volens nolens*, placed. This strikes me as being a thoroughly interesting question, and one that calls for comments that I cannot give in full here. The value of N does, naturally, play a vital role here. Consider, for instance, the second of the examples analysed above. If N is large, a player who unilaterally allows himself a probability higher than x/N of participating in the game hardly affects his expectation of gain. Thus, the strategy of eliminating oneself is only justifiable when N is not too large. It is also the case when N is large but one is dealing with a latent group of the federative type (in Olson's sense). The overall number of pupils who finish is, for example, a group of this type. I have the impression that out of the 20 pupils involved, only 2 will have anything to gain from 'investing' in (for instance) a class preparing them for a *Grande École*, self-eliminating strategies will probably be seen to emerge. The fact that there are a significant number of last-stage classes does not alter this situation in any way. In other words, the conclusions that may be drawn from the preceding examples may, in certain circumstances, be taken also to refer to cases in which N is large.

11 Cf. Arrow, *Essays in the Theory of Risk-Bearing*.

12 If we still presume that the players wish to maximise their expectation of gain, and that they are indifferent to the structure of the lottery proposed.

13 In what follows I have only considered what I termed above *quarrelsome* frustration.

14 George C. Homans, 'Social behaviour as exchange', *The American*

Journal of Sociology, 62 (1958), pp. 697–706. See also W. G. Runciman, 'Justice, congruence and Professor Homans', *Archives Européennes de Sociologie*, VIII, 1 (1967), pp. 115–28, and Lucien Karpik, 'Trois concepts sociologiques: le project de reference, le statut social et le bilan individuel', ibid., VI, 2.

15 Where the hypothesis is that the members of each of the two categories reckon that those of the other will behave as they do.

16 As regards this notion, see François Bourricaud, 'Contre le sociologisme une critique et des propositions', *Revue Française de Sociologie* XVI (1975), supplement, pp. 583–603.

17 Christopher Jencks, *Inequality, a Reassessment of the Effect of Family and Schooling in America* (Basic Books, New York, 1972); Richard A. Easterlin, 'Does money buy happiness?', *The Public Interest* 30 (1972), pp. 3–10. See also Victor R. Fuchs, 'Redefining poverty and redistribution of income', *The Public Interest*, 8 (1967), pp. 88–95. This article perhaps dispenses once and for all with the doctrine according to which there exists a maximum tolerable dispersion of the distribution of goods.

18 David Easton, *A Systems Analysis of Political Life* (Wiley, New York and Amsterdam, 1965).

8

The Political Economy of Peasant Society

SAMUEL POPKIN

INTRODUCTION

Historically the rise of strong central states, the expansion of markets and the growth of cities have been accompanied by major changes in the form of peasant villages. Whereas most of the world's peasantry today live in open villages with individual tax-paying, few restrictions on landowning, imprecise notions of village citizenship, and private land, most of the world peasantry once lived in closed villages with collective responsibility for taxes, restrictions on landowning, a well-defined concept of village citizenship and land that was owned or managed by the village.

Explanations of how and why closed villages have changed are fundamental to theories about statemaking and the transition from feudalism to capitalism, studies of the effect of colonialism and the commercialization of agriculture on peasants around the world and even to analyses of collective agriculture in communist countries.

Here I shall criticize a widely accepted interpretation of these phenomena which I call the moral economy approach and present an alternative that I shall call the political economy approach.

The moral economy approach focuses on the relations between economic and social institutions. It is an economic approach not because it uses the methods of modern economists, but because it addresses important issues about markets and other economic institutions. Indeed moral economists would argue that the methods of modern economists are not even applicable to the study of villages in pre-capitalist settings; pre-capitalist peasants, in this view, are without the possessive individualism assumed to be created by capitalism, when peasants are forced into market relations by the externally induced destruction of their pre-capitalist institutions.

It is a moral approach not because it assumes peasants were necessarily more moral in precapitalist days but because it assumes

This essay was first published in S. Popkin, *The Rational Peasant* (University of California Press, 1979), pp. 35–72, © 1979 The Regents of the University of California.

that under earlier institutions the calculus governing behavior led to more moral outcomes than under the institutions of capitalism.

The moral economy approach is a set of assertions about villages, markets (and patron–client relations) based on assumptions about peasant goals and behaviors. The approach is found in the works of such contemporary social scientists as Eric Wolf, James Scott and Joel Migdal. It also recalls writers of anti-market sentiment such as continental (anti-Marxist) economists like Karl Polanyi and some (but not all) scholars of a Marxist persuasion such as Eric Hobsbawm.

In the moral economy approach, markets are assumed to be a last resort for peasants whose livelihood was guaranteed as a right of membership in their community. With peasant needs guaranteed within their institutions, Karl Polanyi wrote, 'the alleged propensity of man to barter, truck and exchange is almost entirely apocryphal.'[1] With livelihood guaranteed, and with peasant needs implicitly assumed to be fixed, if there is to be a labor market, 'traditional institutions must be destroyed and prevented from reforming.[2] The moral economy approach assumes, then, that markets and capitalist institutions are imposed on an unwilling peasantry. For example, Eric Hobsbawm discusses rural protest in nineteenth-century Spain:

> The best explanation is, that the rise of social revolutionism was the consequence of the introduction of capitalist legal and social relationships. . . . It is hardly necessary to analyze the inevitably cataclysmic consequences of so unprecedented an economic revolution on the peasantry. *The rise of social revolutionism followed naturally.*[3]

Destruction of the peasant's institutional context for assuring livelihood and reducing risk create the tensions, then, that lead to peasant involvement in rebellion and revolution. Resources managed as a village and distributed regularly are assumed to be managed in a redistributive fashion. The communal management of property and other procedures is equated with a collective orientation which is assumed to stand in stark contrast to the possessive individualism of markets and capitalism.

The moral economy approach leaves unconsidered the procedures by which the norms supposedly governing behavior in these villages were decided, how conflicts among the norms were adjudicated or how the minimum subsistence floor was decided upon. There is no consideration of conflicts between public and private means of assuring survival for peasants and no consideration of free-rider problems in the workings of villages

I argue that village resources and institutions are treated by peasants as collective goods, and that peasants apply the same investment logic to villages that they apply to markets. The uncertainties of long-term dependence upon village institutions leads to a preference for private long-term investments and short run maximization behavior about village resources. Village norms are malleable and shift with considerations of changes in the relative power of groups and individuals and are affected by strategic interaction within the village, particularly the free-rider problem.

If free-rider problems exist, if collective interests do not mean that peasants had a collective rationality, then the structure of peasant society will reflect the problems of coordinating mechanisms for the provision of collective goods. Villages have never worked as well as moral economists assume; in many situations there are village arrangements that could, if enacted, leave all better off, that are not enacted because of the problem of free riders. There are times when many collective goods (including insurance or welfare schemes) will be provided by small groups, although large groups could do better – because neither the necessary skills nor incentive systems exist to maintain larger groups (or because cautious peasants, seeking to avert the risks posed by concentrating resources in the hands of another peasant are unwilling to invest their resources in large-scale projects).

There are conflicts within villages, then, between public and private interests and conflicts over the distribution of charges assessed on the village by outside powers and over the distribution of resources are frequent. Unless there is widespread consensus on exactly how to assess and distribute, favoritism and personal profit may influence leadership decisions. Peasant institutions, therefore, have a built-in tension: the benefits of valuable villagewide services and leadership versus the chance of personal loss from power concentrated in the hands of another peasant.

In a world of local institutions, uncertain leadership, cautious investors and a weak central state, village citizenship can have great motive force because membership in a village is a benefit – a license to participate in the economy of the village – in and of itself. The village need not provide welfare or insurance to be important to peasant survival; citizenship alone can bind a peasant to a village.

Further if there is distrust and suspicion among peasants, if expanding the land under cultivation requires additional collective projects, or if it is difficult to learn the rules of collective action and cooperation within a village, there may emerge a large group of peasants who are considered 'outsiders' and who are never granted full rights within the village. The presence of outsiders who lead

lives as second-class citizens reminds us that there can be stratification even with a frontier of available land. Land may even be
worthless if there is no village to provide such collective goods as
self-defense, irrigation or religious rites.

Moral economists have argued that the procedures within pre-
capitalist, closed (or corporate) villages, where land is held in
common and taxes are paid by the village, led to internal leveling
and redistribution, and to villagewide insurance and welfare systems that provided subsistence guarantees for poorer villagers. In
contrast I show that the calculations of peasants driven by motives
of survival in a risky environment led not to subsistence floors and
extensive villagewide insurance schemes, but to procedures that
generated and reinforced inequality within the village.

The core assumptions of both the moral economy and political
economy approaches to peasant society have been identified above.
Building on the political economy assumptions, hypotheses will be
developed about villages and patron-client relationships. Contrasting
political economy predictions with those of the moral economists,
and drawing on suggestive evidence from various peasant societies,
this examination of the inner workings of village and patron-client
relationships will demonstrate the need for important revisions in
previous interpretations of the effects on peasant society of commercial agriculture, the growth of central states, and colonialism. In
particular, precisely because insurance, welfare, and subsistence
guarantees within precapitalist villages are *limited*, a change in
village structures – from closed to open villages – does not necessarily,
as moral economists have asserted, result in a loss of these supports,
although it may change their nature. Nor is the development
of linkages between the village and the wider system always – and
only – initiated from outside the village, as they have further
assumed.

Because villages do not provide extensive insurance or welfare,
there does not have to be a crisis before peasants will involve
themselves in commercial agriculture; their involvement is generally not a last-gasp response to declining situations, *but a response
to a new opportunities*. Indeed, the expansion of markets is frequently of particular benefit to poorer peasants, while it is large
lords and patrons who prevent market involvement by peasants in
order to protect their own control of the economy. These alternate
views of the village and of patron-client relations generate a different analysis of peasant protests and rebellions – one that empha-

sizes the benefits, as well as the hazards, of markets and national development; one that stresses individual, instead of group, benefits and losses.

Procedures for distributing both land and tax assessments within the villages favored the wealthier peasants, and both insurance and welfare at the village level were limited. In part because of village procedures, these villages contained large numbers of persons with minimal rights and with standards of living far below what the more substantial villagers would tolerate for themselves. Because of the limited extent of insurance and this large underclass with few political or economic rights, the transition from closed to open villages did not invariably lower the levels of peasant welfare or insurance. Further, the limited abilities of peasants to generate villagewide insurance and welfare and the large underclass within the villages help explain the attractiveness to peasants of those religious and political movements that could provide the leadership necessary for increased production and for insurance and welfare.

Because moral economists have viewed closed villages as stable and autonomous, the process by which linkages develop between village and supravillage authorities has been described as 'penetration'. The metaphor of penetration has emphasized outside initiation and the need for force to overcome collective resistance by the village to new linkages. This reflects a misunderstanding of the internal dynamics of villages and the role which external authorities played in regulating village life and protecting the poor within villages. It also neglects the divergence between collective and individual interests and the fact that the initiators were frequently villagers seeking outside allies in local power struggles.

When problems of organization within villages are carefully examined, it becomes clear that many innovations fail (or are not adopted) not because of a positive regard for tradition or aversion to risk, but because low-quality leadership and mutual distrust preclude the requisite cost-sharing or coordination among peasants. As agricultural techniques improve, problems of coordination limit investment in, and productivity of, communal land and help explain the transfer of communal lands to private ownership.

Moral economists have interpreted the stability of patron–client ties in terms of the patron's guarantee of short-term subsistence floors for clients. In the political economy view, not only the stability of the ties but the level of the floor itself is a function of the patron's ability to keep relations dyadic, that is, to prevent collective bargaining by a united clientele or to foreclose alternate options which increase the bargaining power of peasants. In order to maintain dyadic ties and foreclose other options, the patron is often the one who prevents the spread of literacy, forcibly keeps peasants from direct involvement in markets, and rejects innovations for raising total production if the new methods have the potential to decrease peasant dependence. Given these patron strategies, central states sometimes can increase their own revenue by overthrowing patrons and raising total production enough to benefit both themselves and the peasantry. And political and religious movements can gain peasant support by providing peasants with incentives to overthrow patrons and enter the market on their own.

The extension of the authority of central states is not necessarily a threat to peasant subsistence. The extension of state authority and the expansion of markets invariably benefit landless peasants because the expanded mobility of labor breaks down some of the coercion used against them by peasants who control land. Whether or not tenants and smallholders benefit from the expansion of states and markets depends on ancillary institutions such as courts, taxation, and titling procedures. These institutions determine entry costs into markets and the distribution of risks and benefits from new commercial opportunities.

Moral economists have viewed peasant political and religious protests as last-gasp, defensive reactions of a dying class. They continually use terms like *decline, crisis, imbalances, decay, loss of legitimacy*, or the *erosion of traditional bonds* to describe the conditions under which protests will occur. On the contrary, I argue that short-term declines or drops are neither necessary nor sufficient for protests, that even without any drop in welfare peasants seek individual or collective means to improve their situation. Protests are collective actions and depend on the ability of a group or class to organize and make demands. Thus, many movements are an expression of 'green power', a reflection of the peasants' growing ability to organize and struggle for rights and privileges previously denied them. Peasant struggles are frequently battles to tame markets and bureaucracies, not movements to restore 'traditional' systems.

VILLAGES

Corporate villages existed throughout most of Europe until the nineteenth or early twentieth century and are still common in parts of Asia and Latin America.[1] In contrast to the 'open' villages more

common throughout the world today, members of corporate villages had a well-defined notion of village 'citizenship', of who
belonged to the village corporation; they regulated the local economy; and they imposed certain forms of discipline on inhabitants,
particularly in relation to the decisions and coordination involved
in open-field agriculture, where plots are intermingled, scattered,
and unfenced.

The degree of involvement of the corporate village in the economic activities of its members varied according to the nature of the
supravillage institutions and according to the nature of local agriculture, but the differences were of degree and not of kind. Where
there were communal pastures, the village decided how many
animals each family could pasture; where the fields belonging to
each family were intermingled and unfenced, the village determined
the times for planting, harvesting, and grazing; where there was
irrigated agriculture, the village decided when the fields would be
flooded and apportioned the work of maintaining the common
irrigation works. The village invariably collected, and frequently
assessed on its inhabitants, land and head taxes and decided which
men would meet the village quotas for labor and military drafts.
The village headman or chief mediated between a village council
and the local lord or bureaucrat, and the headman, together with
the council, adjudicated conflicts between members of the village.
The village also distributed those portions of farmland owned or
managed by the village (communal land) and supervised local
religious life. Often the village would even hire and fire priests.

The communal pasturage and farmland, the local collection and
distribution of taxes, and the many coordinated activities that were
a part of a open-field agriculture have always fascinated observers
of these corporate villages. The extent of interaction among villagers, in marked contrast to modern open villages, has made it
appear as if there were a special mentality and logic to them. As a
result, they frequently have served (as Jerome Blum notes) as a
launching pad for romantic theories about society. The Russian
corporate village or *mir*, Baron Haxthausen wrote in 1847, was the
bulwark that would save Russia from the abhorrent changes being
wrought in the West by individualism and industrialization;
because of the *mir*, Russia, in contrast to Western Europe, had
'naught to fear from pauperism, the proletariat, and the doctrines
of communism and socialism.'[5] From a markedly different but no
less rhapsodic view point, Spanish anarchism was supposed to

reflect a tradition of spontaneous mass action that had characterized the corporate world of the Spanish pueblo. Anarchism was viewed as the product of the irreconcilable conflict between capitalism and primitive communalism.[6] In the words of Gerald Brenan, 'The pueblo was recognized as being the great repository of the virtues of the race, the source from which everything that was sane and healthy sprang. No act in which it did not take part had its roots in national life.'[7]

Nineteenth-century German and Danish scholars saw the corporate village as a vestige of ancient agrarian communism which they claimed could be traced back to Tacitus and Caesar.[8] In France, such villages, Emile de Lavelye argued, had secured for French people 'from the most remote times the enjoyment of liberty, equality and order, and as great a degree of happiness as is compatible with human destinies.'[9] And in Vietnam, Le Thanh Khoi stated that the Vietnamese village 'anchored to the soil at the dawn of history . . . was not touched by the [Chinese] conquerors, and has constituted, behind its bamboo hedge, the anonymous and unseizable retreat where the national spirit is concentrated.'[10]

It is directly upon assumptions about the performance of corporate villages that much of moral economy theory rests. Moral economists, implicitly perceive the change from closed to open villages, with their free land markets and individualistic production, as the peasantry's fall from grace. The transition to open villages is assumed to entail a loss of protection (welfare and insurance) from the village and a change in peasant mentality from a collective orientation to an individualistic, market orientation.

At key points in their analyses, moral economists make direct predictions about village outcomes from their assumptions about shared individual goals. To cite one example, since every peasant is assumed by moral economists to be interested in minimizing risk or maximizing security, it is further assumed from this common individual goal that *villages* also will operate to minimize risk or maximize security. These direct leaps from common interest to collective outcome assume, in effect, a collective rationality among the peasantry. Yet the moral economists' inferences do not follow either from the investment logic that they themselves suggest applies to markets or even from investment logic as amended to take account of long- and short-term investments and gambles.

The validity of moral economy arguments rests on the extent to which income floors are provided within corporate villages. These floors depend on the common insurance and welfare that peasants within such villages are able to provide. Insurance and welfare schemes are limited by several factors. (1) Free-rider problems mean there are risks in investing in mutual enterprises at the expense of private investments. (2) Highly visible and defensible standards not open to ambiguity, misinterpretation, or welfare cheating must be used as the means test to determine eligibility for village assistance. (3) Village leaders use village office as a means of securing and protecting individual fortunes, and village insurance schemes are limited to assets with which leaders cannot abscond; indeed, the transaction costs involved in villagewide insurance schemes appear to have been so high that peasants adopted individual means of protection from crop failure which cut total village production by more than 10 per cent. In other words, the moral economy predictions about collective security, based on assumptions of collective rationality, are borne out partially at best: village processes are shaped and restricted by individual self-interest, the difficulty of ranking needs, the desire of individual peasants to raise their own subsistence level at the expense of others, aversion to risk, leadership interest in profits, and the free-rider problem. Let us examine some of these processes more closely.

There is substantial agreement between moral and political economists that peasants are preoccupied with the constant threat of falling below the subsistence level. Thus, the main focus of the comparisons between the two approaches is on the production, consumption, and exchange of material goods. On the production side, organization and financing of both private and public goods are examined; specifically, explanations of taxation, village finance, insurance programs, leadership, and innovation are considered and contrasted. On the consumption side, access to goods as manifested in village citizenship, the distribution of communal resources, and the provision of welfare are compared. Market exchanges, alliances, and patron–client relationships also are examined. A major consequence of these relationships, stratification, is discussed as well.

Taxation

Romantic scholarship to the contrary, corporate villages had their origins not in a primitive communal mentality, but in the problems of taxation confronting both peasants and supravillage authorities – be they feudal or bureaucratic – during (and after) the Middle Ages. Accurate production figures were not easily obtained, and central states (or feudal lords) had difficulty collecting reliable information as a basis for taxing the means of production, such as manpower and land, for each family (costly information). Conversely, peasants often found it difficult to have their tax records adjusted to accurately reflect the number of workers and the amount of land they controlled (costly access). When households lost workers to disease, war, or migration, there often would be land on which the family owed taxes, but which the family could not farm with the available labor. In times of unsteady labor supply, such land could not always be rented to meet the tax bill, nor could it be easily transferred to someone else if transfer (among freemen or serfs) were costly or if long-term sales contracts were difficult to enforce. Both states or lords and peasants were then faced with the problem of stabilizing tax flows. Instead of keeping tax records on the number of adults and the amount of land in each family, records were kept by the corporate village. A number of peasants were responsible for meeting head and land tax bills and for filling labor and military drafts from within the village. In some countries and in some centuries, the lands also were controlled by the village and reallocated periodically; in other cases, the lands were all or partially private.[11]

Although it was generally feudal lords who established corporate villages to supervise their peasants, coordinate agriculture and exact obligations, there were apparently enough benefits from belonging to a village and paying taxes as a corporate group that peasants were willing to enter corporate villages voluntarily[12] for the benefits of life within a political unit with rights before the state, and often with a constitution.[13]

That these intravillage tax procedures benefit the poor is an explicit claim of moral economists. For example, Scott argues that 'since villages and not individuals were taxed, one might expect the better off to pay something more than an equal share.'[14] Similarly, Migdal claims that paying taxes as a village aided 'not the wealthy who could have paid their taxes on an individual basis just as easily, but the man who did poorly this harvest. The village political leadership could compensate for his inability to pay by making slightly higher demands on others.'[15]

If there were widespread agreement that those less able to pay should be helped when tax and labor responsibilities were distributed, and if there were widespread agreement on how to assess the ability to pay, one would expect, at the least, that the rich would pay more in absolute terms; indeed, one might even predict a progressive tax system in which the rich paid not just more money than the poor, or not just the same percentage of their income in tax, but a higher percentage of their income in tax. And certainly the subsistence ethic should at least express itself in a tax 'floor', an income below which no taxes would be collected from the villagers as long as the village's total tax bill could be met by other villagers above that 'floor'.

This, however, raises the same questions posed earlier: how is ability to pay – or 'needs' – assessed? Arguing from the assumptions of political economy, one would expect that peasants, instead of readily agreeing about need, ability to pay, or standards, would hide their wealth from common scrutiny and thus make it even more difficult to decide who is better off and able to pay a larger share of the load. Indeed, there is commonly a 'cult of poverty': 'Peasants . . . hide wealth to avoid "claims of friends", taxes and contributions.'[16]

When peasants seek to maximize long-run welfare through family and savings, rather than relying on the long-run viability of their village institutions or of any particular rules for determining need or ability to pay, they will hide wealth and there will be struggles in which each person attempts to minimize his own tax. In such a situation, the only stable systems for allocating taxes would be those based not on abstract or complex standards of need, but on criteria that are highly visible and easily defensible. Although systems that share the tax equally are regressive, they are, in fact, based on such visible and defensible criteria. The only groups commonly granted tax relief, for example, are the aged, widowed and orphaned, whose conditions can be easily verified. Both rich and poor can expect to benefit from such rules of exemption during the life cycle. Aside from the aged, widowed and orphaned, the only other clear case would be when 'all is gone', where there is nothing left to conceal. In Vietnam, as we shall see, peasants typically were expected by fellow villagers to pay their own taxes even if it meant selling or mortgaging land, entering into debt-slavery, or breaking up the family. Members of a family might help one another avoid onerous declines due to tax demands in bad years, but village rules in Vietnam (and in the other areas) show no evidence that the village as a village compensated for or eased the burden of individual households in a bad year.[17]

Aside from tax relief for easily identified categories, there is no evidence of the actual use of progressive taxes or of tax floors within pre-capitalist villages. Head taxes, assessed according to the total number of males in the village, were divided equally among male inhabitants. Land taxes, assessed on the total area of land in each of several quality grades, were paid equally if there was village ownership or by the individual owners in the case of private land. There is no evidence that owners of large tracts of land paid more taxes per acre or hectare than did small landowners. Neither capitation nor land taxes were paid in a way that provided either floors or leveling.[18] Instead, there is a clear pattern of opposition to progressive taxes by village leaders eager to minimize their own share of the taxes and to ensure their short-run welfare at the expense of the poor. Occasionally when colonial governments sought to implement progressive tax methods, the opposition came from within the village. When the colonial government in Indonesia once attempted to rebate taxes to the poor (after village leaders had assessed an equal tax share on everyone in the village), village leaders resisted and 'the poor and weak continued to pay the highest taxes.'[19]

There are two interpretations possible for this resistance: (1) village officials administer the village for their own private benefit, or (2) it is extremely difficult for villagers with even the best intentions to agree on ability to pay – they therefore tend to rely on easily coordinated strategies to avoid interminable conflict, with the result that taxes tend to be regressive. Although both these possibilities are counterarguments to the moral economy position, both would find support among political economists and both are consistent with the data.

The struggle to minimize individual shares of external demands on the village is even more pronounced with respect to the military draft. Whereas tax systems usually emphasize equal payments by all – without standard deductions, floors, or progressive rules – it is common for labor demands and military drafts to be pushed onto the poorer villagers. In seventeenth-century France, for example, rich peasants so consistently managed to manipulate local selection procedures to avoid military service that lotteries were attempted as a means of ending unfair selections. Even then the rich managed to escape the burden.[20] Although this example suggests that states may sometimes intervene to equalize village procedures, there are also times, as in pre-colonial Vietnam, when a state may support the creation of a privileged class within the village to insure a steady tax return of its own. That is, a progressive tax system may not be in the short-run interest of either the state or the better-off villagers.

Village Citizenship

In their discussions of welfare and insurance in pre-capitalist villages, moral economists imply that 'all villagers' is equivalent to 'all persons'. The two, however, are not synonymous. Common features of pre-capitalist society are a stratum of residents known as 'insiders', who have full citizenship within the village (although not necessarily with decision-making roles), and a stratum of 'outsiders', who are allowed to reside in the geographic confines of the village, but who have fewer rights and benefits than insiders. Some of these 'outsiders' are persons who marry into the village and seek to earn a place within it; others are 'foreigners' who want to live in a better village. Historically, many 'outsiders' have been individuals who were denied full access to village resources by the better-off members of the village. Summarizing the available data for pre-capitalist villages of Europe, Blum notes,

> Nearly everywhere only certain peasants qualified for active membership. Only these people had the right to vote at communal meetings and to make the decisions which affected the lives of all the villagers. They held the communal offices themselves or arranged to have people they wanted in these posts. Often they had either exclusive or superior rights to the use of the common lands and forests of the village. Presumably, all or nearly all the residents of a village once had equal rights, at least ideally, in the use of communal resources and in the conduct of village affairs. When, however, the population of the village grew, pressure on the common lands increased to a point where the more prosperous villagers decided that they had to prohibit or limit the use of communal resources by the poorer peasants of the village. The better-off peasants realized that to ensure their continued control of the village resources they had to restrict the right of active participation in communal decision making, and so they established criteria to determine who should have this privilege.[21]

This serves to emphasize the conflicts of interest inherent in pre-capitalist villages. It does not follow from individual risk minimization or security maximization that villages will function to minimize risk or maximize security for all. As noted earlier, there are conflicts of interest, in addition to common interests, inherent within the village. Coalitions may be organized for the sharing of resources or contributing to village projects (clearing additional land for the additional peasants, for example), but self-interest can lead also to coalitions organized to drive persons from the village or to deprive them of benefits, in which case the 'outsiders' serve as a source of cheap labor for the insiders.

In other words, whereas moral economists predict that better-off villagers will help their less fortunate neighbors when times are bad, the evidence indicates that affluent villagers commonly react by excluding such persons from the village long before everyone is reduced to the cultural minimum or subsistence line.[22] Indeed, it is not unusual for governments to intervene in corporate villages, for the sake of political stability and/or increased tax revenues, to protect the lower strata against expulsion (or landlessness) or to force villagers to clear additional land for laborers or others who are landless.[23]

Such conflicts over village membership serve to emphasize the importance to peasants of control of and access to courts, both within the village and at higher levels of authority. In sixteenth-century Germany, when a class of landless laborers first developed within the villages, it became particularly important for tenants to control the hiring and firing of the priest, for the priest had an important role in adjudicating disputes over village membership.[24] Similarly, in Vietnam access to and the right to use government tribunals and courts was a prized possession, and peasants who lacked the legal status necessary to use these institutions were at a marked disadvantage in local economic and political struggles. In Java, there was a 'complex and rigid system of social stratification based primarily on differential ownership of privately held land and/or rights to communal land'; 20 per cent of what communal land there was generally went to the village head, and many persons had no right to own private land or receive a share of public land.[25] In the German peasant wars of the early sixteenth century, the general pattern during village uprisings was for the lord's tenants in a village to demand that no common land be given to the landless laborers, even though the latter usually were related to the tenants.[26]

Even among 'insiders', it was common for full shares of resources or eligibility for decision-making roles to be restricted to persons of a certain wealth or with a certain amount of land. This again serves to emphasize the risk of contributing to a village welfare system in years when one has a surplus. When a peasant is in need, instead of receiving welfare, he may be excluded from the village.

At the very least, then, all moral economy generalizations about villages as a source of welfare and insurance (and therefore as a source of social stability) must be reexamined in the light of a large population of 'outsiders'. As Blum concludes, 'These restrictions meant that in many places smallholders, cotters, landless laborers, lodgers, servants and hired hands found themselves excluded from active participation in the management of the community, and from the privileges which accompanied active participation.'[27]

The metaphor of corporate village as 'collectivity' should be replaced by the metaphor of the corporate village as a 'corporation'. Membership in a corporate village need not bring any special tax breaks or welfare or insurance to be of value; membership itself – like membership in a guild or even in a stock exchange – is a license to do business and right of access to crucial institutions, both inside the village and in the larger society. The development of institutions for a functioning local economy – courts, festivals, market days, agreements on when to plant – constitutes a valuable patrimony even when there is no communal land owned by the village, and peasants do not share these corporate assets with persons who did not contribute to building the patrimony, especially when denial of access is profitable to the insiders. At times of depopulation, of course, there are reasons to admit persons into the village to help meet the collective tax bills, but there are at other times numerous incentives to keep institutional access restricted and to maintain a stratum of second-class citizens.

Insurance and Welfare

Moral economists stress both insurance and welfare functions of the village. Phrases such as 'risk minimization', 'life chance equalization', and 'community mechanisms to maximize security' all suggest extensive villagewide insurance. Such phrases as 'minimum income', 'guaranteed minimums', 'danger lines', and 'communal welfare' predict not only *insurance*, but actual *welfare* policies that subsidize the less well-off against drops below the danger point. It is important to distinguish clearly between specific risk-sharing mechanisms – that is, insurance – and subsidies – that is, welfare. From political economy assumptions it follows that villagewide insurance schemes will be highly specific and limited due to problems of trust and consensus, and that welfare schemes will be greatly restricted and restrictive. Further, reciprocity will be strict and limited to relative equals, and the village leaders will help less fortunate villagers only if it does not affect the long-run welfare of the better-off villagers. This is not to say that there will be no welfare available to the insiders of the village. Given the problems of conflicting standards and claims of need, however, very little welfare is available for indigents or persons with bad harvests, and village welfare or subsidies are allocated mainly to the aged, widowed, or orphaned – specific categories with claims that are clear, hard to exaggerate, and clearly not due to laziness or mismanagement. Further, the emphasis is on insurance schemes – not welfare – and the extent of such villagewide schemes depends on (1)

whether, and to what extent, past endeavors have been successful;
(2) whether cooperation is expected to continue in the future, so
that a peasant can be certain that his specific need will be recognized when he makes his claim; and (3) whether someone can be
trusted to hold the insurance premiums of all villagers until they are
needed. As expected, there are few insurance schemes that require
peasants to contribute money to a common fund – since someone
can always abscond with the money – and more schemes that are
highly specific, based on strict reciprocity, and require labor (which
is not so easily stolen), such as a plan whereby everyone helps
victims to rebuild after a fire.[28]

Even among the basically solvent insiders, peasants interested in
their long-run security usually make exchanges of a fixed nature
where it is certain that both (all) parties will be able to maintain a
long-run balance. Instead of general welfare or subsidies of the
poor by the affluent, long-term risks will be excluded, and there will
be strict reciprocity if peasants are cautious about welfare and
personal savings in dealings with one another '. . . exchanges and
contracts are likely to be either highly specific, with an understanding of just what it is each party is expected to do, or they involve
people who are in constant contact so that giving and return can be
balanced at short intervals and the advantages to each partner
easily assessed.[29] In other words, as Potter found in Thailand, if
reciprocal obligations are not to be evaded, 'records must be kept
and sanctions exerted; there is nothing loose or informal about this
at all.' Therefore, complex interchanges generally take place among
small groups of four of five households.[30]

We can begin to identify the critical dimensions of insurance and
welfare systems and specify which types are most viable in peasant
society. Schemes can have either fixed or variable returns. The
insurance systems common in peasant society, such as labor
exchanges or burial societies, have fixed returns. In these groups
each peasant receives exactly what he has put into the scheme. Such
organizations derive their value from utilities of scale in peasant
life: eight days of labor at once by many men in a field make a
better rice crop than one man working for eight days, and a few
coins from many persons when a parent dies are more valuable for
meeting religious obligations and avoiding debts than are a few
coins on the many occasions when someone else's parent dies.
Schemes also can have exact exchange or equivalent exchanges.
Peasant exchange groups are generally for exact exchange – labor
for labor, part of someone's pig this month for part of someone
else's pig next month, or money for money – rather than exchanges
where contributions and payouts involve agreeing on a rate of

exchange on more than one item. Schemes can require centralized holdings of liquid assets or decentralized holdings by the members. Peasant schemes generally do not concentrate any abscondable funds; contributions are held by the members and given to the bereaved on the death, or the labor is given to the farmer on the agreed upon day. Further, peasant schemes generally tend to involve small groups in which only self-management with little leadership (or actuarial skills) is required.[31] We can also distinguish among schemes where everyone has a chance of benefiting and schemes in which many persons have little or no probability of any return. Old age, widow, and orphan support are likely to have some potential value for all villagers, whereas subsidies for poor households are less likely to be of benefit to all villagers and thus may require coercion to establish and maintain.

Ironically, one of the most frequently cited examples of a conservative, safety-first strategy followed by peasants – namely, scattered fields – is an individual-level strategy for avoiding risk that suggests that villagewide insurance schemes are not very comprehensive. It is a clear example of a conflict between individual and group rationality whereby each individual, following a safety-first strategy, ends up with less production than he would if the village as a whole could follow an aggregate safety-first strategy.

Peasants throughout the world farm several plots of land at any one time, and the plots usually are scattered throughout that area of the village under cultivation. The scattering of plots substantially reduces the maximum damage that small local disasters or climatic variations can cause in a given season: mildew or rot in one area of the village, an errant herd, an exceptionally light or heavy rain, and similar minidisasters will be less likely to wipe out a peasant's entire crop when fields are scattered. While scattered plots reduce the variance of yield from year to year and thus reduce the probability of losing the entire crop, scattering also cuts the maximum yield per farmer and for the village as a whole. In a series of ingenious and pathbreaking articles, Donald McCloskey has estimated that the scattered (pre-enclosure) fields in England cut total production by 10 to 13 per cent.[32] Why, it must be asked, are peasants close to the danger line willing to throw away 10 per cent of their output?

Consolidated fields with higher average output and higher variance from year to year would be a better strategy for peasants to follow if the village could provide insurance for farmers to compensate for the increased variance of consolidated fields. A village granary or risk pool, if moral economy assumptions were correct, could have prevented the loss in output by providing 'interest-free credit rationed in accord with the publicly known incidence of relatively favorable or unfavorable agricultural conditions.'[33] But who will hold the grain, and who will decide whether a particular loss is due to nature or sloth?

Village-level, safety-first strategies would be both more productive and more secure (and would be adopted!) if, *and only if*, the moral economy assumptions about villagers were correct. In fact, individual-level, safety-first strategies are followed, and this is one of the most important challenges to moral economy conceptions of the village.

Indeed, plot consolidation is a subject worthy of far more attention than it has received from scholars of all persuasions, for it raises a plethora of important issues about markets, risk and sharing. Scattered plots are often more desirable than a single plot per family when there is no reliable widespread insurance system. However, centuries of division sometimes lead to scattering in the extreme. In Greece, for example, Kenneth Thompson found that the number and dispersion of plots belonging to the typical family was far greater than that needed for insurance value and that a majority of villagers in eighteen villages favored a program of plot consolidation to increase production, decrease family friction over inheritances, reduce violence over access to inside plots, and put land consumed by paths and boundaries back into production. But this majority of villagers believed that a voluntary program of consolidation would not work because the differences in fertility and soil type as well as the problems of accurately evaluating the yield (and variance) of plots made weighting systems for establishing equivalences difficult to establish, and there was little willingness to trust any committee of villagers to arrive at an equitable consolidation. For that reason, the general feeling was that compulsory consolidation was the only way to proceed.[34]

The complex problem of trading and consolidating parcels arises whenever an inheritance is shared among more than one offspring. Michael Lipton describes an Indian village where the farmland runs down the side of a long slope. Soil quality varies from top to bottom of the slope, but varies little along a contour of the slope. If plots were divided horizontally along the contours of the hill, plowing would be easier and cheaper, and average output would be higher. Each father, however, avoids the problem of equating contours with different averages and variances by dividing the patrimony into vertical strips: 'This saddles each generation of sons with longer, thinner sloping strips, increasingly costly and inconvenient to plough properly, i.e., repeatedly and across the slope.'[35] The very lack of insurance and the difficulties of comparing plots mean that for every generation the share of land occupied by partitions increases, as does the gap between actual and potential production.[36]

It is enlightening to examine the procedures used in European medieval villages to govern harvests and gleaning, for they provide valuable insights into the difficulties of developing workable procedures for stabilizing incomes. They also illustrate the conflicts between the tenants of the manor and the cotters, or laborers, who lived in the villages and worked for the tenants – and the mistrust and suspicion of the poor within the village.

There were three basic stages to the harvest. First, the grain was reaped with sickles and bound into sheaves. Then stalks that had not been bundled or somehow had been missed were raked or gathered along with fallen grains. Then the remaining grains that had fallen or had been missed in corners of the field were gleaned. The timing of harvest, and the need for an adequate supply of labor at the very moment of harvest, were crucial for the tenants. If the reaping were begun too soon, grain would spoil or sour. If the harvest were begun a few days too late, many kernels would fall from the stalks.[37]

Since not all fields ripened on the same day, there were usually at any one time during the harvest fields already reaped and ready for raking (or even for gleaning) and fields just about to ripen. The by-laws of twelfth- and thirteenth-century English villages provided for enforced cooperation among tenants and laborers to insure that no man's reap would be delayed for the sake of another man's raking or gleaning. Village by-laws stated that no one offered reaping work at a minimum wage set by the village could leave the village to work elsewhere (without substantial fines), and no one offered work as a reaper could work as a raker – tenants could not even rake their own fields if a fellow tenant wanted to hire them to reap.[38]

Village rules, then, insured that everyone had a chance to complete his first stage of harvesting before anyone finished his second stage; they provided some income stabilization for the tenant class as well. An alternative way of sharing labor between reaping and raking would have been via internal bidding for labor through price competition, that is, a labor market. If laborers and tenants were simply allowed to work for whoever paid best, this would also have had the effect of spacing the harvest, for persons with no grain reaped would have been willing to pay more for workers than would persons concerned with the secondary raking. However, the labor-market approach would have benefited the laborers at the expense of tenants, who would have had to pay more for laborers. The rules were consciously designed 'in the interests of those hiring labor'.[39]

Not even in the case of gleaning – picking up of fallen grains after reaping and raking – is there evidence of village procedures to protect the poor and provide them with floors. Blackstone wrote, 'By the common law and custom of England the poor are allowed to enter and glean upon another's ground after the harvest without being guilty of trespass.' Ault found, however, that there is no mention of such right in *any* medieval English village by-laws or procedures.[40] Further, medieval village rules as well as Roman, Salic and French law all vested the right to glean solely with the owner of the grain.[41]

People sometimes were given the chance to glean any last bits of grain from the fields before animals were set loose to pasture on the stubble and droppings. Even here, however, a strong distrust and suspicion of the poor and the weakness of village commitment to their welfare are evident. Typically, in France and England it was only when outside authority, such as a lord or priest, intervened that the poor were given any time in the field before the animals. Even with outside intervention, gleaning was limited only to those (again, the old, widowed and orphaned) who had passed inspection by bailiffs or who had a letter from the curé certifying their status.[42]

The extensive use of credit and interest rates in pre-capitalist village society contradicts moral economy predictions. How credit is rationed and distributed within the village is a clear test of whether or not need-criteria are being used in the allocation of resources. Bidding for credit – that is, the use of market-determined interest rates – is evidence of a system in which persons are concerned with maximizing the productivity of their resources, and it is in conflict with maximizing the welfare of the poor. Yet throughout Vietnamese history, attempts to limit the (legal) interest rates charged within villages always failed. Not only does a system of credit and competitive interest rates allocate resources in an economic and not a welfare fashion, but it also channels most credit to persons with fixed collateral, such as land. It simply was not common in pre-capitalist society for persons to be extended resources solely on their personal pledge. The general rule was that people without fixed assets could borrow money only if a person was given as collateral. In Thailand, for example, 'there was no organized police force, and it was easy for the debtor to abscond. . . . The best security for a loan . . . was to have the debtor or his child or his wife living and serving in the creditor's household.'[43]

The problem of credit and the related problem of debt bondage in cases where there is no fixed collateral are worth emphasizing. It is often argued that the existence of a wide-open frontier benefits peasants – they can always flee to new areas if the demands of the lord become too onerous. The obverse, however, is seldom noted: if it is possible for peasants to flee, then lords (and other peasants), unless they are unaware of this possibility, will adapt their credit charges to this risk, and credit for persons with no fixed assets will depend on such practices as debt bondage.[44]

Further, a lack of land may mean not only denial of credit, but second-class citizenship as well. It is clear that in many areas pre-capitalist villages were organized around land and that only land-owners had rights as insiders. Today in open villages, when a village patrimony consists of organization to allocate responsibilities for irrigation canals and dams, the landless may have no role in the central core of village society and therefore be looked down on by other peasants. In an open village in Thailand, for example, Potter found that village organization focused on canal work and that the landless did not participate in this activity; they were therefore 'really not full citizens of the community' and were 'not considered of much account at village meetings.'[45]

Limited and specified reciprocities, low levels of welfare and insurance, outsiders, and the prevalence of market-determined credit rates (usury), all challenge the basis of moral economy claims about village welfare and insurance systems. This also means, as we shall see, that the decay of traditional welfare functions under the stress of capitalism and colonialism does not alone account for the rise of new political and religious movements in Vietnam. The successful movements in that country were able to win much of their following merely by providing leadership to extend and improve the insurance and welfare available in the pre-capitalist village, not by restoring old patterns.

Village Finance

Given the importance of insurance and welfare (or loans) to peasants, given also the need for such village-level projects as irrigation and flood control, there is potential value in a village reserve that will be used for public works or for persons in need. The maintenance of such a reserve is consistent with the moral economy approach to the village and necessary for insurance and welfare: since all peasants would have an interest in such a reserve, the village could be expected to provide reserves for specified needs. However, the conflict between individual and group interests points to the possibility that cash reserves will be maintained only when village officials can be trusted not to abscond, that any system of community finance may be manipulated to benefit the leaders at the expense of the village, and that villagewide sources of credit may be opposed by persons seeking to maintain some villagers in a dependent position.

In fact, village reserves are seldom maintained, and public works are instead financed on a project-by-project basis. As we shall see, during the colonial period (the only period for which the evidence is clear), the systems for raising money to finance village projects in Vietnam were consistently manipulated by village leaders to make a personal profit for themselves at the expense of the village treasury. Furthermore, attempts to develop village granaries as a source of low-cost credit for the poor floundered on village squabbling over claims of theft, and attempts to extend agricultural credit to the poor were either blocked or captured by village leaders for their own profit.

Distribution of Resources

The fact that villages typically manage considerable agricultural resources – including pastureland, cropland, forests and irrigation water – that are allocated among villagers on a periodic basis is often taken as *prima facie* evidence of progressive redistribution. Periodically allocating resources, however, is not necessarily equivalent to a leveling or welfare function. If, as moral economists state, there is leveling within villages, or if villages maximize security, minimize risk, or keep persons above a minimum level or danger line, there should be evidence of such considerations at work in the distribution of communal lands, particularly when large amounts of cropland are allocated periodically to individuals by the village leaders. In addition to reserving corners for the widowed, aged, and/or orphaned, there should be evidence of consideration given to households in trouble. If the village is to be progressive, the two areas where progressive principles should be most in evidence are taxation and the distribution of resources.

The alternate, political economy assumptions lead to the prediction that progressive principles will be reflected in the distribution of resources only when there is long-run faith in the institution of the village, when 'need' is easily operationalized and measured, and when village leaders believe it to be in their long-run interests to support progressive rules – that is, when they feel that their long-run security is better served by supporting progressive rules than by maximizing their current share of resources and diverting their current surplus into private investments designed to promote future security. Even with long-run faith in the village's survival and viability, and even with agreed-on standards of need, it is still possible that village leaders may think it better to maximize current shares of community resources and prepare for the future through private investment of those shares. The uncertain prospect of future community guarantees will be balanced against current wealth converted into private preparations for the future.

As noted, many village inhabitants were 'outsiders' excluded from shares of community resources. Moreover, indirect evidence suggests that it was rare, even among 'insiders', for resources to be distributed in a progressive fashion. Sabean notes that peasant revolts in early modern Europe had their basis in communal life and in 'the desire of one faction in the village to control access to resources within the village.'[46] Indeed, it is frequently the state that intervenes to enforce redistribution of village-owned lands when one group in the village has excluded others from access to the resources.[47]

This type of evidence strongly suggests short-run maximization behavior *vis-à-vis* village resources – that in general peasants struggle for as large an immediate share of village resources as they can get (whether or not they invest or gamble, long run or short run, with their shares). Such short-run maximization behavior, in turn, leads to the expectation that factions and coalitions will be highly unstable and subject to change, and that fixed *ascriptive* rules will be used for the actual allocation process.

Fixed ascriptive rules may be the only way to avoid interminable conflict when dividing the pie. Benjamin Ward has shown that any question of dividing a pie is a voter's (Arrow) paradox.[48] That is, no matter what plan is proposed to a group for dividing up a resource, if the decision is to be made by majority rule, there is *always* another plan that can defeat the current plan. This is sometimes called the problem of 'cyclical majorities', for plan *A* can get more votes than plan *B*, which can get more votes than plan *C*, but plan *C* may then get more votes than plan *A*. Purely on a majority-vote basis, then, it is impossible to reach a final outcome, to find a plan that will defeat all others. In such situations, control of the agenda becomes crucial because the order in which a fixed set of plans is offered in pair-wise competition will determine the final winners. Indeed, in Vietnamese villages, resources were allocated among insiders by their rank in the village, and rank was determined largely by age, wealth, and education. In other cases, resources are allocated by lottery, by turn, or even by rotation based on the position of the sun.[49] Shares may well have been of equal size in many medieval villages, but this is clearly not a progressive principle. On the contrary, if shares are of equal size, and if every male is given an equal size share, then inequality among families and households is reinforced.

Thus, the ranking systems within villages, so often pictured as rankings of prestige, are also rank orders of access to village resources. We shall observe, however, that although the ascriptive system was regressive, and although the ranking system for allocating resources in Vietnamese villages accentuated inequality, the ascriptive nature of the system helped to stabilize the system of distribution.

Leadership

Moral economy interpretations of village decision making stress consensus and systematic participation in the decision process by all villagers. They also stress the leveling function of the demands for feasts and expenditures placed on villagers who seek the 'prestige' of a leadership role. I stress the small size of the decision-making group and interpret the emphasis on consensus as an attempt by the elite to close ranks and keep their disputes from the wider village. Moreover, the main motivation for assuming a leadership role is not prestige, but gain. Viewed in this light, the feasts and expenditures required of officials are investments, the costs of which prevent many villagers from assuming any role in village leadership or decision making.

The emphasis on unanimity in decision making is widely noted in the literature on villages; this emphasis often is interpreted as evidence of a strong underlying consensus. It may also mean, however, that the elite decision-making body is trying to iron out all conflict internally in order to avoid splits in its ranks and appeals to less powerful villagers. The emphasis on consensus within the elite also can mean that there is a high degree of distrust and suspicion among its members, and that unit veto rules are the only rules that can maintain a stable peace among them. The distrust interpretation of elite consensus is supported by the fact that actual village decision making is generally limited to councils comprised of no more than twelve to fifteen members (whose deliberations may or may not be presented to all other villagers for approval).[50]

This distrust is also evident in the frequent concern that the headman or chief, who is the link between village councils and the outside authorities, be a lesser person who can be controlled by the council, who will not bring in powerful outsiders to support him in local disputes, or who will not use outside connections to control village resources.[51]

Members of village councils everywhere can and do collude with one another to their common advantage and at the expense of the village. It is equally clear that village officeholding is also often looked on as a way to make money or at least to protect fortunes. Indeed, it is stressed in accounts of prestige economies that peasants will even go into debt to provide feasts and otherwise purchase higher offices in the village. How and why, it should be asked, would conservative, 'safety-first' peasants spend so much money, if they were not going to get it back? How are the loans repaid? As Barth has noted, 'over a longer period of time, a chief certainly expects to derive material advantage from his state.'[52] Furthermore, the requirement that persons must give feasts or sponsor festivals *before* attaining high office sets a high entry cost which precludes from office persons who cannot afford the expense or to whom the rich will not lend money. Thus, in many instances, 'to the poor man, the higher offices are not open.'[53]

(That peasants value feasts is clear; that they consider the best system for providing feasts one in which the rich pay for them is less clear. During the Viet Minh period in Central Vietnam, 1945–1954, feasts were forbidden in most villages; they represented 'feudalism' and the old, superstitious ways. After 1954, when the Viet Minh cadres had left the area, the old notables made an effort to reinstitute the old system of feasts paid for and officiated over by (rich) notables. However, there was widespread opposition from among less well-off peasants at the attempted reinstatement of these privileges. In many villages, the protests prevented the old elite from taking control of the feasts, and rent from a piece of communal land was allocated or a tax was instituted to pay for them. With public finance of the feasts, it was no longer necessary to let the rich officiate at them. Now a man of virtue and prestige could be selected by acclaim to officiate at the feast, regardless of his personal wealth. 'In the old days,' one peasant recounted, 'only the rich could officiate at the feast and have the honor of eating the head of the pig. Now any man of virtue and prestige can eat the head of the pig.')

But ceding village offices to the most well-off villagers may not be objectionable to other villagers. A well-off villager, for example, may be content to maintain his fortune rather than seek additional gain by manipulating village affairs; another might be satisfied with enhancement of reputation for the personal credit that it will bring with others. Indeed, if a stable rotation of high office can be arranged among a small number of villagers, a general balance of power may severely limit the short-run (individual as opposed to class) economic payoffs of office holding. Moreover, a person with fixed collateral is less likely to abscond with the tax money. As Potter found, 'villagers prefer to have wealthy men as village leaders on the theory that, since they already have money, they are less likely to run off with funds entrusted to them.'[54]

In short, the same considerations of investment and profit govern peasant attitudes about village offices as govern their other decisions about security and investment.

Stratification

If, as moral economists state, villages provided viable insurance and welfare, if there were leveling functions, and if it were easy for peasants to flee to pre-colonial frontiers and clear new land whenever demands of villages or lords became exorbitant, there would be little or no stratification in pre-capitalist villages. Stratification among peasants would originate with capitalism and markets. But stratification does exist in pre-capitalist society: '[In the medieval village, there] was clear social stratification by the time we have written records. . . . The division between rich and middle peasants with land and equipment (especially plough teams) adequate for subsistence and poor or landless peasants without enough land for subsistence is found very early.'[55] 'Polarization of fortunes,' then, 'could not simply have resulted from competition in production for the market.'[56]

Stratification occurred before production for markets because peasants were interested in individual security and approached villages as sources of gain, just as they did markets. Stratification is inherent in the procedures used in many, if not all, village societies. Village welfare and insurance systems were limited, and the use of credit as an alternative added to stratification. Village procedures were not progressively redistributive, but favored the rich. Village power was used to control other peasants, as in Russia, where peasants who complained about village officials were sent to the army or to Siberia.[57] Village leaders, furthermore, could use the power that went with their control of village resources to prevent other peasants from opening new lands, so that a source of cheap labor would be available for the better-off peasants.[58]

As Weisser has noted in his reassessment of the Spanish pueblo,

'Even in the primitive, pre-industrial world, economic differentia-
tion was so pronounced as to make absurd the notion that communalism was a dominant mode of economic relations either during or
long before the advent of the modern era.'[59]

During the colonial period, stratification increased in many parts
of the world, including Vietnam, because the richer villagers had
increased opportunities for profit. But at the core were the same
mechanisms of control and stratification as in pre-colonial and pre-
capitalist Vietnam: allocation of village resources and charges,
control of bottlenecks in the local production process, the
manipulation of outside connections. Colonialism and capitalism
exacerbate, but they do not create economic competition and stratification. Stratification, as Jay noted in Indonesia, is part of village
politics and economics:

> The power and prestige that can be derived from village office
> holding. . . . are considerable. The attached land rights afford
> control over a relatively substantial amount of land, which in
> turn permits the establishment of a number of power relation-
> ships with sharecroppers. . . . Control over largess of central
> government gives him opportunities to select friends as
> agents.[60]

Alliances, Markets and Innovations

Evaluation of such phenomena as the development of alliances
between villagers and outsiders; the expansion of land, capital and
commodity markets; the adoption of innovations; and the use of
supravillage institutions are largely determined by one's view of the
corporate village. The moral economy view implies that these
changes are the products of powerful outside forces that penetrate
the village. The metaphor of 'penetration' overlooks the internal
limitations of the corporate framework and underestimates the
desire of peasants to raise their income beyond the levels possible
within corporate villages. Indeed, if village cooperation worked as
well as moral economists claim, why should there be any opposition to outside alliances or to innovations that might raise total
village output by increasing the supply of credit, gaining the support of powerful outsiders, or in other ways helping the village as a
whole to cope with common crises? Even if villages provided ample
protection for the poor and insurance against disasters, why would
those preclude an interest in opportunities for advancement beyond
the income levels possible in a corporate village or an internal

initiative for market development and innovation? Moral economists, however, see peasants as aiming for an income to meet
culturally defined needs or to discharge ceremonial and social
obligations. In this view, peasants are striving for a 'target income';
when they reach this level (which they achieve within the village),
they have no further concern with raising production or acquiring
goods unavailable within the village. The peasant does not acquire
new wants; he is 'pulled from the ideal of self-sufficiency by market
forces only to the extent that they permit him to purchase certain
"traditional" goods.'[61]

The idealization of the corporate village and the accompanying
view of the peasant's wants as fixed and met within the village, thus
leads, as I have noted, to a view of commercialization and market
development as the peasantry's fall from grace. As Jan DeVries has
so aptly phrased it, 'Being content with a caricature . . . can only
result in a misspecification of the historic and potential role of
peasants in economic development.'[62]

There is most certainly internal opposition to innovation,
alliances, and markets, but there is also internal initiative for such
changes. There are, in fact, serious conflicts among members of the
elite about the distribution of benefits from outside opportunities,
conflicts between classes about opportunities for laborers, and free-
rider problems that must be overcome for innovations to be
adopted. The expansion of labor markets, for example, brings clear
benefits to poor peasants, and it is the rich who often collude to
keep the poor from markets. In medieval villages, as we have seen,
labor mobility was controlled, when possible, in order to depress
wages. In Morelos, Mexico, the arrival of haciendas was a benefit
to peasants in many villages, not a threat to well-running corporate
villages with strong subsistence guarantees for all. Before the
advent of the hacienda, villagers suffered debt, slavery, and exploitation at the hands of local leaders. The introduction of the
hacienda, however, led to a wage spiral between competing
demands of the hacienda and the *caciques*.[63]

With its passive connotations, the concept of 'penetration'
implies that the initiative for alliance comes from powerful outsiders. Although the village resists, it finally is broken down and
entered. In both pre-colonial and colonial periods, however, the
initiators of alliances are often local notables looking for external
allies to strengthen their hands in village power struggles.

Frequently, there is strong opposition to allowing persons living
in adjacent areas to own land in villages when such ownership
would threaten the village balance of power and the distribution of

resources and charges within the village. To prevent or impede bankers, moneylenders and bureaucrats from owning land in a village, of course, limits the availability of credit (by making mortgages less valuable) and therefore sometimes limits total productivity. However, small landowners oppose the entrance into their economies of larger, more powerful persons when institutional realities are such that these persons could manipulate taxes, titles and village resources to the detriment of the small landowners. In fifteenth- and sixteenth-century Wallachia (Romania), nobles could get rights to use communal lands in villages only when a villager would form an alliance with them and take money to adopt them as 'brothers'. With their wealth and political weight, the nobles then were able to dominate the entire community.[64]

Opposition to outside alliances, I hypothesize, is tied to the quality of land titles. When there is private land with secure title, the opposition to outside landownership becomes far less pronounced; the attractions of credit begin to outweigh the potential threats to smallholders from the entrance into their village economies of moneylenders, bureaucrats and other foreign landowners. (Of course, there are also numerous attempts by tenants and laborers to prevent landowners from importing tenants and laborers from outside the village.)

Like alliances with outsiders, the advent of new supravillage institutions also can change the power balance within villages; likewise, while some villagers will want to take advantage of these institutions, others will want to prevent villagers from using them. During the colonial period, the new court systems using the laws and languages of the colonizers often had considerable influence on village affairs. Persons who could afford the costs of entry to these institutions (that is, who could afford lawyers or who could speak the new language) had an advantage over adversaries who could not afford the new, higher costs. But the impact of new institutions is not automatic – alliances require at least two parties, and institutions have to be used if they are to have influence. In Mysore, for example, the modern courts established near the village of Namhalli around 1820 had negligible impact on the political and economic life of the village for over a century. No one used the new courts, and 'as long as they were avoided by the villagers', they could have only the smallest effect on village life.[65]

Just as peasants are not necessarily averse to new outside alliances or institutions, they are not hostile to innovations from which they expect personal gain. Even the simplest of innovations, however, such as the planting of peas or beans, which might look virtually costless and without risk to an outside observer, can require extensive cooperation within the village if peasants are to be assured of realizing the fruits of their labor. Caution based on concern for reaping the fruits frequently is misinterpreted by social scientists as caution based on a peasant belief in a fixed (that is, a constant pie) social product. In this view, peasants resist innovation because, given fixed total production, the gain of any one family will come at the expense of other families.[66]

But distrust of innovation is not due to a belief that there is a constant pie or that one person's gain is another's loss. Even when there is an obvious increase in the total product, peasants will be suspicious and distrustful because they will be concerned with getting gains commensurate with their efforts. The types of innovations likely to be adopted, therefore, are those that make it possible for peasants to believe that they, rather than someone else, will enjoy the fruits of their labor.

For English peasants of the thirteenth century, for example, supplementary crops of peas and beans were of obvious dietary value. Further, they required no milling, they could be picked and eaten green, and in a few minutes enough could be gathered for an entire family meal. However, field peas grew so tall that persons were able to hide among them; since they were generally planted in an area separate from the great fields, this meant a great potential for theft. For the growing of legumes to be possible, it was therefore necessary to find a way to insure that everyone would reap the benefits of their own investment in legumes and to control suspicion and conflict. The solution to this problem (and other similar problems) was centered on the bell tower. By agreeing that persons could be in the pea and bean fields only at a specified hour of the day – clearly marked for all by the bell, which the priest would ring – suspicion could be reduced from twenty-four hours a day of worry to one hour. That is, during legume time, someone from every family could watch over the family crop; at all other hours, any person carrying legumes could be presumed by all to be a thief.[67]

Much evidence cited as opposition to innovation is no more than individual economic evaluation, that is, rejection based on cost and risk – particularly cost or risk not obvious to the outside observer.[68] In a village which had no rules for regulating pea fields, for example, it would be easy for a social scientist to ignore potential thefts and to conclude that peasants were not growing beans because they were averse to risk or resistant to innovation. Peas and beans, in fact, require innovations that are relatively easy to make within villages. Once the basic procedures to safeguard legumes from theft have been developed, each family can decide on its own whether or not to grow these crops, with no need to consider the decisions of the other families.

In the village mode of production, however, there are clearly times when individual innovations have serious consequences for others (externalities) and require universal adoption. If there is village irrigation and all fields must be flooded at once, it is impractical to shift to a new crop that requires irrigation at a time different from the crop currently raised by other villagers. If all draft animals are allowed to roam freely in all fields after the harvest, a villager who adopts a new harvest technique may leave behind less stubble in his fields; thus, either he receives a 'free ride' unless all shift at once, or he is forced to use the same harvest technique as other villagers. Such shifts in agricultural technique are made difficult by distrust and conflict within the village, and would be less time-consuming if there were actually a moral economy.[69]

The problems of coordination and decision making within the village also help explain why there is a shift from communal to private property enabling peasants to respond favorably to land, commodity, and capital markets. Peasants are not always 'victims' of markets. When they have secure land titles and therefore outsiders are less able to manipulate the lands and taxes of villagers, peasants respond – without crisis or subsistence threat – to the opportunities for advancement and security afforded them by enlarged land, credit, and commodity markets.

Problems of coordination and investment invariably tend to break down communal rotation systems where they have existed. As agricultural techniques develop and intensify, greater investment in the land is required. To receive maximum benefits from irrigation, for example, countless hours of fine grading of the land is required. If communal coordination could insure that everyone would do the same quality of work, agricultural development and land rotation would not be incompatible. In fact, in Vietnam communal land was generally less productive because peasants did not want to 'set a banquet for someone else to eat'. And more generally, the development of agricultural techniques and investments (whether due to the 'push' of population growth or the 'pull' of market opportunity), such as planting long-range crops like coffee, leads to a situation of de facto private, unrotated land.[70] Because of the problems of communal decision making and coordination, private land is more productive and generally can support a larger population at a higher level than can communal land.

As land rotations break down and private property develops, the extension of land markets can occur in at least two ways. Localized, internal village land markets develop among insiders whenever there is private property, or even unrotated communal land. Whenever outside credit becomes available and peasants have individual land titles, a more general land market develops in which outsiders also can buy and sell parcels within the village. Whenever it is assumed that corporate villages successfully provided a culturally defined 'target income' and that peasants were content (and not pursuing means to raise production) the development of land markets is assumed to be a disaster to the peasantry and is viewed as a product of outside social forces tearing asunder common property. As noted, there were serious limitations on the productivity of communal land, whether or not it was rotated, and the development of land markets and the related extension of commodity markets generally had support among large segments of the peasantry and, in most cases, increased subsistence floors.

The belief that private property and commercialization are deleterious to the peasants goes back, it would appear, to a view of the English enclosure movement that sees in the conversion of common village fields to private, fenced lands the creation of a reserve army of floating laborers upon whose backs the industrial revolution was built. This view of the English enclosures as 'sheep eating men' is a false model to apply to other countries, and it does not even fit with the evidence from England. The English enclosure movement was neither as deleterious to peasants as often assumed nor directly applicable to commercialization in other countries today.

Instead of making all-encompassing generalizations about commercialization or new market opportunities, attention must be paid to the particular crops being cultivated, the specific demands for labor, the potential economies of scale, access to credit and control of marketing arrangements, all of which determine the distribution of benefits. There are indeed times when new markets and increased commercialization will be deleterious to a large part of the rural population. When English lands were enclosed in order to change from growing grain to raising sheep, some people were driven off the land, for sheep require less labor than most grains. But the majority, probably 90 per cent, of enclosed land was not for permanent pasturage, but for grain to take advantage of rising grain prices, to allow farmers to improve their cattle and plough animals by selective breeding (impossible without fences), and to make investments that led to more intensive use of the land:

> Mental habits die hard, and it is still thought – and taught – that as a result of enclosure and the introduction of the turnip (one of the most labour-consuming of all the crops in the

farmer's calendar) agricultural output rose while the labour force fell – or, as some would say 'fled'. Agricultural output certainly rose but there is no reason to think that the labour force engaged in agricultural operations fell; the contribution of the Agricultural Revolution was not to release labour for industry, but to make possible a greater output without making a correspondingly greater demand upon the available labour supply.[71]

There was, to be sure, great rural poverty in England during the time of enclosure. But there was also substantial population growth, and the incidence of rural poverty was correlated not with enclosure, but with the lack of nonagricultural employment. Poverty and the industrial revolution may have risen in the same decades, but they rose in different areas.[72]

Enclosures for wheat, then, were the predominant form in England, and they were labor intensive, increasing the carrying capacity of the land: 'There is no doubt that enclosure and the improvements which it made possible roused ambitions in the ordinary farmer for the first time, and that the fresh opportunities, suddenly opened up, brought into action stores of human energy never previously tapped. The psychological effect of change doubled and trebled the force of the original stimulus.'[73]

Even if the English enclosure movement had not benefited smallholders, it would be a poor model to apply in other cases. Whereas in most of Asia there are no fences, perhaps half the cost of enclosure in England went into fencing to keep livestock apart. Since small holdings require proportionally more fence per unit of land than do large holdings, the initial cost per acre was higher for smallholders than for farmers with more land and was a major reason why smallholders (as opposed to the landless 40 to 50 per cent, who certainly benefited on the whole) did not always gain as much, proportionately, as large landowners.[74]

Even more to the point, the enclosure movement is a bad paradigm because it was administered so fairly, compared to many colonial or contemporary situations. The key determinant of the fate of peasants in open land markets is not the vagaries of commercial agriculture, but the chances which accrue to better educated villagers, who are able to manipulate colonial institutions by registering the land of other villagers in their own name or by using the courts to claim land belonging to others. What is so remarkable about the English enclosure, to a scholar studying mainly contemporary situations, is how much attention (relatively) was given to protecting the rights of smallholders in England.[75]

Just as persistent a myth as that of the enclosure movement as a giant swindle is the notion that small, local commodity markets provide more certain subsistence for peasants than do national or international markets. Certainly as transportation improves and markets reach into once-remote areas, there is generally an increase in stratification. But given the lack of village aid for persons with bad harvests, the tenancy that results from selling land in bad years may not be such a bad alternative to wage slavery, infanticide, or selling of children. When village production can enter a regional or national market, the pool of potential creditors is expanded because the land now has value to outsiders. More important is the fact that, while exposure to international and national markets does subject peasants to new and different kinds of uncertainty, larger markets tend to maintain steadier prices and far more certain supplies of food over time; in England, 'improved transportation reduced risk by increasing the varieties of weather and soil represented in a single market area and therefore decreasing the variability of prices for the market as a whole.'[76] When markets expand, supplies of grain begin to even out, one area's good year canceling another area's bad year. With expansion, then, the actual 'insurance value of money', that is, the probability that money saved in a good year will find food to buy in a bad year, itself increases and peasants have a form of protection which they did not have within smaller market areas.

PATRON–CLIENT RELATIONS

A direct comparison of the moral economy and political economy assumptions reveals important differences in expectations for three aspects of the patron–client relation – the terms of exchange, maintenance of dependency, and distribution of resources.

While moral economists assume a fixed, culturally given subsistence level (target income), I assume that the subsistence level is endogenous and variable. Peasants, that is, will try to raise their share of production, through either individual or group bargaining, according to the risk involved.

If the legitimacy of patron or lord depended on a fixed notion of subsistence, and if pre-capitalist society generally provided subsistence for all, then a drastic reduction in the man/land ratio would have no effect on tenants or clients. In fact, however, throughout the pre-capitalist and colonial world, whenever plagues have drastically reduced the number of tenants on the great estates or holdings, demands for higher wages and better terms of exchange have followed. In fourteenth-century England, 'the immediate impact of the Black Death had been that both agricultural and other workers demanded, *according to the strength of their bargaining power*, up to twice or even three times their previous wages.'[77]

Similarly, in Japan during the 1920s, conflict between landlords and tenants was most common in the villages near urban and industrial centers. This was not because the movement of landlords into the cities had left peasants more unprotected and with less favorable terms of exchange than in the past. All generalizations to the contrary, absentee landlords at this time were more forgiving in bad years, rented larger plots, charged lower rents and evicted tenants less often than resident landlords.[78] Tenancy disputes were centered in these areas not because of negative impacts of absenteeism or commercialization, but because opportunities in factories had drawn laborers out of agriculture, reducing competition for tenancies. Thus, although conditions of tenancy were comparatively good around urban and industrial centers, protest and militancy were widespread, for there was little fear of reprisal.[79] Subsistence, therefore, is not fixed at a culturally given level. Economic shares are based on the terms of exchange, and protest frequently occurs when the balance of exchange is *improving* in favor of the tenant.

Among the many limits on tenant bargaining powers were the feudal laws that required lords to return runaways and antipoaching agreements to prevent bidding among lords for the services of tenants. Such attempts at collusion even extended – when the relative power of the lords *vis-à-vis* the central authorities was high – to limiting the emergence of cities and market areas because cities and markets would benefit clients at the lord's expense.[80]

Within their own domains or estates, it was common for lords to monopolize crucial bottlenecks in the production process in order to maintain control over tenants. At one time or another, mills, ovens and bulls were all preserved as monopolies by European lords. By forcibly maintaining such monopolies (killing all other bulls, for example), lords were not only able to provide a service for their tenants, but they were also able to shift the transaction costs to those who must come to the lords for a vital service. Thus, for example, 'it is no wonder that in a society where bread was so scarce and uncertain the term "keeper of the loaves", *hlaford*, came to mean, in Anglo-Saxon, "master" or lord.'[81]

If lords are an important 'functional', 'legitimate' part of peasant livelihood, then whenever there is a chance to increase production by upgrading the 'human capital' of the tenants, lords logically should do so. In fact, there are many occasions when lords will not risk their position by allowing tenants access to new skills which would raise total output if these skills can also enhance leadership ability and give peasants new options independent of the lord. It is clearly the case that tenants can be forcibly prevented from acquiring skills that increase production but threaten dependency. In Peru, 'mestizo overlords regarded the peasants as little better than animals and actively discouraged education or the use of Spanish on the sound assumption that it might create aspirations beyond servile labor.'[82] Literacy is particularly threatening because it increases the probability that peasants on estates will be able to take advantage of favorable national political climates to move against lords, and because it undercuts the dependence of peasants on lords. John Gitlitz, discussing the threat of mass literacy to Peruvian haciendas, notes that a literate person

> ... can read the papers, follow national political events, and more readily recognize the availability and relative power of differing potential allies. Finally, on the estate, he can ... [help] those among his comrades who are illiterate to deal with the outside world. He can read them the directions for the use of pesticides or interpret orders from the sub-prefect. In short, he can to some extent replace the haciendado.[83]

The very process of production, then, can reflect a divergence between providing the best guarantees for clients and maximizing dependence on lords. To maintain control of serfs, a twelfth-century Chinese book advised, 'one should not allow them to have fields and gardens of their own, for if one does, they immediately become filled with greedy schemes.'[84] Peasants are often forcibly blocked from the market for the same reasons: development of market skills can help the peasant to demand more, or even to do without his patron.

When they were able to do so, large estate owners in colonial Southeast Asia forcibly prevented peasants in their domains from selling paddy, buffalo or even garden produce on their own.[85] In amassing their estates and maintaining forced dependencies, they relied on the sociological incompetence of most peasants, their lack of the linguistic and legal-political skills needed to work with the colonial power structure.[86]

Although the self-image of the patron was that of a patriarchal, all-encompassing father figure, he himself often lacked the managerial competence to perform such a role for large numbers of tenants concentrated on estates scattered over many villages. The use of intermediaries and agents and the requirements that harvesting be done only in the presence of the owner or agent severely strained relations. Even in the best of circumstances, the patriarch–distant relative analogy often is depicted in an overly positive light. As described in ideal form by a Vietnamese estate owner,

> In the past the relationship between the landlord and his tenants was paternalistic. The landlord considered the tenant as an inferior member of his extended family. When the tenant's father died, it was the duty of the landlord to give money to the tenant for the funeral; if his wife was pregnant, the landlord gave money for the birth; if he was in financial ruin, the landlord gave assistance; therefore, the tenant *had* to behave as an inferior member of the extended family.[87]

It is true that landlords preferred multistranded relationships because they allowed them to maintain their monopoly position and the tenant's dependence. Without opportunities to build up reserves of their own, tenants would have to come to the landlord – and be in his good graces – for any unusual expense. Tenants, on the other hand, generally preferred many single-stranded relationships rather than an all-encompassing 'feudal' relationship with one lord. Peasants in commercial areas of Burma, for example, preferred not to borrow money from their estate owners if they had jewelry or cattle for security.[88] Dependence also meant subjugation. As Alexander Woodside has noted, this 'inferior member of the extended family' model was 'symbolically infantile. . . . The economic value of these positions fluctuated with the prosperity of rural harvests but their social value had always been monotonously degraded.'[89] And Chinese peasants, both tenants and smallholders, had an expression which emphasized the importance of maintaining some autonomy and maneuvering room in their relations with landlords: 'Embrace Buddha's leg only in time of need' (Look to a benefactor only when one is in difficulty).[90]

Peasants, as we shall see, can overthrow lords and increase their security by changing modes of production and by reorganizing agricultural institutions to remove monopolies and overcome linguistic and legal barriers which put them at a disadvantage in the marketplace. The central state is not automatically a threat to the peasantry; on the contrary, it can be an ally in the process. As Robert Brenner noted for seventeenth-century France, 'strong peasant property and [the] absolutist state developed in mutual dependence upon one another. The state increased its power by virtue of its ability to get between the landlord and the peasants, to ensure peasant freedom, hereditability and fixed rents, and thus to use peasant production . . . as the direct source of revenue for royal strength and autonomy.'[91] In twentieth-century Japan, landlords became less important to tenant prosperity as state agricultural services provided farming advice, local officials settled disputes, and the government issued disaster relief.[92]

In moral economy terms, lords will strengthen their position and create the highest general level of security by distributing resources equally among all peasants on their lands. I predict unequal distribution. Given political economy assumptions about gain and individual approaches to security, there will be substantial conflicts of interest among peasants, and lords will take advantage of these conflicts to increase their own profits. Lords pursue divide-and-conquer strategies that capitalize on competition and conflicts among peasants, as can be seen in the unequal treatment of clients and tenants.

The patron–client literature does not deal extensively with the distinction between tenant and client, but the distinction between these two types of relations helps clarify the strategies that landlords use. Successful maintenance of a large estate involves limiting the ability of tenants to engage in collective action. A critical component of a strategy to prevent collective action can be, and very often is, the uneven and unequal distribution of patronage and incentives. The clients in reality are usually a small subset of tenants who have curried special position, favor, or treatment from the landlord through special services. These special services often include acting as 'strikebreaker' or keeping the landlord informed about the activities of other tenants. In China, the subset of tenants who helped the landlords to control other tenants were referred to by the latter as 'dog's leg';[93] in colonial Vietnam, clients were known to other tenants as 'basket carriers' and 'servile flatterers of the rich'.[94]

Within villages or on large estates, lords or notables are usually the arbiters of disputes among peasants. This control of arbitration helps to divide and conquer the peasants, pitting them against one another for future considerations. Notables or lords also control the allocation of scarce resources that put peasants into competition. Indeed, a scarcity of crucial resources can aid the lord by increasing tension among tenants and, therefore, the competition for special treatment.

The very existence of a class of landless laborers in a peasant society suggests that there are critical weaknesses in the moral economy views of the village and of patron–client relations. The concept of common moral expectation and universe appears to conflict with the hostility so often encountered between laborer and tenant. Much of landlord 'exploitation' is facilitated by the uneven distribution of resources (which leads to laborers and tenants, instead of a single class of tenants). The lack of common moral solidarity among the peasantry means competition among peasants for land and credit and a waiting source of men willing to help the landlord evict a tenant who makes trouble.[95]

CONCLUSION

I have made assumptions about individual behavior that are different from those of the moral economists. These assumptions have drawn attention to different features of villages and patron–client ties and have led to questions about the quality of welfare and insurance embedded in both villages and vertical patron–client ties. This, in turn, has demonstrated that there is more potential value to markets *relative to the actual performance level* of these other institutions. Commercialization of agriculture and the development of strong central authorities are not wholly deleterious to peasants, although they may dramatically alter peasant society. This is not because capitalism and/or colonialism are necessarily more benevolent than moral economists assume, but because traditional institutions are harsher and work less well than they believe.

Depending on the specific institutional context, commercialization can be good or bad for peasants. In many cases the shift to narrow contractual ties with landlords increases both peasant security and his opportunity to benefit from markets. The protection and material assistance of the past carried an onerous burden, for often it was based on dependencies that resulted in low production plateaus, enforced ignorance, and limited skills. In Latin America, 'the patron held life-or-death judicial authority over his dependent serfs, and the murder of peasants or the violation of their wives and daughters was not uncommon.'[96] As long ago as the fifth century, a monk described the transformation that overcame freemen who became part of estates: 'all these people who settled on the big estates underwent a strange transformation as if they had drunk of Circe's cup, for the rich began to treat as their own property these strangers.'[97]

Single-stranded relationships may be far more secure for the peasant because there may be less coercion, an absence of monopolies, competition among landlords, and less need for submission of self. The development of an independent trading class can give small peasants easy, low-risk access to international markets and a way of escaping the domination of large lords who use coercion to control the economy despite inefficient practices. The growth of independent small traders like the Chinese in Vietnam, for example, is opposed not by peasants but by large landowners. In particular, erosion of the 'traditional' terms of exchange between landlord and tenant is not the only way for peasants to turn against large lords. It is not the case that if the patron guarantees the traditional subsistence level, peasants will cede him continuous legitimacy; peasants can and do fight for autonomy when better alternatives exist in the market. There are often better opportunities for peasants in markets than under lords, and markets can reduce the bargaining power of the lords.[98] Indeed, it was not uncommon in Europe for men to buy their way out of clientage for the security and freedom of markets.[99]

One need only note the land rush in the new areas of Cochinchina after the French made it habitable to see that markets can be an enormous opportunity for the poor, a chance to escape onerous dependencies and establish themselves, as well as to develop and rely on a more extensive family network than was possible in dependent subsistence. Throughout the world, peasants have fought for access to markets not as a last gasp when all else has failed them, but when they were secure enough to want to raise their economic level and 'redefine' cultural standards! In medieval England, when peasant conditions were comparatively secure,

> The essential quarrel between the peasantry and the aristocracy was about access to the market. It was not that the peasants were worried about the impact of the market in a disintegrating sense upon their community; what they wanted was to be able to put their produce on the market and to have a freer market in land which would enable them to take advantage of the benefits of the market.[100]

The rise of strong central states and the growth of a market economy, then, even in the guise of colonialism (and compradore capitalism), cannot be directly equated with a decline in peasant welfare due to the destruction of traditional villages and/or elite bonds. In the short run, local village elites with the skills to ally themselves with outside powers may reap the greatest benefits from new institutional arrangements, but in the longer run new elites emerge who form alliances with the peasantry against both feudalism and colonialism.[101]

Indirectly, peasants clearly benefit from the growth of law and order and its resulting stability, as well as improvements in communications. The numerous and onerous taxes of the colonial period – as applied by village elites – increased stratification in the majority of countries, but the colonial infrastructure also led to wider systems of trade, credit and communications that helped keep peasants alive during local famines. As Day has noted of Java, local crop failures were so serious in pre-colonial times before there was a developed communications and trade network 'because it was impossible to supply a deficit in one part of the country by drawing on the surplus which might exist in another.'[102] Colonialism was ugly, but the quality of the minimum subsistence floor improved in most countries.[103]

NOTES

1 K. Polanyi, *The Great Transformation* (Rineholt, New York, 1957), p. 44.
2 Ibid., p. 163.
3 E. Hobsbawm, *Primitive Rebels* (W. W. Norton, New York, 1965), p. 80. Emphasis added.
4 J. Blum, 'The European village as a community, origins and functions', *Agricultural History*, 45 (1971), pp. 157–78; idem, 'The internal structure and polity of the European village community from the fifteenth to the nineteenth century', *Journal of Modern History* , 43 (1971), pp. 541–76; E. Wolf, 'Closed corporate communities in Meso America and Java', *Southwestern Journal of Anthropology*, 13 (1957), pp. 1–18; idem, 'Types of Latin American peasantry: A preliminary discussion', *American Anthropologist*, 57 (1955), pp. 452–71.
5 J. Blum, *Lord and Peasant in Russia: From the Ninth to the Nineteenth Century* (Princeton University Press, Princeton, N.J., 1961), pp. 508–9.
6 M. Weisser, *Peasants of the Montes* (University of Chicago Press, Chicago, 1976), pp. 6, 120.
7 Ibid., p. 7.
8 Blum, 'European village', pp. 157–8.
9 Blum, 'Internal structure and polity', p. 541.
10 Le Thanh Khoi, *Le Vietnam: Histoire et Civilisation* (Les Editions de Minuit, Paris, 1955), p. 133.
11 Blum, *Lord and Peasant*, pp. 506–21, is the best source.
12 Ibid., p. 514.
13 Blum, 'European village', p. 162.
14 J. C. Scott, *The Moral Economy of the Peasant* (Yale University Press, New Haven, 1976), p. 54.
15 J. Migdal, *Peasants, Politics and Revolution* (Princeton University Press, Princeton, N.J., 1974), p. 82.
16 O. Lewis, *Life in a Mexican Village: Tepotzlan Restudied* (University of Illinois Press, Urbana, 1951), p. 54. This is but one of many formulations of the cult of poverty.

17 Sometimes on the precolonial frontier, landless persons with no money and no property had their taxes paid for them by the village (or rich men) in exchange for labor services, but this was more like servitude or debt bondage than the adjustments suggested by the arguments of moral economists.

18 If all taxes were land taxes (in other words, if there were no head taxes at all), then there would have been some floor. Additionally the ratio of head taxes to land taxes has important distributional consequences.

19 C. Day, *The Dutch in Java* (Oxford University Press, New York, 1966), p. 187. 'Poor' is defined by landholdings.

20 Blum, 'Internal structure and polity', p. 547. See also, Joan Rockwell 'The Danish Peasant Village', *Journal of Peasant Studies*, 1 (1974), pp. 409–61. But it is possible to devise visible and defensible rules for conscription. Under these rules, one son, either the youngest or the eldest (depending on the country), would be exempt from drafts to ensure family continuity. There would still be potential for conflict any time a family had two sons drafted before all other families had one son drafted. (If a couple with two sons sends one of them to live with a childless relative, do both sons get exemptions?)

21 Blum, 'Internal structure and polity', p. 549. The evidence from the Cochinchina region of Vietnam is consistent with a hypothesis different from Blum's: access to full participation in the village always may have been limited for the profit of insiders, even when there was no population pressure. However, there are not enough data to test alternate explanations for the origins of outsiders.

22 Similarly, in today's peasant world, castes, families, and villages can redefine their boundaries and make new demarcations between insiders and outsiders. Further, persons of substance can avoid responsibility while maintaining a moral front by adapting the posture that they fulfil obligations to their employees and retainers and should, therefore, not be held responsible for the problems of others. During Jan Breman's fieldwork in India, 'a grandfather, a father, and two daughters returned to the village in mid-season. They suffered from typhoid fever and had been sent away from the brickyard so as not to infect the other laborers. Gravely ill and penniless, they had found their way back. . . . Once they were in Chikhilgam, not one of the farmers for whom members of this household sometimes worked gave them any aid. I found these people in their hut, uncared for and without food, lying on jute bags. Two of them died of the fever the next day.' J. Breman, *Patronage and Exploitation* (University of California Press, Berkeley and Los Angeles, 1974), p. 252.

23 Blum, *Lord and Peasant*, pp. 516, 519.

24 D. Sabean, 'Family and land tenure: a case study of conflict in the German Peasants' War (1525), *Peasant Studies Newsletter*, 3 (1974), pp. 1–20.

25 B. White, 'Production and reproduction in a Javanese village', PhD dissertation, Department of Anthropology, Columbia University,

1976, pp. 71–2. White also notes that the notion of work-spreading implied by involution should not be taken to imply that scarce opportunities were relatively evenly distributed (p. 74).

26 D. Sabean, 'German agrarian institutions at the beginning of the sixteenth century: Upper Swabia as an example', *Journal of Peasant Studies*, 3 (1975), October, pp. 76–88.

27 Blum, 'Internal structure and polity', p. 550.

28 Although Blum ('Internal structure and polity', p. 546) says that the community provided 'welfare services', his examples are chiefly of the kinds of insurance discussed here.

29 E. Colson, *Tradition and Contract* (Aldine, Chicago, 1974), p. 50.

30 J. Potter, *Thai Peasant Social Structure* (University of Chicago Press, Chicago, 1976), pp. 163, 171.

31 There can be large groups with little management required for tasks with large economies of scale, like a bucket brigade, or where only low-quality labor is required. Agricultural development and refinement of techniques often lead to smaller exchange groups because higher quality labor input, and thus more vigilance against slackers, is required.

32 D. McCloskey, 'English open fields as behavior toward risk', in P. Uselding (ed.), *Research in Economic History*, vol. 1 (JAI Press, Greenwich, 1976), pp. 124–5.

33 S. Fenoaltea, 'Fenoaltea on open fields: a reply', *Explorations in Economic History*, 14 (1977), p. 405. Fenoaltea argues that since such insurance was possible, scattering was not due to the absence of insurance. I obviously disagree.

34 K. Thompson, *Farm Fragmentation in Greece* (monograph no. 5, Center of Economic Research, Athens, 1963), pp. 40, 69, 86, 187, 207, 243.

35 M. Lipton, 'The theory of the optimising peasant', *Journal of Development Studies*, 4 (1968), p. 339; this article should be considered must reading for scholars in the field, especially for its critique of the free-market laissez-faire approach to peasant economies.

36 Ibid., p. 339.

37 W. O. Ault, *Open Field Farming in Medieval England* (George Allen and Unwin, London, 1972), p. 28. The word *gleaning* generally refers to both the secondary gathering of grain and the later picking-over of fields for the last remnants. Here, however, *raking* refers to the secondary gathering, while *gleaning* refers to that collection of grain not shared with the farmer in control of the fields.

38 Ibid., pp. 19, 29–30, 33, and W. O. Ault, 'By-laws of gleaning and the problems of harvest', *Economic History Review*, 14, 2nd ser. (1961–62), pp. 217–19.

39 Ibid., 'By-laws of gleaning', p. 217. Note that a system of maximum wages (which was tried) would not be as effective because it would be harder to enforce. A tenant who secretly overpaid a laborer would not easily be detected; neither the farmer nor the laborer would have an incentive to disclose an otherwise undetectable transgression. Third

parties, however, can easily see whether a person is reaping or raking, and laws giving precedence to reaping over raking are, therefore, more effective in the absence of class solidarity among tenants. After the Black Death, limitations on outside work became unenforceable.

40 Ibid., *Open Field Farming*, p. 31.

41 P. De Gruilly, *Le droit du glanage* (V. Giard et E. Briere, Paris, 1912), pp. 35, 50; Ault, *Open Field Farming*, p. 37, and 'By-laws of gleaning', p. 215.

42 Ault, 'By-laws', p. 214, and *Open Field Farming*, pp. 30, 31; De Gruilly, *Le droit du glanage*, pp. 35, 51, 70, 71; G. Homans, *English Villagers of the Thirteenth Century* (W. W. Norton, New York, 1975), p. 103. In the thirteenth century, French priests apparently demanded and received a share of the glean; this tithing of the glean elicited a strong rebuke from Pope Clement IV (De Gruilly, p. 45). Biblical law enjoins owners to leave something for orphans, widows, and outsiders. While it is not clear how these laws were enforced (or if they were), it would appear that rabbis, like priests and lords, tried to protect the floors for the poorest (De Gruilly, pp. 24, 28), for there are numerous legal opinions and arguments in the Talmud about, for example, forgotten or neglected grain, about grain hidden by harvesters, or even about grain that falls on anthills (De Gruilly, pp. 26–8).

43 Rabibhadana, *The Organization of Thai Society in the Early Bangkok Period, 1782–1873*, Southeast Asia Data Paper no. 74 (Cornell University Press, Ithaca, 1969), p. 110.

44 Practices sometimes assumed by some to be unjust, immoral, and exploitative were thus a common feature of pre-capitalist society: 'A man who surrenders his child for a loan or one who sells his birthright for a mess of pottage are extreme examples. The needs of the weaker party have allowed the stronger to impose an exchange that violates the true value of things; the bargain is unjust and extortionary' (J. C. Scott, 'Explanation in Rural Class Relations: A Victim's Perspective', *Comparative Politics*, 7 (1975), pp. 489–532.

As Lucien Hanks has noted of Thailand today, 'The departing ones recognize their peripheral position under a given roof, since the most dispensable person had to be chosen from among many, yet leaving for a better opportunity in another area also signifies a parent's concern for a child's well-being. A Bang-Chan rice grower, telling of his childhood, upbraided his parents for refusing to give him into the care of a powerful government official who wished to adopt him. The storyteller commented, 'My parents could not have loved me very much' (L. Hanks, *Rice and Man: Agricultural Ecology in Southeast Asia* (Aldine Press, Chicago, 1972), p. 88).

45 Potter, *Thai Peasant Social Structure*, p. 55.

46 D. Sabean, 'The communal basis of pre-1880 peasant uprisings in Western Europe, *Comparative Politics*, 8 (1976), pp. 355–65.

47 Blum, *Lord and Peasant*, p. 519.

48 B. Ward, 'Majority rule and allocation', *Journal of Conflict Resolution*, 4 (1961), pp. 379–89.
49 Rockwell, 'Danish Peasant Village', p. 417.
50 F. G. Bailey, 'Decisions by consensus in councils and committees with special reference to village and local government in India', Association of Social Anthropologists of the Commonwealth, monograph no. 2: *Political Systems and the Distribution of Power* (Tavistock Publications, London, 1965), pp. 1–20.
51 There will also be times when the potential for profit in the linkage role is clearly less than the level of demands on the role made by powerful outsiders and/or powerful insiders. (See Blum, 'Internal structure and polity', pp. 557–60, and *Lord and Peasant*, p. 523.)
52 F. Barth, 'Segmentary opposition and the theory of games: A study of Pathan organizations', *Journal of the Royal Anthropological Institute of Great Britain and Ireland*, 89 (1959), pp. 5–21.
53 C. Wagley, 'Economics of a Guatemalan Village', *Memoirs of the American Anthropological Association*, 58 (1941), p. 76.
54 Potter, *Thai Peasant Social Structure*, p. 52. Note that both moral economists and political economists agree that there is value in prestige. What needs more development is when leadership will content itself with prestige and when leaders expect a more direct and immediate payoff.
55 R. Hilton, 'Medieval peasants – any lesson? *Journal of Peasant Studies*, 1 (1974), January, pp. 209–10.
56 R. Hilton, *Bond Men Made Free: Medieval Peasant Movements and the English Rising of 1381* (Temple Smith, London, 1973), pp. 32–3.
57 Blum, 'Internal structure and polity', p. 575.
58 O. Lewis, *Pedro Martinez: A Mexican Peasant and His Family* (Random House, New York, 1964), p. 7 is but one example of this.
59 Weisser, *Peasants of the Montes*, p. 48. Surveying the evidence on stratification, Weisser notes that 'the division between rich and poor, between those who work and those who are idle, was probably greater in the [sixteenth century] past than in the present' (p. 37).
60 R. Jay, 'Local government in rural central Java', *Far Eastern Quarterly*, 15 (1956), February, p. 226. Assuming the presence of work-sharing and corporate mechanisms, J. C. Scott and B. J. Kerkvliet argue that 'the typical Javanese village . . . by having avoiding [sic] glaring income differentials, has greatly tempered the local face of class antagonisms' ('The politics of survival: peasant response to "progress" in Southeast Asia', *Journal of Southeast Asian Studies*, 4 (1973), p. 254). Ann Stoler, in contrast, has noted that the 'concept of "shared poverty" . . . obscures the fact that Javanese society has always been stratified . . . through differential access to strategic resources. It is surprising, then, that the shared poverty concept remains the most popularly held characterization of Javanese rural society, despite the existence of many studies which document the

more relevant theme of class stratification based on differential access to land' ('Class structure and female autonomy in rural Java', *Signs*, Special Issue: *Women and National Development*, 3 (1977), Autumn, pp. 78–9).

61 J. DeVries, 'Peasant demand patterns and economic development: Friesland, 1550–1750', in E. L. Janes and W. Parker (eds), *European Peasants and Their Markets* (Princeton University Press, Princeton, 1975).

62 Ibid., p. 234.

63 O. Lewis, *Tepotzlan: Village in Mexico* (Henry Holt and Co., New York, 1960), pp. 18–20.

64 D. Chirot, *Social Change in a Peripheral Society* (Academic Press, New York, 1976), p. 46.

65 A. Beals, 'Interplay among Factors of Change in a Mysore Village', in M. Marriott (ed.), *Village India* (University of Chicago Press, Chicago, 1955), p. 91.

66 These views generally derive from the work of George Foster, particularly 'Peasant society and the image of limited good', *American Anthropologist*, 67 (1965), pp. 293–315, and 'Interpersonal relations in peasant society', *Human Organization*, 19 (1960–61), pp. 174–80; see also J. C. Scott and B. J. Kerkvliet, 'The politics of survival: peasant response to "progress" in Southeast Asia', p. 243.

67 Ault, *Open Field Farming*, pp. 39–40; Homans, *English Villagers*, p. 103. The same sorts of rules were used to regulate the removal of grain from the field and to decrease suspicion of laborers; grain could be removed only by cart, only between certain hours, and not by laborers. Ault (p. 40) also suggests that the poor may have some rights to gather the peas of others. This example demonstrates how technology, that is, bell towers, can increase community. It also suggests the value of the political (or, in this case religious) entrepreneur who can increase productivity and build organization around such collective goods as the bell tower. (And even if the priest – before ringing the bell – ate everyone else's peas, how much can one person eat?)

68 A. H. Niehoff and J. C. Andersen, 'Peasant fatalism and socioeconomic innovation' (*Human Organization*, 25 (1966), pp. 273–82) is a wonderful analysis of this common phenomenon.

69 See, for example, Blum, 'Internal structure and polity', p. 569.

70 Chirot, *Social Change in a Peripheral Society*, p. 21; J. DeVries, *The Economy of Europe in an Age of Crisis, 1600–1750* (Cambridge University Press, Cambridge, 1976), pp. 41–2; Blum, *Lord and Peasant*, p. 328; S. R. Ortiz, *Uncertainties in Peasant Farming: A Columbian Case* (Humanities Press, New York, 1973), pp. 85–132.

71 J. D. Chambers and G. E. Mingay, *The Agricultural Revolution, 1750–1880* (B. T. Batsford, London, 1970), p. 3.

72 Ibid., p. 103. A. Appleby's 'Agrarian capitalism or seigneurial reaction? the Northwest of England, 1500–1700', *American Historical Review*, 80 (1975), pp. 574–94 is a valuable introduction to the debates over the reasons for rural poverty during enclosure.

73 Joan Thirsk, *English Peasant Farming* (Routledge and Kegan Paul,

London, 1957), p. 296. 'Nor was it the land alone which underwent improvement, but living conditions also. In Messingham, the wealth which flowed into the village after enclosure and the warping of the land was partly used to convert the mud and straw covered huts into brick and tile cottages.'

74 D. McCloskey, 'Economics of enclosure: A market analysis', in W. N. Parker and E. L. Jones (eds), *European Peasants and Their Markets* (Princeton University Press, Princeton, 1975), pp. 144–6. I am grateful to Donald McCloskey for reminding me (personal communication, April 1978) that 'a smallholder of land benefits from an improvement in technique in the village even if he does not undertake it. The value of his land rises because it can be used by others (the buyers) with the new technique.' Thus, even a technique which smallholders cannot afford themselves may still benefit them by making it possible for them to survive a bad year by selling a small corner of their now-more-valuable land instead of selling all of their land or some of their children instead.

75 Chambers and Mingay, *Agricultural Revolution*, pp. 85–90. The impact of views of the enclosure movement on analysis of contemporary situations is clearly demonstrated in Scott's discussion of the green revolution in the Punjab region of India. '*As in England*, the transition has not been peaceful. The lower 20 per cent of the labor force is perhaps worse off than before and open conflict between landowners' and laborers' factions is common . . . almost all the new profits have gone to those who control land and capital. . . . A portion of the tenants and smallholders *forced off* the land have been absorbed into the agrarian labor force, another portion into the secondary industries of processing, transport, and marketing created by the agricultural boom, and still another substantial portion into the growing industrial sector of the region. It would seem, thus far at least, that the Punjab has experienced a successful shift to productive, capitalist agriculture. The "success" has eliminated many of the traditional securities for the rural poor and has particularly damaged those at the very bottom of the social structure but it has provided enough economic safety valves to absorb much of the peasantry' (Scott, *Moral Economy*, p. 208; emphasis added). Scott is wrong for the Punjab as well as for England. There has been a large influx of laborers into the Punjab from other provinces because the green revolution has been labor intensive. There has been a 'discernible and unparalleled improvement in employment opportunities and earnings of the agricultural laborers' and an upward shift in income for almost all the farmers in the state. 'There are no facts to support that in Punjab evictions took place due to green revolution technology' (S. S. Johl, 'Gains of the Green Revolution: how they have been shared in Punjab', *Journal of Development Studies*, 11 (1975), July, pp. 182–5). The green revolution, however, is by no means the panacea suggested by some of its more ardent enthusiasts.

76 McCloskey, 'English open fields', p. 129.

77 Hilton, *Bond Men Made Free*, p. 154 (emphasis added). See also E. Tuma, *Twenty-six Centuries of Agrarian Reform* (University of California Press, Berkeley and Los Angeles, 1965), p. 42; J. Blum, R. Cameron and T. Bames, *The Emergence of the European World*, 2nd edn (Little, Brown, Boston, 1967), p. 37; H. Alavi, 'Peasants and revolution', in J. Saville and R. Miliband (eds), *The Socialist Register* (Merlin Press, London, 1965), p. 266; Sabean, 'German agrarian institutions', p. 80.

78 A. Waswo, *Japanese Landlords: The Decline of a Rural Elite* (University of California Press, Berkeley and Los Angeles, 1977), pp. 88–9. Although absentee landlords in Japan at this time provided more secure floors, they were less likely or able than resident landlords to carry out projects that would raise productivity and increase the shares of both landlords and tenants.

79 Ibid., pp. 102–3; J. Gitlitz, 'Haciendad, comunidad and peasant protest in Northern Peru', PhD dissertation, Political Science Department, University of North Carolina, Chapel Hill, 1975, p. 426.

80 Jerome Blum, 'The rise of serfdom in Eastern Europe', *American Historical Review*, 42 (1957), pp. 820–34; Hilton, *Bond Men Made Free*, p. 152; Breman, *Patronage and Exploitation*, pp. 64–5; Mark Elvin, *The Pattern of the Chinese Past* (Stanford University Press, Stanford, 1973), pp. 71–3.

81 R. Lopez, *The Commercial Revolution of the Middle Ages, 950–1350* (Prentice-Hall, Englewood Cliffs, N.J., 1971), p. 17. G. C. Coulton, *The Medieval Village* (At the University Press, Cambridge, 1926), p. 56, discusses common monopolies.

82 J. Paige, *Agrarian Revolution: Social Movements and Export Agriculture in the Underdeveloped World* (Free Press, New York, 1975), p. 167.

83 Gitlitz, 'Haciendad, comunidad and peasant protests', p. 436. He notes also the important role of army veterans in uprisings on the haciendas studied. Veterans home from the Seven Years' War also played an important role in English food riots by 'providing a disciplined core of militants able to defy the military, and by giving direction to the disorders' (Walter J. Shelton, *English Hunger and Industrial Disorders* (Macmillan, London, 1973), p. 3.

84 Quoted by Elvin, *Pattern of the Chinese Past*, p. 77. See also Paige, *Agrarian Revolution: Social Movements and Export Agriculture in the Underdeveloped World*, p. 171.

85 For estates on private lands of Java, see S. Kartodirdjo, *Protest Movements in Rural Java: A Study of Agrarian Unrest in the Nineteenth and Early Twentieth Centuries* (Oxford University Press, Singapore, 1973), pp. 24–30. See also Breman, *Patronage and Exploitation*, pp. 5–6, 10.

86 M. Adas, *The Burma Delta: Economic Development and Social Change on an Asian Rice Frontier, 1852–1941* (University of Wisconsin Press, Madison, 1974), pp. 141–2.

87 R. Sansom, *The Economics of Insurgency in the Mekong Delta of Vietnam* (MIT Press, Cambridge, Mass., 1970), p. 29. Emphasis in original.
88 Adas, *Burma Delta*, p. 137.
89 A. Woodside, *Community and Revolution in Modern Vietnam* (Houghton Mifflin, Boston, 1976), pp. 257–8.
90 R. Thaxton, 'The world turned downside up', *Modern China*, 3 (1977), pp. 185–228, 194.
91 R. Brenner, 'Agrarian class structure and economic development in pre-industrial Europe', *Past and Present*, 70 (1976), p. 71. The importance to states which benefit from increased development and peasants who secure their families and are more able to control their offspring of hereditability should not be overlooked. A major peasant demand in Germany during peasant uprisings was for hereditary tenure. (David Sabean, 'Family and land tenure', p. 5.)
92 Waswo, *Japanese Landlords*, pp. 92–3.
93 W. Hinton, *Fanshen* (Random House Vintage Books, New York, 1968), pp. 112–17.
94 Author's interviews.
95 Alavi's 'Peasants and revolution' is the seminal statement on these class conflicts in agriculture. See also Tuma, *Twenty-six Centuries*, p. 72; Breman, *Patronage and Exploitation*, p. 56; and Gitlitz, 'Hacienda, comunidad and peasant protest', p. 14. At times, however, peasants did maintain solidarity against lords and denied them the power to bring in new tenants. As long as effective boycotts of new tenants were maintained, the newcomers could not survive, particularly when other farmers refused to help extinguish the fires set on unwanted tenants' lands. (Blum, 'Internal structure and polity', p. 522.) Today, agricultural laborers may boycott or otherwise use collective action against tenants who try to use labor-saving means of harvesting or threshing their crops. Such strategies generally fail, however, because those hiring the labor use divide-and-conquer strategies against the laborers. Divide-and-conquer strategies seldom require more than paying a few laborers higher wages to switch from knives to sickles and to exclude other laborers from the fields, or demanding free preharvest weeding from small numbers of laborers in exchange for giving them rights to do the entire harvest. (W. A. Collier et al., 'Agricultural technology and institutional change in Java', Staff Paper 75–1, Agricultural Development Council, New York, pp. 169–94; M. Kikuchi et al., 'Evolution of land tenure in a Laguna village', paper no. 77–11, Agricultural Economic Department, International Rice Research Institute, July 1977, pp. 12–14.) The same focus on visible standards is found in conflicts between laborers and tenants, as discussed earlier.
96 Paige, *Agrarian Revolution*, p. 167.
97 Hilton, *Bond Men Made Free*, quoting J. LeGeof, p. 58.
98 See, for example, Blum, 'The rise of serfdom in eastern Europe', p.

816; Breman, *Patronage and Exploitation*, p. 75; Hilton, *Bond Men Made Free*, p. 214.

99 R. Hilton, 'Peasant society, peasant movements and feudalism in Medieval Europe', in Henry Landsberger, *Rural Protest: Peasant Movements and Social Change* (Barnes and Noble, New York, 1973), pp. 67–94, 81; Blum et al., *A History of the Modern World*, p. 23.

100 Hilton, 'Medieval peasants – any lesson?' p. 217.

101 As Weisser notes for Spain, 'anarchism sought to sweep away the remnants of that old system by joining with those elements in the outside world that had begun a similar attack' (*Peasants of the Montes*, p. 117).

102 Day, *Dutch in Java*, p. 25.

103 C. Geertz, *Agricultural Involution: The Process of Ecological Change in Indonesia* (University of California Press, Berkeley and Los Angeles, 1966), p. 80; T. Kessinger, *Vilyatpur 1848–1968* (University of California Press, Berkeley and Los Angeles, 1974), p. 87; C. Robequain, *The Economic Development of French Indochina* (Oxford University Press, London, 1941), p. 328.

ADDITIONAL BIBLIOGRAPHY

J. S. Migdal, 'Why change? toward a new theory of change among individuals in the process of modernization', *World Politics*, 26 (1974), pp. 189–206.

J. C. Scott, 'Patron–client politics and political change in Southeast Asia', *American Political Science Review*, 66 (1972), March, pp. 91–113.

—— 'Peasant revolution: a dismal science', *Comparative Politics*, 9 (1977), pp. 232–48.

—— 'Protest and profanity: agrarian revolt and the Little tradition', part I, *Theory and Society*, 4 (1977), pp. 1–38; part II, ibid., pp. 211–46.

—— and B. J. Kerkvliet, 'How traditional patrons lose legitimacy: a theory with special reference to Southeast Asia', *Cultures et Développement*, 5 (1973).

E. Wolf, 'Aspects of group relations in a complex society: Mexico', *American Anthropologist*, 58 (1956), pp. 1065–78.

—— 'Introduction', in N. Miller and R. Aya (eds), *National Liberation: Revolution in the Third World* (Free Press, New York, 1971).

—— 'Kinship, friendship, and patron–client relations in complex societies', in M. Banton (ed.), *The Social Anthropology of Complex Societies* (ASA Monographs, Tavistock Publications, London, 1966).

—— *Peasants* (Prentice-Hall, Englewood Cliffs, NJ, 1966).

—— 'Peasant rebellion and revolution', in N. Miller and R. Aya (eds), *National Liberation: Revolution in the Third World* (Free Press, New York, 1971).

—— *Peasant Wars of the Twentieth Century* (Harper and Row, New York, 1969).

—— 'Review essay: why cultivators rebel', *American Journal of Sociology*, 83 (1977), pp. 742–50.

9
A Neoclassical Theory of the State

DOUGLASS NORTH

I

The existence of a state is essential for economic growth; the state, however, is the source of man-made economic decline. This paradox should make the study of the state central to economic history: models of the state should be an explicit part of any analysis of secular changes. But while the long path of historical research is strewn with the bones of theories of the state developed by historians and political scientists, economists traditionally have given little attention to the issue.

Recently, however, modern extensions of neoclassical economic theory, which have proven to be powerful tools of analysis, have been applied to a variety of political issues.[1] Neoclassical theory conceived of as a theory of choice has provided at the very least a disciplined and logically consistent approach to a study of the state. This theory offers the promise of developing refutable propositions about nonmarket decision making. In addition, research into economic organization has revealed its close kinship with political organization. A satisfactory theory of the firm would contribute immensely to the development of a theory of the state.[2]

We must, of course, be cautious about the limits of neoclassical theory. Public choice theory – economics applied to politics – has at best had only a modest success in explaining political decision making. Interest group politics cannot effectively explain voting behavior; ideological considerations appear to account for a great many political and judicial decisions.[3] Further, the questions that must be asked are at a different level than the day-to-day political decision-making process. For the economic historian, the key problems are to explain the kind of property rights that come to be specified and enforced by the state and to explain the effectiveness of enforcement; the most interesting challenge is to account for changes in the structure and enforcement of property rights over time.

II

At the outset one is faced with the problem of defining precisely what a state is. Where, for example, does the medieval manor belong on the continuum from the voluntary organization to the state? For the purposes of this work, a state is an organization with a comparative advantage in violence, extending over a geographic area whose boundaries are determined by its power to tax constituents. The essence of property rights is the right to exclude, and an organization which has a comparative advantage in violence is in the position to specify and enforce property rights. In contrast to the theories frequently advanced in the literature of political science, sociology, and anthropology, here the key to understanding the state involves the potential use of violence to gain control over resources. One cannot develop a useful analysis of the state divorced from property rights.[4]

Two general types of explanation for the state exist: a contract theory and a predatory or exploitation theory. Contract theories of the state have a long history. Recently they have been resurrected by neoclassical economists because they are a logical extension of the theorem of exchange, in which the state plays the role of wealth maximizer for society. Because a contract limiting each individual's activity relative to others is essential for there to be economic growth, the contract theory approach offers an explanation for the development of efficient property rights that would promote economic growth.[5]

The predatory or exploitation theory of the state is held by a remarkably varied collection of social scientists, including Marxists (at least in their analysis of the capitalist state) and some neoclassical economists. This view considers the state to be the agency of a group or class; its function, to extract income from the rest of the constituents in the interest of that group or class. The predatory state would specify a set of property rights that maximized the revenue of the group in power, regardless of its impact on the wealth of the society as a whole.

The contract approach may explain why the state potentially can provide a framework for economizing on the use of resources and therefore can promote wealth. As both the third party to every contract and the ultimate source of coercion, however, the state becomes the field on which the battle for control of its decision-making power is fought. All sides wish to be able to redistribute wealth and income in the interest of their own group. While the contract theory explains the gains of initial contracting but not the subsequent maximizing behavior of constituents with diverse interests, the predatory theory ignores the initial gains of contracting and focuses on the extraction of rents from constituents by those who gain control of the state. Nevertheless, the two theories are not inconsistent. It is the distribution of 'violence potential' that reconciles them. The contract theory assumes an equal distribution of violence potential amongst the principals. The predatory theory assumes an unequal distribution.

Property rights that produce sustained economic growth have seldom held sway throughout history, but even the most casual survey of the human experience makes clear that there have been political-economic units that achieved substantial economic growth for long periods of time. By sustained economic growth I mean that output has grown at a more rapid rate than population. This phenomenon is not confined to the two hundred years since the Industrial Revolution. There was an immense accumulation of wealth between the development of agriculture in the eight millennium BC and the *Pax Romana* of the first two centuries AD. It is true that during those centuries whole civilizations declined and disappeared, but there were also civilizations that experienced economic growth for lengthy periods in Mesopotamia, Egypt, Greece, Rhodes, and, of course, the Roman Republic and Empire. There is nothing new about sustained economic growth, then, despite the myth perpetuated by economic historians that it is a creation of the Industrial Revolution. Nor is there anything more inevitable than the ultimate economic decline of political-economic units.

In this chapter I shall develop a simple model of the state in order to explain two aspects that are fundamental to economic history: the widespread tendency of states to produce inefficient property rights and hence fail to achieve sustained growth; and the inherent instability of all states, which leads to economic change and ultimately to economic decline. Initially the model examines a state with a single ruler. However, I shall also explore the tension between ruler and constituents which leads to the dilution of the ruler's control and the emergence of political pluralism.[6]

This model of the state with a wealth- or utility-maximizing ruler has three essential characteristics. One specifies the exchange process between ruler and constituents; the other two specify the conditions that will determine the terms of exchange.

First, the state trades a group of services, which we shall call protection and justice, for revenue. Since there are economies of scale in providing these services, total income in the society is higher as a result of an organization specializing in these services than it would be if each individual in society protected his own property.

Second, the state attempts to act like a discriminating monopolist, separating each group of constituents and devising property rights for each so as to maximize state revenue.

Third, the state is constrained by the opportunity cost of its constituents since there always exist potential rivals to provide the same set of services. The rivals are other states, as well as individuals within the existing political-economic unit who are potential rulers. The degree of monopoly power of the ruler, therefore, is a function of the closeness of substitutes for the various groups of constituents.

By exploring in more depth these three hypotheses, we may not only put flesh on the bare bones of the model but also draw out some useful implications for the economic historian.

III

The basic services that the state provides are the underlying rules of the game. Whether evolving as a body of unwritten customs (as in the feudal manor) or as a written constitution, they have two objectives: one, to specify the fundamental rules of competition and cooperation which will provide a structure of property rights (that is, specify the ownership structure in both factor and product markets) for maximizing the rents accruing to the ruler; two, within the framework of the first objective, to reduce transaction costs in order to foster maximum output of the society and, therefore, increase tax revenues accruing to the state. This second objective will result in the provision of a set of public (or semi-public) goods and services designed to lower the cost of specifying, negotiating, and enforcing contracts which underlie economic exchange. The economies of scale associated with devising a system of law, justice, and defense are the basic underlying source of civilization; and the creation of the state in the millennia following the first economic revolution was the necessary condition for all subsequent economic development. While the ten millennia since the creation of settled agriculture appear in historical retrospect as an endless saga of war and of butchery, exploitation (however defined), enslavement, and mass murder, most often done by the state ruler or his agents, it is still essential to stress the necessity of a state for economic progress. Throughout history, individuals given a choice between a state –

however exploitative it might be – and anarchy, have decided for the former. Almost any set of rules is better than none, and it is not in the ruler's interest to make the rules so unpalatable that initiative is stifled.

There are three important implications of these objectives.

1. Put together, the two are not completely consistent. The second objective implies a completely efficient set of property rights to maximize societal output; the first attempts to specify a set of fundamental rules that will enable the ruler to maximize his own income (or, if we wish to relax the assumption of a single ruler, to maximize the monopoly rents of the group or class of which the ruler is the agent). From the redistributive societies of ancient Egyptian dynasties through the slavery system of the Greek and Roman world to the medieval manor, there was persistent tension between the ownership structure which maximized the rents to the ruler (and his group) and an efficient system that reduced trans-action costs and encouraged economic growth. This fundamental dichotomy is the root cause of the failure of societies to experience sustained economic growth and I shall explore it more precisely later in this chapter.

2. The creation of an infrastructure designed to specify and enforce a body of property rights entails the delegation of power to agents of the ruler. Since the utility function of the agents is not identical with that of the ruler, the ruler will specify a group of rules to attempt to enforce conduct by his agent that will be consistent with his own objectives.[7] There will be, however, a diffusion of the powers of the ruler to the degree that the agents are not perfectly constrained by the rules. The effect will also be a reduction in the monopoly rents of the ruler. We can predict the structure of this bureaucracy by exploring the transaction costs of the several parts of the economy.

3. The services provided by the ruler have differently shaped supply curves. While some services are pure public goods, others have typical U-shaped cost curves reflecting rising average costs beyond some range of output. The cost curve of protection would be relative to the state of military technology and would specify the size of the political-economic unit as 'efficient' when the marginal cost of protection was equal to the incremental tax revenue. From the Greek city-state to the Roman Empire to the small decentralized political organization of the feudal era to the nation state, military technology and changes in military technology have played a major role in shaping the supply curve.[8]

Two partial theories that have been advanced to account for the varying size of the state are consistent with the above stated marginal conditions. Wittfogel's hydraulic society[9] was in effect a natural monopoly, with economies of scale derived from the indivisibility of an integrated water system. Friedman's theory of the size and shape of nations[10] explores the relationship between the type of revenue and the size and shape of nations, arguing that if trade is the major political revenue source the result should be a large nation; that rent should imply small nations; and that labor should imply that nations will have closed boundaries or be culturally homogeneous.

IV

The economy consists of a diverse group of activities with varying production functions reflecting the technology, resource base, and population of the political-economic unit. The ruler will specify a set of property rights designed to maximize his monopoly rents for each separable part of the economy by monitoring and metering the inputs and outputs of each. The costs of measuring the dimensions of the inputs and outputs will dictate the various property rights structure for the diverse sectors of the economy, which therefore will be dependent on the state of the technology of measurement. Common property resources have persisted where the costs of measuring the dimensions of the resources have outweighed the benefits. The development of standardized weights and measurements is almost as old as government and has typically been fostered by the state. Standardization performs the function of lowering transaction costs and of allowing the ruler to extract the maximum amount of rent. The higher the cost of measurement of the multiple dimension of a good or service, the greater the dissipation of rent.[11]

Some of the historical forms of organization employed by the ruler include a loosely organized federal structure of local governors with their own bureaucracy; a centralized bureaucracy directly employed by the ruler; a bailiff system; and tax farming. Despite elaborate efforts at monitoring, in each of these organizational structures the agents of the ruler were imperfectly constrained, and their interests never completely coincided with the ruler's. The result typically was more or less dissipation of the monopoly rents of the rulers to the agents; in some cases there was collusion between agents and constituents to divide up some of the monopoly rents.

V

The ruler always has rivals: competing states or potential rulers within his own state. The latter are analogous to the potential rivals to a monopolist.[12] Where there are no close substitutes, the existing ruler characteristically is a despot, a dictator, or an absolute monarch. The closer the substitutes, the fewer degrees of freedom the ruler possesses, and the greater the percentage of incremental income that will be retained by the constituents. The opportunity cost of each of the various constituents will be different and will dictate the bargaining power each group has in the specification of property rights, as well as the tax burden it will incur. Opportunity costs will also dictate allocation of services provided by the ruler to the degree that they are not pure public goods, since the ruler will provide greater services to those with close alternatives than to those with none.

Constituents may, at some cost, go over to a competing ruler (that is, another existing political-economic unit) or support a competitor for ruler within the existing state.[13] The former alternative depends upon the structure of competitive political units. The more geographically proximate ones of course have an advantage. The ruler's efforts to gain or keep constituents will be determined by the supply curve of protection and the marginal benefits to be derived from additional constituents.

The latter alternative depends upon the relative violence potential of competing constituents. The ruler's own agents may be able to organize opposition and attract supporters from among the constituents by offering a better division of the existing rents. However, other individuals with command over sufficient resources to acquire military capability (or in the feudal world, lords with existing military capability) are potential rivals.

VI

The simple static model just described will give rise to two constraints on the ruler: a competitive constraint and a transaction cost constraint. Both typically produce inefficient property rights. Under the first, the ruler will avoid offending powerful constituents. If the wealth or income of groups with close access to alternative rulers is adversely affected by property rights, the ruler will be threatened. Accordingly, he will agree to a property rights structure favorable to those groups, regardless of its effects upon efficiency.

Efficient property rights may lead to higher income in the state but lower tax revenues for the ruler because of the transaction costs (monitoring, metering, and collecting such taxes) as compared to those of a more inefficient set of property rights. A ruler therefore frequently found it in his interests to grant a monopoly rather than property rights which would lead to more competitive conditions.

These two constraints together account for the wide spread of inefficient property rights. In effect, the property rights structure that will maximize rents to the ruler (or ruling class) is in conflict with that that would produce economic growth.[14] One variant of this is the Marxian notion of the contradictions of the mode of production, in which the ownership structure is incompatible with realizing the potential gain from an evolving set of technological changes. Economic growth is assured when the state behaves as specified in the contract case cited earlier (given reasonable assumptions about individual preferences with respect to savings and the number of children desired). Given the strictures in the foregoing model, however, it is clear that the pure contract case occurs only under the unusual circumstance that the ownership structure specified by the ruler is consistent with the kind of efficiency standards implied by neoclassical growth models (capitalism as described in the *Communist Manifesto*, for example). In effect, an ownership structure that provided incentives for efficient resource allocation (that is, a set of property rights that made the private rate of return on innovation, investment in human capital, and so forth approach the social rate) would be essential. But we should note immediately that the consequences must be destabilizing, since technological change, the spread of more efficient markets, and so forth would alter relative prices and the opportunity cost of constituents and would lead eventually to conflicts with the fundamental ownership structure of property rights.

In short, the process of growth is inherently destabilizing to a state. I shall explore in the next section the adjustment process of a state to such changes.

If, however, growth is destabilizing, so is no growth, when a political-economic unit exists in a world of competing political-economic units. Relatively inefficient property rights threaten the survival of a state in the context of more efficient neighbors, and the ruler faces the choice of extinction or of modifying the fundamental ownership structure to enable the society to reduce transaction costs and raise the rate of growth. Again, however, we must note carefully that the ability to adjust assumes a single ruler and none of the complicating issues posed when there are multiple sources of decision making.[15]

Stagnant states can survive as long as there is no change in the opportunity cost of the constituents at home or in the relative strength of competitor states. This last condition usually implies that the state approaches the status of a monopoly and is surrounded by weak states (and there are no net gains to a ruler in acquiring these states).

VII

The inherent instability of the state as outlined in the previous sections should be evident. Changes in information costs, technology, and population (or relative factor prices in general) are all obvious destabilizing influences. Also significant is the fact that the ruler is mortal.

A change in relative prices that improves the bargaining power of a group of constituents can lead to alteration of the rules to give that group more income, or, alternatively, the constituents can force the ruler to give up some of his rule-making powers. Sometimes the emergence of 'representative' government has come in the face of an external threat to the ruler. The transformation of the Greek city-state from monarchy to oligarchy to democracy (in the case of Athens) occurred as a consequence of a change in military technology (the development of the phalanx) which could only be accomplished with a citizen army; the price the ruler paid was the dilution of his rule-making powers. Similarly in early modern Europe, alterations in military technology (the pike, the longbow, and gunpowder) led in some instances to the delegation of rule-making powers to parliament or Estates General in return for the increased revenue needed for survival.

While changes in military technology were a major (though certainly not the sole) source of the growth of pluralist or representative government in the ancient and medieval world, the modern alterations in control of the state have been associated with the radical change in relative prices stemming from the Second Economic Revolution. The overwhelming dominance of agriculture in production in the Western world prior to the nineteenth century resulted in struggles to control the state being associated with the distribution of landed wealth and income (including the income from trade and shipping of agricultural and resource goods). With the Second Economic Revolution, the decline in the relative importance of land rent (and the landlord), the growth of manufacturing and services, the growing share of income going to labor, and in particular the growing importance of human capital have transformed the structure of production and created new interest groups; further, they are the basis of the struggle to control the state that has been going on in the past century.[16]

VIII

Instability is one thing; the process by which change and adjustment take place is something else. Here the separation between the application of economic principles and the application of other social science and Marxist principles is important. The former principles are inspired by the adjustment process in markets. In this process, changes at the margin lead to instantaneous adjustment. In politics as well as in economics, adjustments will occur only as long as the private returns exceed private costs; otherwise, the free rider problem will prevent adjustment. This condition severely restricts the willingness of constituents to adjust; and while it helps to explain the persistence of inefficient property rights, it obviously cannot explain the action of large groups to alter the property rights structure when private returns are negligible or negative.

Theories originating in the other social sciences and Marxism, on the other hand, account for large group action to alter property rights but have not provided any convincing theoretical underpinning to account for the way by which the free rider problem is overcome.

This theoretical gap is a crucial problem in any explanation of secular change. Causal empiricism provides ample evidence that large groups have sometimes acted to alter the structure of the state; but without some model we are unable to predict when the free rider problem will preclude action and when it will not. The study of ideology and the development of some positive model on the free rider problem are essential preliminaries to formulating a dynamic theory of change in the state.

We should note also the implications of adhering strictly to a neoclassical approach where the free rider problem will prevent large group activity. These implications point up the explanatory power of this neoclassical model at the same time as they delineate its limitations, and in concluding this discussion I wish to dwell briefly on a number of them.

First, the free rider accounts for the stability of states throughout history. The costs to the individual of opposing the coercive forces of the state have traditionally resulted in apathy and acceptance of the state's rules, no matter how oppressive. An historical counter-part of the low voter turnout in many current democracies is the failure of individuals to act as classes and of large groups to overthrow societies in the past. While the significance of this simple observation has not appeared to be properly appreciated in much of the literature on the state, it is amply (though inadvertently) attested to by the immense literature of Marxists on class con-sciousness, class solidarity, and ideology. Lenin and subsequent Marxist activists have been well aware of the very real problem that the free rider posed for Marxist theory and revolutionary practice.

Second, institutional innovation will come from rulers rather than constituents since the latter would always face the free rider problem. The ruler will, on his side, continue to innovate institution-al change to adjust to changing relative prices since he has no free rider problem. Thus a change in the relative scarcity of land and labor which made labor scarcer would lead the ruler to innovate institutional changes to appropriate increased rents from labor. These innovations will be carried out as long as the opportunity costs of labor do not change (that is, there is no change in potential competition from other rulers).

Third, revolutions will be palace revolutions undertaken by the ruler's agents or by a competing ruler or small elite Leninist-type groups.

Fourth, where the ruler is the agent of a group or class, some rules for succession will be devised to minimize the opportunities for disruptive change or revolution upon the death of the ruler. As noted above, disruptive change or revolution will come most likely from the ruler's agents.

The foregoing four points help to explain a great deal about the stability of and the sources of changes in the structure of the state throughout history. Limiting one's analysis to instances where one could identify net private gains (in narrowly construed economic terms) to the actors, however, would put a fatal handicap on the study of structural change of the state. It is necessary to construct a theory of ideology to resolve the free rider dilemma.

NOTES

1 See W. Baumol, *Welfare Economics and a Theory of the State* (Har-vard University Press, Cambridge, Mass., 1952); J. Buchanan and G. Tullock, *The Calculus of Consent* (University of Michigan Press, Ann

Arbor, 1962); A. Downs, *An Economic Theory of Democracy* (Harper and Row, New York, 1957); W. Niskanen, *Bureaucracy and Representative Government* (Aldine Publishing Co., Chicago, 1971); A. Breton, *The Economic Theory of Representative Government* (Aldine Publishing Co., Chicago, 1974).

2 See R. Coase, 'The nature of the firm', *Economica* (1937), November; A. Alchian and H. Demsetz, 'Production, information costs and economic organization', *American Economic Review* (1972), December.

3 Douglass C. North, 'Structure and performance: the task of economic history', *Journal of Economic Literature*, 16 (1978), September, pp. 963–78.

4 In an otherwise interesting analysis of the origins of the state, R. Carniero ('A theory of the origin of the state', *Science*, 169 (1970), pp. 733–8) fails to link the state with the establishment of property rights.

5 The most careful analysis is that of J. R. Umbeck, *A Theory of Property Rights: with Application to the California Gold Rush* (Iowa State University Press, Arnes, Iowa, 1981).

6 The study of legitimacy and alienation is considered elsewhere in the book from which this essay is reprinted. I also neglect in this essay the impact of state policies on fertility and mortality.

7 For a further discussion of agency theory, see M. Jensen and W. Meckling, 'Theory of the firm: managerial behavior, agency costs and ownership structure', *Journal of Financial Economics* (1975), October.

8 One of the most neglected parts of economic history is the study of military technology in relationship to the size of states. While there is an immense literature on military technology itself, it has seldom been explored in terms of its implications for political structure. For an exception to this indictment, see R. Bean, 'War and the birth of the nation-state', *Journal of Economic History* (1973), March.

9 K. Wittfogel, *Oriental Despotism* (Yale University Press, New Haven, 1957).

10 D. Friedman, 'A theory of the size and shape of nations', *Journal of Political Economy* (1977), February.

11 Y. Barzel, 'A theory of rationing by waiting', *Journal of Law and Economics*, (1974), April; S. N. S. Cheung, 'A theory of price control', *Journal of Law and Economics*, (1974), April.

12 For an analysis of the monopoly case, see H. Demsetz, 'Why regulate utilities?', *Journal of Law and Economics*, (1968).

13 These two choices are roughly analogous to Hirschman's Exit and Voice. See A. Hirschman, *Exit, Voice and Loyalty* (Harvard University Press, Cambridge, Mass., 1970).

14 Under the condition of zero transaction costs, the ruler could always devise first an efficient set of rules and then bargain for his rents, but this postulate from welfare economics simply ignores positive transaction costs, which is what the game is all about. Even the most casual observations from history and the contemporary world make clear that 'inefficient' property rights are the rule, not the exception.

15 Gerschenkron's relative backwardness hypothesis makes sense only in this context.
16 The property rights and allocation implications of the rise of pluralism are explored elsewhere. Here I want simply to emphasize that whether constituents bargain with a ruler over property rights or gain some control over rule making power, the result may be the same as far as the efficiency or inefficiency of property rights is concerned and the argument advanced in section vi above still holds. I can make this point more forcefully by the following illustration. In the contemporary world there are immense differences in the control of the state as between the Soviet Union and the United States. The former is certainly close to my model of a single-ruler state; the latter is certainly a pluralist state. In the former, the bargaining over property rights takes place *within* the control structure; in the latter there is a ubiquitous struggle by interest groups to control the state. But I know of no a priori reason on the basis of *this difference alone* to predict the relative efficiency of property rights in one country or the other.

Index